"In this excellent book, Professor Br
working with adolescents and their f
with useful clinical examples, the bri
developed and manualised whilst worn...g

of the increase in mental health difficulties in adolescence, this approac.. p
vides a much needed developmentally sensitive and in-depth brief therapy model.
Highly recommended to clinicians working with adolescents."
—Prof. Alessandra Lemma, Consultant, Anna Freud National Centre for
Children and Families, Psychoanalysis Unit, UCL

"This important and useful book sets time-limited work with adolescents and young
adults in the context of both the specifics of time-limited work and the particulars
of working with young adults. The author sets the work firmly in the developmental
process, which characterises this stage of life. Using the TAPP model, he shows
how this work can be transformative for a young adult, and at times for the therapist
too. He uses many case illustrations, which help the reader to have a lively experience of the work and its value. This book is of use to clinicians working therapeutically with young adults, and for those who offer time-limited work with any age
group. It is also of interest to any thinker who wants to explore this part of the
human condition and the challenges of becoming a person."
—Jan McGregor Hepburn, Psychoanalytic Psychotherapist, Registrar, BPC

"It was a wonderful and thoroughly rewarding experience to immerse myself in
this important book. I enjoyed learning so much about short-term therapies in general and the workings of TAPP. I particularly valued the clinical examples which
were easy to understand and made the theoretical discussions come alive. It is a
remarkable book about a very useful intervention for young people in distress."
—Mark J. Goldblatt, MD, Associate Professor of Psychiatry, PT, Harvard
Medical School; Clinical Associate, McLean Hospital; Faculty, Boston
Psychoanalytic Society and Institute

"Adolescent mental health is one of the pressing public health issues of our time.
Yet contrary to accepted belief, young people do not present with neat diagnostic categories but complex issues best understood within a developmental and
psychosocial context. With a foundation in psychoanalytic thinking and clinical
work, Professor Stephen Briggs provides a rich and detailed understanding of
adolescence in chapters that span development and pathology, the rationale for
brief work, therapeutic priorities, growth and change and endings. The book provides a guide to using TAPP for practitioners in training and psychotherapists
working with young people in all settings, including mental health services."
—Dr Monique Maxwell, Child and Adolescent Psychotherapist,
Leicester CAMHS

Time-Limited Adolescent Psychodynamic Psychotherapy

Time-Limited Adolescent Psychodynamic Psychotherapy: A Developmentally Focussed Psychotherapy for Young People will be an indispensable clinician's guide to the practice of Time-Limited Adolescent Psychodynamic Psychotherapy (TAPP), providing comprehensive instruction on the theory and delivery of this distinctive model of psychotherapy.

TAPP is a manualised, brief, psychodynamic psychotherapy of 20 sessions for young people between approximately 14 and 25 years, combining psychodynamic psychotherapy with psychosocial understanding of adolescent difficulties. It places emphasis on the therapeutic engagement of young people and works with a developmental focus to effect change and growth. Divided into two parts, "Conceptual framework" and "Practice," this book combines digestible scholarly analysis with case studies to effect a one-stop practitioner's guide to TAPP.

Time-Limited Adolescent Psychodynamic Psychotherapy: A Developmentally Focussed Psychotherapy for Young People will be of immense value to clinicians working with young people, researchers engaging with evaluating TAPP and students of psychotherapy.

Stephen Briggs is Professor of Social Work at the University of East London. He is a Member of the Tavistock Society of Psychotherapists and a Fellow of the Academy of Social Sciences. He was formerly a Consultant Social Worker in the Adolescent Department, Tavistock and Portman NHS Foundation Trust.

Time-Limited Adolescent Psychodynamic Psychotherapy

A Developmentally Focussed Psychotherapy for Young People

Stephen Briggs

Routledge
Taylor & Francis Group

LONDON AND NEW YORK

First published 2019
by Routledge
2 Park Square, Milton Park, Abingdon, Oxon OX14 4RN

and by Routledge
52 Vanderbilt Avenue, New York, NY 10017

Routledge is an imprint of the Taylor & Francis Group, an informa
business

British Library Cataloguing-in-Publication Data
A catalogue record for this book is available from the British Library

Library of Congress Cataloging-in-Publication Data
Names: Briggs, Stephen, author.
Title: Time-limited adolescent psychodynamic psychotherapy: a
developmentally focussed psychotherapy for young people/Stephen Briggs.
Description: Abingdon, Oxon; New York, NY: Routledge, 2019. |
Includes bibliographical references and index.
Identifiers: LCCN 2019001322 | ISBN 9781138366640
(hardback: alk. paper) | ISBN 9781138366664 (paperback: alk. paper) |
ISBN 9780429430190 (ebk)
Subjects: | MESH: Psychotherapy, Psychodynamic | Mental Disorders–
therapy | Psychotherapy, Brief | Adolescent
Classification: LCC RC480 | NLM WS 466 | DDC 616.89/14–dc23
LC record available at https://lccn.loc.gov/2019001322

ISBN: 978-1-138-36664-0 (hbk)
ISBN: 978-1-138-36666-4 (pbk)
ISBN: 978-0-429-43019-0 (ebk)

Typeset in Times New Roman
by Deanta Global Publishing Services, Chennai, India

To Matthew, Oliver and Eleanor

Contents

Foreword

I am delighted to welcome readers to this book in which there is so much to learn from Stephen Briggs' long clinical experience and academic immersion in the field of adolescent mental health. We were both fortunate to work for many years in the Adolescent Department of the Tavistock and Portman NHS Foundation Trust, surrounded by colleagues with immense expertise in psychoanalytic approaches to understanding adolescence.

This is a generous book which brings to a wider audience clinical insight and wisdom developed over decades in the Adolescent Department. Since the Department was established in 1959 there has been a growing recognition of the mental health needs of children and young people but sadly no sign that the prevalence of mental health difficulties is decreasing, nor of services being in a position to keep up with demand.

Many adults with mental health difficulties can trace the onset back to the early years of adolescence. This may have been prevented or alleviated with effective intervention in adolescence. Time-Limited Adolescent Psychodynamic Psychotherapy (TAPP) brings together an in-depth psychoanalytical approach with a structure designed to work with the psychic experience of time and change in adolescence and the social world expectations attending the passage into adulthood.

The book provides the reader with a guide to engaging young people in a collaborative, structured approach to psychotherapy closely linked to the developmental process of adolescence. The process is marked by loss as well as the emergence of new possibilities often simultaneously experienced as disturbing and exciting. All relationships may be unsettled during adolescence – in the psyche, in the family, socially – leaving many young people feeling alone and overwhelmed, especially where social structures offer only fragile support. Both the tumult of the inner world and the realities of deprived social contexts for many young people are clearly held in mind throughout the book.

As Stephen Briggs will explain, TAPP grew out of the Adolescent Department approach and specifically the Brief Therapy Workshop, which I founded and chaired from 1996 to 2008, with the remit to develop a time-limited model. Within the Department, the Young People's Consultation Service, a four-session self-referral service, was already well established although generally individual therapies were of variable lengths and did not include a structured time-limited approach beyond this very brief service.

Searching the literature in the 1990s, it was hard to find evidence-based brief psychotherapy models designed specifically for adolescents. One exception was Interpersonal Therapy for Adolescents (IPT-A) (Mufson et al 1994), adapted from the original time-limited model developed for depressed adults. In our workshop, we began work on an assessment-plus-16-session structure with a follow-up appointment some weeks after the ending. The aim was to develop a psycho-analytically based model which could be researched and compared in terms of outcome to other established models of a similar length.

Our workshop discovered that we could work with a wide range of young people and the criteria often set for adult brief therapy models did not apply. We especially needed to work hard in the workshop in thinking through the mount-ing anxiety we and our patients frequently experienced as the end of the therapy drew near. We came to understand that this was a valuable opportunity to focus on central adolescent issues of separation and loss in the therapeutic relationship. For some, the fact that the therapy was circumscribed conveyed hopefulness and confidence in their continuing development. Of course, the outcome for young people may often seem unclear to both the patient and the therapist and here the follow-up appointment proved an important juncture for reflection on what had been helpful and whether further therapy or support was needed.

Many of the key features of the original model are recognisable in TAPP as set out in this book but Stephen Briggs has very significantly extended the reach of the model based on substantial clinical experience well beyond the north London-based Tavistock and Portman NHS Foundation Trust. He sets out clearly and sensitively the steps required to engage and help a wide range of young people in many different settings. His approach emphasises the importance of attending carefully to the developmental process, noting the individual variability and ado-lescent changeability that require acute attention and flexibility of response on the part of the therapist. He is alongside the therapist and helpfully supportive of the doubts, frustrations and misunderstandings which can assail us in working with young people, often mirroring their own experiences. He shows how, by remain-ing curious about our experience with our patients and sharing our work with col-leagues where possible, we can help young people find their own capacity to think through discovering the transformative value of thinking with another.

Louise Lyon
Former Chair, Brief Therapy Workshop,
Adolescent Department, Tavistock and Portman
NHS Foundation Trust, Clinical Psychologist
Psychoanalyst, Member of the British
Psychoanalytic Society

Acknowledgements

Over many years, I was fortunate to work with inspiring colleagues in the Tavistock Clinic's Adolescent Department; the Department's unique approach to working with young people continues to be crucial for working with the problems faced by young people today. In particular, I would like to thank Louise Lyon who has had a pivotal role in developing the model of brief therapy discussed in this book and from whom I learned how to do time-limited psychotherapy. I am indebted to the young people whom I have seen as patients in TAPP therapy. Through providing training and supervision of TAPP, I have enjoyed working with many practitioners in various places across the world, and these experiences have helped me formulate how to communicate the nature and practice of TAPP. I have been sustained in the process of writing by colleagues and friends who have offered stimulating discussions and provided invaluable feedback. I would like to thank William Crouch, Mark Goldblatt, Rebecca Hanson, Jan Hepburn, Alessandra Lemma, Monique Maxwell, Soraya De Negri, Terence Nice and Laurence Spurling. I am grateful to my wife, Beverley, for her enduring support and her understanding of my preoccupation with this book.

Chapter I

Introduction

"Adolescence is one of the most radical of all the developmental periods."
(Anderson & Dartington 1998, p. 2)

Introduction

This book is about an approach to time-limited psychotherapy, Time-Limited Adolescent Psychodynamic Psychotherapy, which is known by its acronym, TAPP. The recent emergence of time-limited approaches for working with young people is clearly a response to current service delivery priorities; time-limited models can be developed as a pragmatic response to demands on services and resource limitations. These factors are present for, and increase the current utility of, TAPP; however, in its concepts and practice, TAPP also takes a more positive approach to time-limited psychotherapy. It aims to increase the engagement of young people in psychotherapy and to provide a structured therapeutic approach, which is highly relevant for young people experiencing the often extended and uncertain transition to adulthood in contemporary social contexts. Relating to the significantly changed social contexts for young people is an important consideration for adolescent psychotherapy.

Discussion of this period of life involves engaging with a fissure that runs through the subject; whilst the term 'adolescence' retains currency for psychological thinking about this period of development, social studies and a significant amount of national and international policy refer to 'youth' and 'young people.' The different terminology highlights an important difference for understanding the age period involved; the idea of an upper age limit of 18 years has been institutionalised, including in mental health services, despite increasing evidence that the period of transition to adulthood – into the twenties – continues the development of 'adolescence' socially, internally and neurologically (Blakemore 2018; McGorry 2018). In contrast, the period of 'youth' is usually taken to extend to the mid-twenties, but can underplay the importance of the changes of early adolescence, following the onset of puberty. In this book the psychological and social are both treated as important aspects of adolescence, that is, of the crucial developmental processes of this period.

In addition to attending to current contexts for young people, TAPP is distinctive in its therapeutic aims. The importance of the developmental process has long been recognised when working therapeutically with young people; it is a crucial and radical process of change and growth. However, in TAPP the emphasis on development is heightened so that the aim of therapy is to focus on an aspect of disturbance in the developmental process for each individual. Working with the structure of the time-limited approach provides therapeutic impetus that enhances opportunities for change, the reduction of problems and the establishment of developmental capacities in the individual that continue after the therapy ends. This approach of TAPP has been found in practice to offer a powerful, often intensive process for growth and change. TAPP is becoming more widely used in the UK and internationally; practitioners are finding it a helpful way of working with young people, and there is now sufficient experience with the approach to justify gathering together experiences, distilling them and making them more widely available in this book.

Adolescent psychotherapy

Providing meaningful and effective therapeutic interventions for young people with mental health difficulties is a vital task. Every generation has its distinctive difficulties with adolescence. Thinking about adolescence is essentially interactive and intergenerational; as in previous generations, adults are worried about and by adolescents, and adolescents are worried about themselves and society. Adolescence is characterised by the intensity of powerful emotions and energies, flowing "when the tide of life is running strongly" (Williams 1978, p. 311), creating tensions between creativity and its counterpart of a more destructive kind. Adults can be disturbed by encountering adolescent emotionality, be caught up with it and defend against it; rivalry is never far away from interactions between adults and young people (Bradley 2017). Society identifies folk devils and experiences moral panics (Cohen 2002). Therefore, thinking about adolescent difficulties necessitates a reflective approach that differentiates concerns and reactions; in psychoanalytic terms, there is always much to think about in the countertransference when working therapeutically with young people.

In order to relate effectively to young people, adolescent psychotherapy requires distinctive skills, training and the adoption of a therapeutic stance that enables orientation to adolescent development and its ambiguities of expression and communication. Adolescence is a radical period of development because the changes that follow puberty are intense and far reaching, involving the loss of childhood relatedness to adults, starting to live in a new, adult, sexual body and re-evaluating relatedness to the self and others. The adolescent process underpins development and drives it; the young person is confronted with the push to progress and the pull to try to hang on to childhood. Being in such a radical process of change means being out of balance, in oneself; the capacity "to bear to continue the experience of being naturally out of balance, as well as an environment that can support this" (Anderson & Dartington 1998, p. 3) enables the young person to grow with the emotional demands of integrating the changes of adolescence into his sense of himself and his relationships with others. Being able to work therapeutically <u>within</u> the developmental process is a different way of working; it makes adolescent psychotherapy distinctive.

Mental health difficulties in adolescence

Globally there is increasing awareness of the importance of recognising mental health difficulties experienced by young people and providing access to appropriate health care; mental health difficulties in adolescence are recognised as a threat to long-term well-being. Steps to reduce societal discrimination, stigma and isolation for people experiencing mental health difficulties are important in creating a climate in which young people can more easily access mental health care. That young people – especially those with the most needs – find it difficult to access, engage in and sustain therapeutic help is a long-standing concern (Baruch 2001; O'Reilly et al 2013).

Concerns about young people's mental health difficulties are heightened by reports that increasing numbers of young people have such difficulties, including depression, self-harm, suicide, eating disorders, anxieties, and the effects of abusive and exploitative relationships. Surveys consistently identify higher numbers of young people reporting mental health difficulties in childhood and adolescence (Pitchforth et al 2018). The increase could be partly explained by young people being more able to recognise and seek help for their difficulties, which indicates that efforts to reduce stigma are having a positive effect; on the other hand, more young people indeed may be experiencing mental health difficulties (Gunnell et al 2018). However, this has created a problem referred to as the 'treatment gap' (Rice et al 2017): "a range of policy reports have identified a persistent gap between identifying the needs of children and young people and their access to timely, high-quality help and support" (CQC 2017, p. 30). Shortfalls in funding, exacerbated during austerity, critically hamper the aim of creating a comprehensive child and adolescent mental health service (CAMHS), whilst transition to adult mental health services results in up to 50% of young people under 25 disengaging (CQC 2018). The quantitative pressure inevitably impacts on quality; high-quality – and thus usually more expensive – interventions are more under pressure than easier, cheaper to deliver interventions. Yet there is a wealth of evidence that more intensive and high-quality interventions can make a difference for young people, not least in preventing disturbances in adolescence from becoming long-term psychosocial and mental health disorders that persist into adulthood (Patton et al 2014).

In these contexts of anxieties about demands and the management of risks, delivery of mental health services for young people conflates factors that are involved in young people's difficulties: diagnosis of mental health disorder, social vulnerability and disturbances emanating from the process of development and change in adolescence. Cottrell and Kraam (2005, p. 115) pointed out over a decade ago that young people in mental health services present "with troubling predicaments, not neat diagnoses". Clinicians in CAMHS and other services working with young people with mental health difficulties, including educational settings, are aware on a daily basis that few young people present with simple, single issues such as depression but many have a complex combination of mental health difficulties, difficulties relating to adolescent development and current life tasks, and social vulnerability, including backgrounds of deprivation of various kinds, having experienced abuse, family disruptions, being in care, being teenage parents, having offended, seeking asylum, being homeless and being discriminated against in black and minority ethnic (BME) communities (CQC 2017, p. 43). Requirements for evidence-based practice also contribute to a simplification of adolescent problems; evidence for effectiveness in interventions, which are usually based on a single issue, primarily depression, contrasts with the complex nature of the problems young people present.

Changing contexts of adolescence

Alongside the changing landscape of the provision of therapeutic interventions for young people, wider social changes have transformed the contexts of adolescence. Throughout the adolescent development period, from societal encouragement of the 'pseudo-sexuality' of pre-pubescent children, with implications for the body and sexuality (Lemma 2015b), to the extended pathways in the transition to adulthood, young people encounter new and different socio-cultural contexts. Thinking about adolescence means paying attention to these changes: new patterns of friendship and ways of relating to others, experiences of intimacy and separateness driven significantly by the impact of online and social media, new vulnerabilities, especially evidenced by concerns about increasing adolescent mental health problems, and new possibilities relating to the body, sexuality and gender. Adolescence is characterised by diversity, socially and culturally; the diversity of ethnic identities demonstrates there are different notions and constructions of adult identity.

Transitions to adulthood create deeply contradictory situations; young people may be psychologically ready to leave home, take up a career and/or enter a sexual partnership, but continue to depend on parental support. It is more realistic to see adolescents moving into adulthood piecemeal or in uneven ways, becoming positioned as 'more adult' in specific domains – such as relationships, employment and becoming a parent (Briggs 2008). Pathways into adulthood have become extended into the third decade, a factor that is not usually represented in services, which have a divide at the age of 18. The exceptions that treat adolescence as a discrete entity and provide services beyond 18 demonstrate a more adolescent-centred approach, supporting the integrity of this most crucial developmental period and allowing professionals to develop the specialised skills needed for working with young people (McGorry 2018). Transformation of the social context has generated new and different psychological tasks and has required specific qualities to negotiate transitions that have become extended, less structured, 'disembedded,' and more uncertain (Côté 2014; Furlong & Cartmel 2007).

Time-limited psychotherapy for young people

Short-term or time-limited psychotherapies have been demanded increasingly for mental health services working in these contexts; when developed to meet economic constraints shorter therapies are attractive, but perhaps for the wrong kinds of reasons (Lemma et al 2011); on the other hand, some reasons for developing time-limited therapies may be thought of as 'better' ones. These include helping young people engage in therapy, providing structured interventions to meet the needs of young people experiencing fragmentation during the transition to adulthood and addressing the kind of predicaments that young people bring to therapy. Some psychoanalytically oriented interventions have recently been developed, notably Short-Term Psychoanalytic Psychotherapy (STPP) (Catty 2016), and Mentalisation-Based Therapy for Adolescents (MBT-A) (Rossouw & Fonagy 2012). This is a relatively new development; apart from the work of Shefler (2000) it is hard to find earlier models of time-limited psychotherapy designed specifically for young people. Despite the wide recognition of the importance of therapeutic interventions for young people, there are relatively few evidenced psychodynamic interventions (Abbass et al 2013); there continues to be the need to develop interventions that are effective, meaningful and relevant for young people. Interventions for adolescents that can be delivered in the context of the limited resources of public services, as well as in the private sector, are urgently needed.

Time-Limited Adolescent Psychodynamic Psychotherapy (TAPP): origins and overview

TAPP is for adolescents and young adults in the age range of 14–25. The age range reflects the key objective of providing a therapeutic approach that maintains the integrity of the period of adolescent development, including taking account of the extended transitions to adulthood when adolescent development continues to be a process in which the young person is involved. The age range is that of the United Nations definition of youth (UNESCO 2018). In practice, TAPP is for young people whose difficulties can be related to problems and disturbances of the adolescent developmental process, and for whom an individual psychotherapy is indicated. TAPP is a structured therapy which consists of three phases: engagement and assessment, consisting of four sessions at weekly intervals; treatment, of 16 weekly sessions; and post-treatment review, with a minimum of one session six to eight weeks after the end of treatment. The aim is not to try to solve all problems in 20 sessions; a focus for therapy is identified with the aim of harnessing the power of the adolescent developmental process to generate change and growth. A therapeutic focus on developmental difficulty and disturbance aims to recover the individual's capacity to meet developmental challenges. Therapeutic structures of time and focus are used to help young people manage transitions in their often complex, confusing and fragmentary social and cultural contexts. TAPP is a psychodynamic approach, based on a psychoanalytic understanding of adolescent development and therapeutic relationships, and focuses on emotionality and relatedness. It is a depth therapy, working with unconscious processes and in the therapeutic relationship with transference and counter-transference to effect internal change. Engagement of young people in the therapeutic relationship is critical and this is facilitated in TAPP by working with the young person's active involvement in identifying a developmental focus; it aims to help the young person develop an interest in his own life and difficulties. TAPP works with the social and cultural experiences of adolescence, and explores the meaning of the social and cultural contexts in young people's development and in understanding the difficulties that have brought them to therapy.

TAPP has its origins in the Brief Therapy Workshop in the Tavistock Clinic's Adolescent Department, when in the mid-1990s, Louise Lyon brought her expertise in brief therapy to establish the Brief Therapy Workshop. This was simultaneously a departure from and application of the Adolescent Department's model of psychotherapy, applying the core principles of the individual psychotherapy approach to the task of developing a shorter, time-limited model; similar developments had occurred in family therapy, group therapy and very brief psychotherapy consultations in the Young People's Consultation Service (Young & Lowe 2012; Lyon 2004). The Adolescent Department's approach emphasised reaching out to young people in difficulties through thinking psychoanalytically about the adolescent developmental process (Anderson & Dartington 1998). It was rooted in a multi-disciplinary approach; distinguished clinicians developed a distinctive model of psychotherapy which drew, in the hands of various clinicians, on Klein and post-Kleinian, Winnicottian and Freudian approaches, of which the post-Kleinian work of Wilfred Bion was especially influential. It applied an experiential process for engaging adolescents in therapy, including, for example, an initial assessment process consisting of four weekly meetings. Psychotherapy was usually open-ended, frequently involved more than one session a week and some young people were offered and received intensive psychotherapy of three or more sessions a week.

Throughout the history of brief psychotherapy, the development of a time-limited model has divided opinion. The members of the Brief Therapy Workshop consisted of a mixed group of staff and trainees, very much like the model that had earlier been used for the development of adult brief psychotherapy by David Malan (see Chapter 2). The approach was based on the Adolescent Department's emphasis on the adolescent developmental process and aimed to identify how the individual's difficulties or presenting problems and symptoms could be thought of in terms of an impasse in development. The aim was to work in depth with the transference and counter-transference. A striking feature observed through clinical experience was that the developmental issue, identified as a focus for time-limited psychotherapy, came to be replicated in the transference especially in the process of termination. The TAPP model, which initially used the acronym TPP-A, was discussed in publications (Briggs 2010a; Briggs & Lyon 2011; Briggs & Lyon 2012).

TAPP has evolved significantly in recent years, through practice in a range of different settings, whilst retaining the key features developed in the Brief Therapy Workshop, including the timescale and the concept of developmental focus. In current practice the focus on engagement has been extended, as has working with different kinds of developmental focus, and with diverse therapeutic aims for young people with different needs and difficulties. In current practice, the psychosocial dimension is important, relating the therapeutic approach to the young person's internal and developmental difficulties and disturbances to contemporary issues for adolescents and the psychological tasks they face in negotiating the complicated pathways to adulthood. TAPP is used widely CAMHS by psychotherapists working in primary care, educational settings, voluntary organisations and private practice, in the UK and other countries. Challenges provided by new and different issues that young people present, as well as applications of the model in different settings, continue to expand and refine how TAPP is delivered (Briggs et al 2015). The approach is for the model to be replicable and evidence based. Service evaluations show that TAPP effectively engages young people in therapy and that problems and risks are reduced (Briggs et al 2018). Therapists can now train to become TAPP practitioners and supervisors through following a training programme which is accredited by the British Psychoanalytic Council (BPC). It is widely felt by those participating in these training courses that TAPP succeeds in making sense of the task of engaging with and thinking about young people's difficulties and providing a structure for intervention that is helpful and effective. This book aims to distil what has been learnt from applying TAPP, so as to make these lessons more widely available to practitioners working with young people in all settings.

The scope and limitations of this book

The book is written primarily for practitioners: psychotherapists working with young people in all settings including mental health services, educational, primary care, volunteer sector organisations and private practice. Many of these practitioners are required by their organisations to work with a time-limited approach; others are able to combine applying TAPP with longer-term psychotherapy. The book provides a detailed account of how to undertake therapy using the TAPP approach; this involves detailed accounts of the key practice issues throughout the TAPP process, from the first meeting to the post-treatment review. It is in one sense a manual. Therapy manuals can attract strong views, for and against. There are different kinds of manuals, but this book's approach to manualisation is to articulate principles and practice rather than to be prescriptive. TAPP requires the creative processes of a skilled therapist to work inside a clear and meaningful structure provided by the time-limited therapeutic frame. Key aspects of TAPP require emphasis, including the process of assessment and engagement, the identification of a developmental focus, working with this in the treatment phase, identifying and maintaining the therapeutic stance and techniques and working with termination. Case examples are used extensively to demonstrate applications in practice. In that the book can be thought of as a manual for TAPP, in addition to being a guide for practitioners, it also provides a protocol for research into the effectiveness of the intervention, through the articulation of the aims, rationale and practice of TAPP; therefore, the book is also intended for use by researchers evaluating the effectiveness of TAPP.

Psychotherapy practice routinely involves learning from experience, from personal analysis and supervision, as well as from theory and clinical discussions. These are all important to learning and practicing TAPP. Training as a TAPP practitioner involves in-depth, regular weekly supervision, individually or in a small group, of the treatment of two TAPP cases. Supervision aims to clarify the dynamics and emotionality in the therapeutic relationship and to help the therapist to attain and maintain optimal sensitivity to the patient, whilst working with the TAPP structure, and to meet the demands of working with a time-limited therapy. TAPP is demanding of the therapist in the sense that there can be a great deal of clinical material, often seeming ambiguous, to keep in mind and to think about; working with the counter-transference is therefore a crucial part of the process. Supervision and small reflective seminar groups form essential aspects of the approach for new and experienced TAPP practitioners. This continues the model used in the Brief Therapy Workshop where the process of therapy was discussed in a weekly seminar group.

In TAPP, therefore, as in all psychoanalytic therapy, learning from experience and from cases is at the heart of the process. Learning from cases has a privileged place in psychoanalysis and psychoanalytic psychotherapy; working with individual cases is what psychotherapists 'do.' Freud thought his case studies "read like novellas, and that they, so to speak, lack the serious stamp of science". However, he added – importantly – that it is "the nature of the subject, rather than my predilection, that is responsible for the result" (Gay 1988, p. 89). This is not, by the way, to enter the controversial arena of the scientific merits, or limitations, of single case studies; cases are being thought of here in the exemplary and illustrative senses. The experience of individual cases is the starting point for clinical discussion and theory development; they illustrate assertions and theories, and they bring alive descriptions of methods and techniques. Description of case examples is used extensively in this book; some cases are followed throughout the TAPP process from assessment to the end of treatment. They are used to demonstrate methods and to be exemplars of the kinds of cases that are worked with in TAPP, and of the processes that ensue.

The book engages in some wider discussions in relation to theory and practice; these are relevant to TAPP, underpin practice and have further implications.

Firstly, TAPP is discussed in relation to brief psychodynamic psychotherapy, and the discussion over many generations now of time and duration in psychotherapy. The history and development of brief therapy as a genre, and the debates and controversies that have accompanied it, make an important theme which has not often been studied. 'Brief' and 'short-term' are relative terms, and, like many kinds of identity, are defined at least partly in relationship to something 'other,' which, in this case, is long-term or open-ended psychodynamic or psychoanalytic psychotherapy. Most time-limited therapies are short-term, or brief. However, it is possible to find time-limited therapies that cannot really be described as short-term, and short-term therapies that are not time-limited. In the classic canon of psychoanalysis, Freud's case of the Wolf-man ended up time-limited, when, in the fifth year of treatment, he set a termination date, one year ahead, to the patient's outrage; his aim was to more effectively mobilise the patient's associa-tions. Much more recently, Shaw (2014) has discussed a time-limited intensive treatment of a patient seen three times weekly for two years. Neither of these can reasonably be called 'brief' or 'short-term.' Some short-term psychotherapies, such as Davanloo's (2000) more recent work, do not have a time limit but rather an expectation of work being of brief duration. Brief therapy developed in the UK with Malan's (1976) work in the 1960s and 1970s, and in the USA through Sifneos (1972), followed by key contributions by Strupp and Binder (1984) and, more recently, by Stadter (2009); developments in thinking about brief therapy and debates about method form an important background to current practice. The more recent development of brief and time-limited methods for young people do need to be related to the broader conceptual frameworks for brief and longer-term therapy. The position taken by TAPP is that these are complementary rather than alternatives; brief work differs from longer-term work in its aims as well as duration.

Secondly, the book engages in thinking about how contemporary contexts for young people have an impact on psychotherapy. As introduced earlier in this chapter, unprecedented social changes have transformed the social and cultural worlds young people live in and created new contexts for development, including the impacts of diverse ethnicities, different approaches to gender and sexuality and the presence of an online virtual world which is important for many young people. How social changes impact the adolescent developmental process and changes in conceptualising adolescent subjectivity are crucial areas that require new integrations of theory for practice. Applications of theories of development, from psychoanalysis and social theories, and their impact on thinking and inter-ventions is an important, and exciting, new development in psychotherapy for young people. How the development of subjectivity – probably a better term to use than 'identity' in these contexts – can be understood and worked with has wider implications for practice and continues to develop my earlier discussions of this subject (Briggs 2008).

Thirdly, discussion of the approach of TAPP leads to consideration of adoles-cent psychotherapy as a distinctive method with specific skills and techniques.

Working with the adolescent developmental process in the therapeutic process is a critical aspect for adolescent psychotherapy. The therapeutic relationship holds adolescent conflicts about becoming more separate from adult figures, anxieties about dependency and being close to others. Understanding anxieties, how young people communicate them, and defences against the pains of development is only really possible within a framework where the developmental process is held centrally in mind. This has to be related to thinking about risks and the new contexts for adolescence, and to working with parents. The skills, knowledge and understanding needed for this work can easily be lost, when adolescence is subsumed within child or adult structures in organisations. A significant amount of knowledge about adolescent psychotherapy has been gained over time, and this benefits from being thought about, reviewed and reconsidered.

Fourthly, as adolescent psychotherapy continues to develop with changing contexts and aims, developments within psychoanalytic thinking and clinical practice are contributing to new ways of working. One important strand of this is the emergence of new thinking about subjectivity in the analytic process, which, to an extent, transcends previous demarcation lines, or 'schools.' Alongside major differences, there are points of correspondence between post-Kleinian, Independent (following Winnicott) and Lacanian thinking about the growth of subjectivity in psychotherapy; thinking across different schools of thought enriches and opens possibilities for new and more effective ways of working. The discussion here draws on White (2007), in particular, and her description of the movement within psychoanalytic practice towards process models of mind and self, more open concepts of subjectivity and the conceptualisation of the psychoanalytic process as "a dynamic interchange between two engaged subjects in which new and unexpected configurations and development may emerge" (White 2007, p. 203). Cahn's (1998) exploration of the Lacanian idea of subjectification (becoming a subject) adds to a thinking about the adolescent process that resonates with the question of developing subjectivity in contemporary society. The work of Britton, Ogden, Benjamin and Ferro are noted particularly as having developed new aspects of thinking about the therapeutic relationship and the transference–counter-transference field. There is affinity between these ideas and the priorities of TAPP, that is, emphasis on the relational and intersubjective, a therapeutic process that starts with understanding the differences in the room, and what is always an inter-generational therapy. These ideas help to articulate processes in TAPP and adolescent psychotherapy and contribute to the development of the theory and practice of TAPP.

Outline of the book

The book is structured in two parts. Part I consists of three chapters that form the conceptual, underpinning framework for TAPP. Each of these chapters develops one of the key areas discussed above. First, Chapter 2 reviews the development of brief psychodynamic psychotherapy; primarily, this is about adult psychotherapy, and the relevance of these methods for working with young people needs to be considered. The most important contributions by Malan, Balint, Mann, Davanloo, Strupp and Binder, and Stadter are discussed; from these have developed the key parameters for brief psychotherapy: aims, focus, technique, selection of patients and how to handle termination. Differences of approach and how these influence the practice of brief and time-limited therapy are discussed and related to accounts of current practice. Recent developments in psychoanalytic practice and theory open up new ways of conceptualising the aims, methods and scope of time-limited therapy.

Chapter 3 explores thinking about adolescence; taking as the starting point that adolescence has both enduring aspects and aspects that are new with every generation, the chapter explores the development of current thinking about adolescence. This entails discussion of how psychoanalytic thinking, as it has developed over time, theorises the adolescent process; it also entails drawing upon social theories to make sense of the psychosocial nature of adolescence and to assist thinking about the changing nature of the transition to adulthood, diversity, new ways of experiencing the body, including sex and sexuality, and relating through online and social media. The aim is to understand the meaning and implications of these changes and how they have an impact on developing subjectivity during adolescence.

Chapter 4 discusses the development of adolescent psychotherapy. It explores how psychotherapy with young people has developed over time starting with classical psychoanalytic sources: Anna Freud, Donald Winnicott and Moses Laufer. It explores key tensions and dilemmas in current theory and practice, including consideration of what is distinctive and different in psychotherapy with young people. The important considerations of thinking about assessing risks and working with parents are included here. Recent developments in psychoanalytic practice are discussed in relation to their implications for methods and aims in working with young people, and to how psychotherapy can be relevant for contemporary young people and take into account social changes.

In Part II, Chapters 5 to 11 provide a detailed study of TAPP aims, methods and practice. The chapters each describe a key aspect of the approach. Chapter 5 provides an overview of the aims and rationale. Chapters 6 and 7 focus on the assessment and engagement phase; Chapter 6 focuses on processes and the therapeutic relationship in this phase whilst Chapter 7 discusses identifying, discussing and agreeing on a developmental focus. The following four chapters discuss the treatment phase. Chapter 8 discusses therapeutic priorities with a detailed discussion of the therapeutic relationship and working with transference and counter-transference. This draws upon recent psychoanalytic thinking to elaborate understanding the tensions, aims and emotionality of the relationship. Chapter 9 discusses working with the developmental focus. Case examples, which illustrate throughout, are here particularly important for describing and explaining the interrelationship between the focus, the young person's development and the therapeutic relationship. Chapter 10 focuses on the important ending phase.

The dynamic potential for change in the ending phase is a key feature of TAPP, and means, often, working with and containing intense feelings and responses to separation and loss. Chapter 11 is a discussion of the kinds of growth and change that are experienced in TAPP and how these relate to the aim of TAPP in restoring and supporting the developmental process.

The aim is that the book forms a whole, in terms of locating the practice of time-limited psychotherapy with young people in its theoretical and practice contexts. Each chapter could be read individually, if preferred. The three conceptual chapters in Part I can be read as individual essays. Practitioners in training can use each of the chapters in Part II to work with the aspect of the TAPP process being described therein. The whole book is cross referenced.

A note on style

Reluctantly, but for clarity, and where the sense is generic, I have used the male pronoun when referring to young people in therapy, and therapists are referred to by the female pronoun, including in the case examples. There is tension over whether to use the term 'adolescent' or 'young person'; 'adolescent' can have a somewhat pejorative meaning, whilst its use is current in the context of services, as in 'child and adolescent mental health service.' To be inclusive of all in this age range, young people in adolescence and young adults, I have used the term 'young people.' 'Adolescent' is used to describe the developmental processes throughout the period, including for young adults. I refer to young people in therapy as 'patients,' rather than using other terms such as 'client' whilst recognising different usage in various settings. Neither term is satisfactory; 'patient' is passive and medicalised, whilst 'client' has a business sector tone.

Describing cases presents some complex difficulties descriptively and ethically. I have preferred where possible to illustrate processes in therapy through detailed description of interactions in therapy sessions, rather than summaries, as this gives an authentic flavour of the therapy. Protecting confidentiality and anonymity means that cases in the book are either fictionalised or composite; that is, they do not represent any one actual case but present a narrative taken from several in similar situations. Underpinning these cases, from which the descriptions are extrapolated, are actual cases, and the aim is to present these in a way that retains the authenticity of individual processes. Adolescent therapy involves specificities of time and place, gender, ethnicity, social class, education and family composition; however, the aim here has been to provide possibilities for replication and applicability by emphasising some frequently encountered experiences, dynamics and relationships. Approximately an equal number of cases of male and female case examples are provided.

Part I

Conceptual framework

Chapter 2

Time-Limited Psychodynamic Psychotherapy

History and current practice

And the stars we think we see on moonless nights
are long extinguished. And of course,
this very moment as you read this line,
is literally gone before you know it.

From The Present, Michael Donaghy (2014)

Where there is no time, there is no cause, and so, at depth, life is inconsequential.

David Bell (2007, p. 81)

Introduction: time, duration and the 'secret' of brief therapy

Time and duration are crucial and long-contested issues in psychoanalysis. The existential issue of passing time is related – perhaps obliquely at first glance – to the question of duration of psychotherapy. The questions of what can be done, in what way, on what time scale and at what costs and benefits are implicit, if not always explicit. All psychotherapy is time-limited, of course, though it is not always brief or short-term. David Malan, whose significant role in the development of time-limited psychotherapy is discussed below, asked "why is it that the secret of brief psychotherapy keeps getting lost?" (Malan 1963); being timely evaporates into timelessness. On the other hand, contemporary social demands for instant everything denigrate the value of taking one's time, not rushing and crafting something deeper and – possibly – more enduring. Michael Donaghy and David Bell, in different ways, are contributing to thinking about time passing, the contrast between living in time and timelessness, the problem of finity, the vitality of growth and development, and the inevitability of death. These existential – perhaps grand – themes underpin considerations about the duration of psychotherapy and its content, both brief and long-term.

Malan's puzzlement about the disappearing secret of brief therapy refers to the repeatedly contested views about the duration of psychotherapy. Malan's view was that changes in Freud's methods initiated longer therapies, through the adoption of 'free-floating attention,' which, as Freud described in Little Hans, meant taking an observational stance:

> ...not to try to understand everything at once but to give a kind of unbiased attention to every point that arises and await further developments.
>
> (Freud 1909, p. 207)

Neutrality and abstinence are required of the analyst to eschew conscious expectation – "memory and desire" as Bion (1970) later described it – to achieve the analytic position, and to avoid 'suggestion':

> ...the attitude which the analytic physician could most advantageously adopt was to surrender himself to his own unconscious mental activity, in a state of evenly suspended attention, to avoid so far as possible...the construction of conscious expectations...to catch the drift of the patient's unconscious with his own unconscious.
>
> (Freud 1923, p. 239)

For Malan, the whole edifice of psychotherapy became misconstrued:

> It needs to be stated categorically that in the early part of the [20th] century, Freud unwittingly took a wrong turn which led to disastrous consequences for the future of psychotherapy. This was to react to increasing resistance with increased passivity.
>
> (Malan & Osimo 1992, in Coren 2010, p. 12)

The analyst's passivity was thus felt to prevent purposeful therapeutic work, extend the duration of therapy and create therapeutic timelessness rather than face the reality of time (Mann 1973). Whether working with free association and free-floating attention constitutes passivity is highly questionable; the therapist's mind is, or ought to be, extremely active. Fuelling this controversy is the contradiction between Freud's views on technique and his experiences of doing brief psychotherapy, which were an analysis of Gustav Mahler in one session of four hours in 1908, Bruno Walter in five sessions, and 'Katharina' in one session (see Groves 1996, p. 507). Freud's disputes over technique with Rank and Ferenczi and the impact on analytic orthodox opinion of Alexander and French's (1946) methods for changing the therapeutic frame, with their 'principle of flexibility,' are key moments that have given impetus to brief psychotherapies. The subsequent development of brief therapies shows that the binary of the therapist's 'activity' and 'passivity' is not a decisive distinction between longer and shorter therapies, nor is the analytic position of free-floating attention incommensurate with time-limited work.

At the time that Malan and others were developing new approaches to brief therapy, there was significant opposition within psychoanalysis which favoured long-term psychotherapy. Malan has recently described the opposition he experienced from the British Psychoanalytic Society and within the Tavistock Clinic (Baker 2012), with the effect that brief therapy was starved of referrals. It is perhaps difficult to conceptualise this situation now, some 50 years later, when the converse is mainly true; longer-term work is viewed with suspicion in public health services, where brief methods based on diverse theoretical frameworks are widely practised and highly valued. These form a long list: Cognitive Behavioural Therapy (CBT) especially; Interpersonal Psychotherapy (IPT); Cognitive Analytic Therapy (CAT), which can be claimed as a psychodynamic model; Solution-Focussed Brief Therapy (SFBT); Dialectical Behaviour Therapy (DBT); and Schema-Focussed Therapy (SFT). Psychodynamic therapy has needed to develop brief models to compete and to survive. In the current contexts of evidence-based practice, and austerity, brief therapies are attractive; they meet "the social and economic needs of public and private mental health agencies" (Migone 2014, p. 643).

Evidencing the effectiveness of brief psychodynamic therapy gives reason to suggest that psychodynamic therapies can compete in this crowded field. The effectiveness of brief psychodynamic psychotherapy for adults has been evidenced through several studies. The most recent and comprehensive of these is the Cochrane systematic review and meta-analysis by Abbass et al (2014) of short-term psychodynamic psychotherapy which analysed data from 33 randomised controlled trials (RCTs). The studies included spanned a range of brief psychotherapy models: 11 were based on the Davanloo (1980)/Malan (1979/1995) model, and 6 used either Psychodynamic Interpersonal Therapy (PIT) (Guthrie & Moghavemi 2013) or a conversation model based on Hobson (1985). Other studies referenced the models of Mann (1973), and Strupp and Binder (1984). The number of sessions ranged from 4 to 40. Follow-up data extended from the end of treatment to four years later.

From a meta-analysis of the 33 studies, the review concludes that short-term psychodynamic psychotherapy "may be effective for a very broad range of common mental disorders, with evidence of modest to large treatment effect sizes that increase in long-term follow-up" (Abbass et al 2014, p. 20). Improvements were identified across a range of outcome measures that tested for psychiatric and somatic symptoms, depression, anxiety, interpersonal and social adjustment, reduced self-harm and weight gain in anorexia nervosa. As the authors found the quality of the research in the studies reviewed was variable, they conclude that caution needs to be exercised in interpreting these results.

The most significant developments in brief psychotherapy occurred during a highly productive period in the second half of the last century. On both sides of the Atlantic, between the mid-1950s and the 1980s, several distinctive approaches developed, principally those of Peter Sifneos (1972), David Malan (1963, 1976), Habib Davanloo (1978, 1980, 1990), James Mann (1973) and Hans Strupp and Jeffrey Binder (1984). These models remain key reference points for current practice. They showed that brief psychotherapy could be defined, and differentiated from longer-term therapy, and they establish the key parameters for the practice of brief therapy; the aims and constraints of brief therapy; the selection of suitable patients; the identification of a focus for intervention; the techniques that may differ from those used in long-term therapy; and how to work with the process of termination. There are two key issues when considering these approaches from the perspective of current practice. Firstly, though these models of brief psychotherapy contain some similar and overlapping features, there are also important differences between them. Secondly, though current brief psychotherapy relies on and has developed from these original approaches, current psychodynamic practice is significantly different from that at the time these models were being developed. Both these issues need exploration to understand current practices of brief psychodynamic psychotherapy. Therefore, in this chapter, I will discuss the development of brief psychodynamic psychotherapy by discussing the models developed by Malan, Mann, Davanloo and Strupp and Binder with emphasis on identifying what they have in common, and in what ways they differ. Secondly, I will assess how recent developments, especially in theorising the therapeutic relationship and therapeutic action, have influenced current practice of brief psychotherapy. Finally, I will summarise issues and priorities in current practice.

David Malan's 'radical' approach

Malan was a member of Michael Balint's focal psychotherapy workshop in the Tavistiock Clinic's Adult Department in the 1950s; later he led the Brief Psychotherapy Workshop (Baker 2012, p. 30). His scientific background – he had been a research chemist – gave him a leaning towards empiricism and a contemporary-sounding emphasis on outcome; he "painstakingly gathered, collated, researched and presented evidence for the validity of brief psychodynamic psychotherapy" (Baker 2012, p. 26) and reported both successful and unsuccessful outcomes.

Malan described two approaches to brief psychotherapy, which he called conservative and radical. The conservative approach eschewed making interpretations, especially of the negative transference, for fear of leaving the patient with an unresolved transference neurosis. However, the cases seen in the Brief Therapy Workshop showed that working in depth was possible and was not damaging. The full range of psychoanalytic techniques was used with these patients, including transference interpretations. This was "a radical technique of brief therapy leading to radical outcome" (Malan 1976, p. 351), which aimed to "resolve either the patient's central problem or at least an important aspect of his psychopathology" (Malan 1976, p. 248).

This radical – and ambitious – aim had implications for the selection of patients and the identification of a focus for therapy. Malan's model is amongst the more exclusive for patient selection (Stadter 2009). Key factors for inclusion, based on the findings of the two studies (Malan 1963, 1976), were the patient's motivation for insight and his capacity to make use of the interpretive method that Malan favoured. A crucial part of the assessment process was to offer a 'trial interpretation,' which aimed to deepen rapport, to assess the patient's capacity to use interpretations and to test hypotheses about the patient's difficulties (Malan 1976, p. 252).

Malan's study of the cases seen in the Brief Therapy Workshop showed that the technique used in radical brief therapy involved all the interpretations used in analysis, "including interpretation of dreams and fantasies, analysis of resistance, interpretation of the transference and the link between the transference and childhood" (Malan 1976, p. 47). Interpretations had to be used appropriately; Malan emphasised the importance of timing and cautioned against making interpretations before the transference has developed (Malan 1976, p. 261), and against ill-chosen, badly timed interpretations, that is, ones that "face the patient with feelings he is not ready to cope with" (ibid, p. 252). The privileging of interpretations does not equate to the frequency of making them; Migone (2014, p. 644) gives an example: "I can recall a videotape of a brief therapy conducted by Malan, who remained completely silent for most of a session." Malan's emphasis on activity – contrasting what he thought was analytic passivity – was guided by the need for intensity: "The aim of every moment of every session is to put the patient in touch with as much of his true feelings as he can bear" (Malan 1979/1995, p. 74).

Malan and Sifneos: motivation and focus

Peter Sifneos (1967, 1972) reached conclusions similar to those of Malan about motivation and patient selection, though working independently in Boston. Sifneos developed two approaches to brief psychotherapy, called 'anxiety-provoking' and 'anxiety-suppressing.' Anxiety-provoking brief therapy, which has similarities to Malan's radical approach, aimed to achieve deep change for some carefully selected patients who demonstrated motivation for change and who were assessed as having sufficient strengths to withstand the rigours of the method. Sifneos, like Malan, used repeated assessment interviews to assess motivation (Groves 1996, p. 402).

Sifneos worked with a narrow focus: problems in mourning a death, Oedipal issues manifesting as conflicts in triangular love relationships or inability to complete projects because of fear of success (Groves 1996, p. 5). Despite the restricted focus, the aim of solving emotional problems gave the patient a learning experience that was transferable, after the therapy ended, to emotional problems experienced beyond the focus of the therapy. Sifneos discussed the focus and the educational aim of the therapy explicitly with the patient at the beginning of therapy to obtain his agreement (Sifneos 1968; Malan 1976, p. 33). This collaborative approach and learning from the experience – we might now say its internalisation – have become important factors within current brief therapy approaches. In contrast, Malan would "hold the focus without explicitly defining it for the patient" (Groves 1996, p. 5). The focus is identified by the therapist as "some circumscribed aspect of psychopathology, formulated in terms of a basic interpretation, which it seems feasible to try and work through in a short time" (Malan 1976, p. 256). The therapist then assesses the patient's ability to think of his problems in emotional terms, his strength to face disturbing material, his response to interpretations and the motivation to face the stress of therapy (Malan 1976, p. 256).

Malan was to an extent ambivalent about the use of the term 'focus.' He preferred to think about planning a therapy and the need for the therapist to be active in defined ways, to avoid what he thought of as the passivity of longer-term work. Initially, the therapist is active in planning a limited aim for the therapy; in the sessions with the patient, the therapist is active in 'guiding' the patient, through "selective interpretation, selective attention and selective neglect" (Malan 1976, p. 32). Malan endeavoured to address the problem of the tendency towards the conservative or 'superficial' approach to brief therapy, which risks losing the possibility of working with "deeper foci" (Malan 1976, p. 37). Malan used French's term, 'nuclear conflict,' to indicate working with greater depth; he identified cases where the patient's nuclear conflict was formulated at the Oedipal level but permitted deep work within a short time scale. One example was a case called the "Neurasthenic's Husband," where in the 13th and penultimate session, the therapist interprets the (paternal) transference in depth in relation to the impending termination; the patient is demonstrably moved by the new understanding that he experiences (Malan 1976, pp. 35–36).

Malan and Balint: interpretative and non-interpretive techniques

Michael Balint, Malan's mentor, has been accredited with the "intuitive brilliance" that was complemented by Malan's systematic, scientific approach; there was an undercurrent of tension between the two (Gustafson 1981). Balint's contributions to the development of brief therapy grew from his analytic work on regression (Balint 1979) and his work with GPs that led to the development of 'Balint groups' (Balint 1957). Because of the importance to the subsequent development of brief therapy, it is important to include Balint's contributions here. In comparison with Malan's interpretive centred approach, Balint had a different view of therapeutic action based on interpersonal relatedness.

Balint was significantly influenced by Ferenczi, his fellow Hungarian and analyst; most accounts of the origins of brief psychotherapy identify the importance of Ferenczi (Coren 2010; Groves 1996; Stadter 2009). As Balint (1979) recounts in detail, Ferenczi had a significant disagreement with Freud over technique and method. Ferenczi advocated an active technique, through which, to speed up the analytic process at certain points in an analysis, the aim was to expose the patient to situations that increased tensions and thus stimulated the emergence of repressed material. In Ferenczi's later work, the emphasis switched from activity to the 'principle of relaxation,' which meant responding positively to the patient's expectations and needs, once these had been understood. Ferenczi's innovations conflicted with Freud's position on technique, summarised as the 'principle of abstinence' (Freud 1912), in which the analyst was cautioned to maintain sympathetic objectivity and interpret the transference. Ferenczi thought that deeply distressed or disturbed patients needed actively expressed support and encouragement; remote objectivity could retraumatise them (Coren 2010, p. 22).

Balint's approach to identifying the focus for brief work was different from Malan's. Balint juxtaposed the systematic way of forming a focus, as described by Malan, with an intuitive component based on his 'flash technique' developed through his work with GPs. Balint considered Malan's discussion of the focus as gradually emerging, until it crystallised, through the joint work of the patient and therapist to be partially, but not wholly, accurate. A second method was the tuning in, a flash of understanding, like a meeting of two minds, that could be put concisely into words (Balint et al 1972, p. 151). Balint emphasised "interpersonal flexibility and existential staying-with-the-patient" (Gustafson 1981, p. 89). The very detailed discussion of the patient Mr Baker, in Balint et al (1972), who is also discussed by Malan as 'the stationery manufacturer' (Malan 1976, p. 305ff), demonstrates Balint's way of working through understanding and accepting the patient's projections. A simple example is that in the second session, Balint told the patient that his feelings were important, and he could use Balint as a "sounding board."

> …in order that his fleeting ideas, fantasies, and emotions should be reflected back to him so that instead of vanishing into limbo they should make some impression upon him
>
> (Balint et al 1972, p. 23, quoted in Smith 2006, p. 267)

Psychic change comes from the experience of the therapist's handling of these experiences. This draws on and has some similarities with Alexander and French's (1946) "corrective emotional experience," and foreshadows later developments in object relations and interpersonal psychotherapy, as well as brief therapy applying this approach.

Malan triangles

Malan's enduring legacy is the method of working with the 'Malan triangles.' He claimed only that he brought together the two triangles: Ezriel's (1952) triangle of conflict and Menninger's (1958) triangle of insight; he preferred the term 'triangle of person' for the latter, as he thought both were triangles of insight (Malan 1979/1995, p. 90). The triangle of conflict consists of defence, anxiety and hidden feeling, or impulse. The triangle of person represents three links: past relationship (usually parent or sibling) to present relationship with another (O/P link); past relationship to transference relationship (T/P link); and present/other to transference (O/T link). The triangles stood on an apex to represent the aim of reaching beneath the defence and anxiety to access the hidden feeling and trace this back to its origin in the past. The two triangles account for "almost every intervention that a therapist makes" (Malan 1979/1995, p. 91) and the skill is in working out which parts of the triangle to include in any interpretation. The therapist therefore works with the matrix of both triangles, in each moment of each session:

> The strategic aims of psychoanalytic therapy can therefore be stated relatively simply as (1) to clarify the nature of the defence, the anxiety and the impulse, (2) to clarify this in all three main areas: current, past and transference, and (3) to make links among these three areas.
>
> (Malan 1976, p. 260)

Though primarily developed within Malan's use of the Freudian paradigm, it can be applied using other approaches; for example, Hinshelwood (1995), from a Kleinian perspective, discusses a triangle of three kinds of object relationship: the current life situation, the infantile object relations and the transference relationship. The potential for using the two triangles to consider the quality of relationships and relatedness makes them applicable, to an extent, in interpersonal and object-relational approaches. They constitute an organising principle for the method developed by Davanloo, Intensive Short-Term Dynamic Psychotherapy (ISTDP) and his "second generation" followers, and are found too in the object relations theory of Stadter (2009), discussed later in this chapter.

Termination and time limit

Malan had an uncomplicated approach to termination. Experiences in the Brief Therapy Workshop led to his preference of setting a time limit from the beginning as an end date, rather than as a set number of sessions. He thought the advantages of this were that there was no need to keep count of the sessions, and it "removes at one stroke all sorts of complications to do with whether or not to make up sessions that were missed, and having to judge whether absences were due to reality or to acting out" (Malan 1976, p. 257). The length of therapy was usually 20 sessions, though this was extended to 30 for trainees to give "opportunity to make up for mistakes that may hold up the work for several sessions" (ibid); but Malan thought there was "no special magic in any particular number of sessions" (1976, p. 40).

Setting a time limit from the beginning "highlights the termination issue from the very beginning" and this is "beneficial." Working with the transference and having the confidence to use transference interpretations facilitate working through the patient's anger and disappointment. Malan offered informal follow-up sessions after the end of the therapy, wherever possible. He argued this was not clinically harmful, as "to [the patient's] unconscious the last regular session is the end of the relationship" (Malan 1976, p. 41). In this respect, he disagreed with James Mann, as is discussed below.

The different emphases of Malan and Balint are picked up in other contributions to the development of brief therapy. The classical psychoanalytic approach is found in Davanloo's work, whilst the interpersonal and object relations perspectives of Mann and the Vanderbilt group, Strupp and Binder, have points of connection with Balint. The object relations approach of Stadter explicitly combines both.

James Mann: time, separation and termination

Mann's Time-Limited Psychotherapy (TLP) consists of two key constructs: the concept of time and a focus on what he called the *central issue*, or core problem, of the patient's "present and chronically endured pain." The model consists of 12 sessions exactly, with no follow-up. It has therefore "a specific structural framework with a precise, predetermined goal and a predetermined time limit that is the same in each case" (Mann 1991, p. 26).

Mann turned to time-limited methods in 1962, when, in the Boston University School of Medicine, there was an increasing waiting list for patients for psychotherapy. Cases were routinely seen on an open-ended basis; as many were seen by residents in training and on rotation, patients experienced changes of therapist twice a year. He found that as patients appeared unperturbed by changes of therapist the transference to the institution appeared to be more significant than to the therapist. Thus, experiences of separation and loss were absorbed in the institution and patients' dependency needs were gratified. Mann's time-limited model thus aimed pragmatically to reduce waiting lists and to address, rather than avoid, experiences of separation for therapists and patients in ending therapy.

Time

The concept of time is one of Mann's key concepts; in time-limited therapy, "the meaning of time is the lever that motivates and moves the patient" (Mann 1996, p. 78). Time-limited therapy addresses both child and adult time. Child time is subject to omnipotent fantasies of timelessness, the timelessness of the unconscious, and the pleasure principle. Adult time is that of the reality principle, finite and leading inexorably to death, as symbolised by familiar images of death as Old Father Time, a grinning skeleton with a scythe. As facing reality and death is difficult, there is a strong pull to "escape the strictures of time" and with it, reality: "time always represents the reality principle and the time to wake up is connected with the father" (Mann 1973, p. 4).

Mann used Winnicott's (1955) discussion of the infant's development of a sense of time in the depressive position, linked with weaning, and the capacity to let go of objects in contrast to the fantasies of never separating, of the mother and infant being endlessly united. The concept of time is therefore a cause of internal conflict; resistance to the realities of adult time by the unconscious pleasure of timelessness is linked to painful experiences of separation. Whilst the reality of the ticking clock – categorical time – is a physical experience, psychological time can expand or contract according to age and mood. In adolescence, time appears to move slowly, whilst in adulthood, it races away; the sense of duration is relative. Memories of good experiences and loved objects, and the capacity to mourn, established initially through the experience of weaning, can provide individuals with internal resources that sustain the capacity to face reality. Mann suggests that all shortened forms of therapy revive the "horror of time," whether or not practitioners recognise it. In time-limited therapy, Mann links the sense of time, and its limits, to experiences of separation and the termination of the therapy.

Mann's view of the meaning of time has similarities with other accounts. Molnos makes time a central consideration of her discussion of brief psychotherapy, contrasting, like Mann, the childhood sense of timelessness with the adult "terror of time's arrow" (1995, p. 7). Stadter (2009) uses a similar duality, referring to "time near", or clock time, and "time far." Recent discussions of time and timelessness include Perelberg's (2007) book on time and memory, in which Bell contrasts feeling oneself existing in time, an important developmental achievement, with a sense of imminent catastrophe, which leads to the creation of a timeless world where nothing happens and time stands still (Bell 2007, p. 65). Bergson's concept of duration, of subjective time, is not linear as a clock ticking, but is a complex relational process of life, mixing together past and present, that also links time and memory (Guerlac 2006).

The question of time in Mann's time-limited psychotherapy relates closely to the duration of therapy, the process of termination, the focus, or *central issue*, and the selection of suitable patients. Patients are selected for the 12 weekly sessions on the basis that they have a capacity to tolerate separation and loss, and that the therapist has a "clear understanding of the patient's capacity to engage and disengage quickly" (Mann 1973, p. 40). This criterion cuts across diagnostic groups, and Mann includes some borderline patients, though usually these would be referred for long-term therapy after TLP. The purpose of TLP in these cases is to enable the patient to engage constructively in longer-term psychotherapy, to reduce defensive manipulation and effectively to speed up the initial processes of engagement that "often consumes one or two years of therapeutic groundwork" (Mann 1991, p. 12). Suitable patients are usually amongst the better functioning, in order to tolerate the brief engagement and the impact of termination. Patients will need to have sufficient ego strength to negotiate a treatment agreement and treatment schedule (Mann 1996, p. 79).

The central issue and termination

The focus for TLP, the central issue, in each case, consists of "the patient's chronic and presently endured pain" (Mann 1991, p. 19). The patient is trapped in time. The pain is experienced as always having been there, is there now and is expected to be there in the future; there is a "conviction that nothing about the self can change" (Mann 1991, p. 19). Mann's formulation of the central issue has similarities with the "core conflictual relationship theme" (Luborsky et al 1994) or the point of maximum pain (Hinshelwood 1995). Its formulation facilitates working towards deepening the capacity for intimacy and the toleration of separation and separateness. Time and the central issue:

> ...cannot help but bring to the forefront of the treatment process the major pain that human beings suffer, namely the wish to be as one with another but also the absolute necessity to learn how to tolerate separation and loss without undue damage to one's feelings about the self.
>
> (Mann 1973, p. 42)

In each case, the central issue is formulated as a short statement that links "time, affects and the negative image of the self" (Mann 1991, p. 23). The link with time is typically through a phrase like 'now and always'. Mann gives many examples, for example:

> You have had many difficult times in your life, and you have struggled quite successfully with them; however what hurts and has always hurt is your feeling that you have been cheated, and as a result you feel helpless.
>
> (1991, p. 39)

Throughout the TLP therapy, the therapist aims to maintain the focus on the central issue and will interrupt when the patient moves away from this. The therapist is urged to deal "insistently" with the patient's reactions to termination in the last three or four sessions, when "the definitive work of resolution" of the central issue takes place, through understanding the dynamic events and the feelings accompanying these, in fantasy and behaviour, in sadness, grief, anger and guilt: "The central issue is experienced *in vivo* within the transference and must be resolved as much as possible" (Mann 1991, p. 38). Resolution is through interpretation, using the Malan triangles, in "living, existential terms" (ibidibid) relating to relationships in the past and present, and in the therapeutic relationship.

Mann emphasised the painful difficulties of termination for both patient and therapist, in all therapies and especially in time-limited therapy: it is "intensely affect-laden" (1996, p. 90). Acutely, Mann draws attention to the parallel unconscious experience of the therapist facing, like the patient, a separation without resolution. Mann signals the importance of counter-transference reactions that

> ...press towards a reluctance to fully face the termination process or even towards actions which will serve to continue the treatment and not bring it to its agreed upon end. The patient is the major loser if this happens.
>
> (1973, p. 41)

It is "absolutely incumbent" on the therapist to deal with all painful aspects of the ending; by doing so the patient can internalise the therapist as more positive than the original ambivalent object. This moves the experience of separation from one that is unbearable and must be defended against to one which is "a genuine maturational event" (Mann 1996, p. 91). For the patient, a satisfactory ending is one in which he feels sad: "sadness in place of depression allows for separation without self-injury" (1991, p. 39). The potential for growth and development is located in working with the ending and the depressive feelings that can ensue, and with which the patient can leave the therapy.

Davanloo and Intensive Short-Term Dynamic Psychotherapy

Intensive Short-Term Dynamic Psychotherapy is almost the converse of Mann's TLP; it has no time limit, it does not work through termination, there are few restrictions on selecting suitable patients in terms of diagnostic categories and its techniques are distinctly different, including its own version of transference and the virtual absence of discussion of counter-transference. Davanloo (1980, 1990, 2000) divides opinion; his method excited Malan (1979/1995), who said, "Freud discovered the unconscious and Davanloo discovered how to use it therapeutically" (Osimo & Stein 2012, p. 12). In his later work, Malan adopted Habib Davanloo's approach and subsequently collaborated with some of Davanloo's followers, notably Patricia Coughlin Della Selva (Malan & Coughlin Della Selva 2006) and Ferrucio Osimo (Malan & Osimo 1992). Undeniably, Davanloo has had a significant and widespread influence on the practice of short-term psychotherapy, but his methods have been criticised as confrontational and abrasive (Baker 2012), and as using "bulldozer techniques":

> What can be seen as potentially disquieting is the frequent repetition of an interpretation until the patient is ground into submission and agrees with the therapist.
>
> (Coren 2010, p. 36)

Davanloo's method involves the early detection of manifestations of resistance and the repeated focus on the patient's defences of vagueness, passivity and withdrawal, in order to "unlock the unconscious" (Davanloo 1990, p. 217). His method can indeed appear abrasive, especially when his work is accessed through reading excerpts from transcripts of video recorded sessions. However, more detailed reading of whole sessions in Davanloo's transcripts, or seeing and hearing the video itself, can modify this impression. Molnos (1995, p. 50) suggests that there is a contrast between the audible warmth of the words and their brusqueness on the printed page; this combination can, however, sow confusion or promote manipulation.

The patient is divided in Davanloo's view; a part of him resists treatment, whilst another part wants to be better, and this latter part makes an "unconscious therapeutic alliance" (Davanloo 2000). Whilst Davanloo's focus on the resistance and the defences has a relentless quality (he referred to himself as a "relentless healer" [Strupp & Binder 1984, p. 19]), the therapeutic alliance holds the patient through communicating respect and care. Thus, there is a sense of collaboration between the patient and therapist working together on the defences. Coughlin Della Selva described this duality as:

> The therapist communicates the utmost care and respect for the patient as a human being, whilst maintaining an attitude of disrespect and intolerance for the defences that cripple the patient's functioning and perpetuate his suffering.
>
> (Malan & Coughlin Della Selva 2006, p. 19)

The procedure involved a technique for the "rapid uncovering or unlocking of the unconscious" (Davanloo 1990, p. 217), by following a "central dynamic sequence." This involved using pressure to elicit how the patient resists and defends against directly experiencing emotions. This will "intensify intrapsychic conflicts, generate complex transference feelings and speed up the process of therapy" (Malan & Coughlin Della Selva 2006, p. 19). Davanloo (1990, p. 219) describes the sequence as more like a spiral than a linear process, adapted to meet the needs of different patients. Coughlin Della Selva (2006, p. 26) suggests that for highly responsive patients, the process mobilises the "healing forces" (unconscious therapeutic alliance) and leads to direct experience of feelings towards loved others that have hitherto been avoided. In most patients, the process results in intense, complex transference feelings, and the "crystallisation of resistance" (ibid), which is addressed through a "head-on collision." It is in this phase that the therapist uses "very loaded language" (Malan & Coughlin Della Selva 2006, p. 26), which is designed to point out to the patient that the resistance aims to defeat the therapy. Whilst the ethics of the approach and the ensuing power relations may – at least – be questioned, there are clearly some patients for whom this approach would be damaging, rather than provoking. It must be noted that Davanloo was not reckless; he assessed the capacity of the patient to withstand the confrontation with the resistance from the beginning, and his use of the "spiral" of the central dynamic sequence in the trial therapy shows him responding to the patient's anxiety with rapidly tuned sensitivity.

The method, which has become known as Intensive Short-Term Dynamic Psychotherapy (ISTDP), claims, firstly, to bring about significant internal or structural changes, and secondly to be applicable to a wide range of patients. Unlike almost all other brief psychotherapy, no time limit is set. The patient is seen until the work was concluded, with both symptomatic and dynamic changes. ISTDP lasts between two and 40 sessions, depending on the patient's pathology. Termination is not viewed as problematic; issues can be addressed quickly; there is no need for working through the termination. ISTDP aims to be inclusive in its approach to selecting suitable patients. In his earlier work, Davanloo thought that motivation and ego strength were important factors when assessing suitability for ISTDP.

He changed his views, which he dates from the late 1970s. From this time, he thought that therapists who could not treat "highly resistant complex patients" sheltered behind the criterion of motivation (Groves 1996, p. 378).

Malan (1979/1995, p. 283) was disappointed in his hope that Davanloo's method would revolutionise psychotherapy; he put this down to the therapists':

> ...mistaken idea...they needed to imitate Davanloo's idiosyncratic and abrasive style exactly – which was far from suiting everyone's personality.
> (Malan, quoted in Osimo 2003, p. xi)

Thus, what was needed was "a technique incorporating some of his discoveries which is applicable to a wider range of therapists" (Malan 1995, p. 284). Some therapists continue to follow Davanloo's method as well as his "metapsychology of the unconscious," for example, Hickey (2017); others have adapted the method (Malan & Coughlin Della Selva 2006; Fosha 2000; Osimo 2003). Therefore, a second generation of ISTDP practitioners has now developed different ways of working with resistance, so that whilst maintaining the overall aims of ISTDP, of unlocking the unconscious through actively working on the defences and resistance to emotional experience, they have developed their own styles and methods.

The Vanderbilt group: an interpersonal approach to time-limited psychotherapy

The version of time-limited psychotherapy developed by the Vanderbilt group (Strupp & Binder 1984) is important to consider here because the interpersonal approach that characterised the work of this group provides a different approach to brief psychotherapy than has been considered so far, and it is one which prefigures many future developments. This difference of approach is indicated by its more recent development, in the "third generation" of brief therapy theorists (Stadter 2009). The method draws on Harry Stack Sullivan's (1953) theory of personal relationships, object relations theory, especially through Kernberg (1976), general systems theory (Bateson 1972; Haley 1973; Watzlawick et al 1974) and Spence's (1982) narrative approach: "in [Time-Limited Dynamic Psychotherapy] (TLDP) the patient and therapist are engaged in a joint narration and re-narration of the central interpersonal dilemmas of the patient's life" (Strupp & Binder 1984, p. 69).

Sullivan, in particular, influenced the development of Interpersonal Therapy (IPT) (Klerman et al 1984) and, more recently, Dynamic Interpersonal Therapy (DIT) (Lemma et al 2011). But here, in the work of Strupp and Binder, it is a psychodynamic psychotherapy because it draws on early relationships to understand current interpersonal interactions; it emphasises internal relationships, especially object relationships but also fantasy and dreams, and working with transference and counter-transference is integral to the therapeutic method. It makes use of what Strupp and Binder call "newer conceptions of transference and counter-transference," and the approach to counter-transference is significantly different from other brief therapies discussed thus far. The time-limited model, Time-Limited Dynamic Psychotherapy (TLDP), articulated and practised by this group took account of other brief psychotherapy models, including Sifneos, Mann, Malan and Davanloo, and the work of Alexander and French (1946).

The therapist's stance

The term 'stance' is used to describe the therapist's activity and orientation to time-limited psychotherapy; it encompasses values, beliefs and attitudes, as well as techniques, to provide a complete contrast – antithesis even – to Davanloo's method. Whilst disagreeing with Carl Rogers that the relationship is all, the Vanderbilt approach does hold to the healing power of a good relationship (Strupp & Binder 1984, p. 139); the therapist's activities provide patients with a new and direct experience in relatedness. There are affinities, too, with Fromm; the operating principle for therapy is that "hidden behind the patient's anxieties and self-protective mechanisms lies the hope of a loving and supportive relationship in which one is understood," so the aim is to be "maximally constructive, minimally destructive" (Strupp and Binder 1984, p. 41). This depends on receptivity, respect for the patient and empathy. Confrontation can be valuable but is not to be confused with "overtly pushing, badgering, controlling, exhorting or indoctrinating the patient" (ibid, p. 68). Achieving collaboration between patient and therapist is an important objective. The therapist keeps in mind two questions: "How can I best understand the inner world of the other person?" and "What might be the most constructive intervention at this time?" (ibid p. 41).

Psychotherapy should provide a new and constructive interpersonal experience for the patient (ibid, p. 138) which is accomplished through the analysis of transference and counter-transference in the here-and-now (ibid, p. 139). With echoes of Balint, Strupp (1996, p. 280) thought that the mutative effect of transference interpretation was overrated; it was not so much the interpretation but the whole and cumulative experience of the constructive aspects of the therapeutic experience that was mutative: "what matters is not what the therapist says, but what the patient carries away from the interaction with the therapist" (Strupp and Binder 1984, p. 139). Therefore, working with the transference relationship is the central 'technique' in TLDP in order to understand the affective and relational themes that "unconsciously govern the patient's life" (ibid, p. 145). Transference is seen as:

> ...the enactment of certain internal structured role relationships around which the patient's life is organised and which in turn colour experiences of self and the world.
>
> (ibid, p. 148)

The relational understanding of transference has its counterpart in the way TLDP conceives counter-transference. Groves (1996, p. 250) noted that counter-transference was not often written about in the literature of short-term therapy, and, he adds, "where it is, the quality of the discourse (except by Mann) tends to be mediocre." Strupp and Binder introduce into brief therapy, via the work of Kernberg (1976), the meaning of counter-transference developed by Heimann (1950) and Racker (1968), in which the patient evokes in the therapist aspects of his internal world. Strupp and Binder stop short of attributing this to the mechanism of projective identification, but they conclude that in TLDP the patient and therapist are always "entwined" as "co-participants who are reciprocally influenced by the affective restrictions placed on the relationship by the patient's conflictual modes of relatedness" (Strupp and Binder 1984, p. 148). Thus, the concept of counter-transference should be broadened to:

> ...encompass those therapist actions and reactions (including attitudes and behaviour as well as thoughts feelings and fantasies) that are evoked by the patient's transference enactments.
>
> (ibid, p. 149)

The dynamic focus

In TLDP a dynamic focus is identified in assessment sessions that establish the interpersonal, relational way of working and encourage the patient to relax and explore issues in depth. Assessment is seen as a therapeutic experience in itself (ibid, p. 134), and its purpose (but not its methods) can be compared to the trial interventions of Malan and Davanloo. The dynamic focus is a heuristic device (ibid, p. 21): "a focus does not explain everything: it is a map, not the territory itself" (ibid, p. 105). The dynamic focus is arrived at collaboratively with the patient, as is consistent with the overall approach in TLDP:

> ...the focus ought not to be imposed by the therapist; this would contravene the basic principles of TTDP by augmenting the patient's dependency on a powerful authority figure.
>
> (ibid, p. 67)

The dynamic focus consists of four structural elements, which are called acts of self, expectations about others' reactions, acts of others towards self and acts of self towards self (introject). The process of identifying the focus consists of two steps: firstly, to gather information about recurrent patterns of interpersonal transactions from the flow of the therapeutic dialogue and, secondly, using the four structural elements "to sort, interpret, organise, and assemble these raw data about interpersonal transactions into a coherent outline of a repetitive problematic interpersonal transaction pattern" (ibid, p. 79).

Suitability for TLDP was decided through making an 'interpersonal diagnosis,' understanding how presenting difficulties in cognitive, emotional and behavioural functions are rooted in disturbed interpersonal relationships. Criteria for selection for TLDP are described as the patient having emotional discomfort suitable for psychotherapy; having basic trust; being willing to consider conflicts in interpersonal terms; being willing to examine feelings; and having some capacity for mature relationships. Effectively TLDP is suitable for reasonably well-functioning adults; the case examples which Strupp and Binder use extensively to illustrate their approach show individuals with a capacity to enter into the collaborative process of psychotherapy, which constitutes the essence of the approach.

Time limit and termination

TLDP evolved to consist of 25 weekly sessions, with the time limit set at the beginning of the therapy. Initially, the approach was quite laissez-faire about termination; in the collaborative spirit, a negotiation took place about when to end. Unlike Mann, Strupp and Binder saw "no harm in granting two or three additional sessions," but "there should be no ambiguity about the necessity of exposing the patient to the pain of separation and its aftermath" (1984, p. 257). Working through the relational and interpersonal aspects of the ending in the transference and counter-transference was particularly important, and difficult for both patient and therapist. The threat of separation involved the replaying and enactment of "old problems" (ibid, p. 264).

Current practice of brief psychodynamic psychotherapy

Current practice of brief psychotherapy reflects developments within different psychoanalytic theoretical approaches. They include classical, Freudian psychoanalytic methods, exemplified by applications of Davanloo's method (Hickey 2017), and a range of developing and emerging applications that take account of recent thinking, especially from the perspective – very broadly speaking – of relational, interpersonal and object relations approaches. Aims and desired or expected outcomes reflect changed thinking about therapeutic action, and the contexts in which brief therapy is practised, as has been noted earlier in this chapter, are now characterised by the availability of different modalities of psychological therapies and by emphasis on evidenced outcomes. Reaching out to and providing effective therapy for a wider range of people has also demanded that therapy, delivered within time limits, is offered more inclusively. In these contexts, the relationship between brief psychodynamic psychotherapy and long-term therapy have changed from the earlier antagonism – though this does continue to be a tension within psychoanalytic practice (Stadter 2009) – to become more complementary and interdependent.

Just as Davanloo, on the one hand, and Strupp and Binder, on the other hand, proposed approaches based on different theoretical and, perhaps, philosophical views, so in current practice these mirror, in effect, a division between 'classical' and relational/interpersonal approaches. Davanloo's method, as currently practised (Hickey 2017; Malan & Coughlin Della Selva 2006), best exemplifies the continuing practice based on the classical theory of repression, the uncovering of repressed emotion or conflicts by aiming to remove the crippling effects of defences. Critiques of the method led to the 'softening' of Davanloo's method and in Osimo's experiential method (Osimo & Stein 2012) it embraces a more relational theory of psychopathology and therapeutic change.

Others, who can be thought of as following the interpersonal approach of Strupp and Binder, have developed brief therapy approaches that account for changes in thinking about the therapeutic relationship and the nature of therapeutic action. This includes applying Winnicott's ideas of 'holding,' which supports the infant's sense of 'going on being' by being in the infant's 'otherness of time' (Ogden 2004, p. 1350), and Bion's container–contained relationship (Bion 1962), to extend the thinking that the therapist's emotional experience in the counter-transference is informative of the patient's state of mind. The patient communicates unbearable emotional experiences through projective identification; the therapist is receptive to these through 'reverie,' takes them in and makes sense of them, and returns them to the patient in modified, detoxified, more manageable form. The patient then internalises the named emotion together with the therapist's capacity for thinking about emotional experiences. Reverie, the therapist's ability to make sense of the patient's inchoate feelings, means being able to tolerate 'not knowing' or not reaching conclusions prematurely about the meaning.

There are several key reference points for the theoretical changes that have developed from within these different schools of thought (White 2007; Lemma 2015a): Daniel Stern's (2004) theory of implicit relational knowing, with the emphasis on change through 'now moments' or moments of meeting, rather than on interpretation; the different understanding of the Third by Ogden (1994) and Benjamin (1988); Benjamin's (2018) re-thinking of the therapeutic relationship, "beyond doer and done-to"; and Britton's (1998) concept of the third position. Benjamin's thinking about the therapeutic relationship, in particular, provides a challenge to the practice of brief psychotherapy; the process of recognition of the other moves "us out of tendencies towards control and submission" (Benjamin 2018, p. 78). Here there arises a stark choice; whereas Davanloo's supporters emphasise that the outcomes justify the means of the relentlessness of the method, for Benjamin, and other relational/interpersonal theorists, real therapeutic change depends on the means, that is, the engagement with the nature of the relationship itself, based on beliefs in and practice of mutual recognition. Emphasis on therapeutic action as consisting of processes of creating meaning, leading to narrative transformations and the development of symbolic capacity, posits the unconscious as to an extent emergent, or co-created, rather than pre-formed but hidden from sight and awareness (Ferro 2004; Donnel Stern 2010).

Though the implications of recent theorisation of the therapeutic process and relationships have not been fully discussed in the brief therapy literature, there are several accounts that explore aspects of these: Bravesmith 2010; Laor 2001; Coren 2010; Smith 2010; Lemma et al 2011 for the model of DIT; and Guthrie and Moghavemi 2013 for Psychodynamic Interpersonal Therapy (PIT). Probably the most comprehensive account is by Stadter (2009, 2016), who approaches brief therapy mainly from an object relations perspective. Stadter demonstrates the integration of recent theoretical approaches, especially concerning the therapeutic relationship, with the parameters of brief therapy established by the earlier generation of brief therapy theorists. He builds on the approach of Strupp and Binder, which he admires, and he also draws on Balint.

Stadter (2016) works from the basis that two kinds of unconscious co-exist; the dynamic unconscious, as described by Freud, which can be "revealed" behind defences, and the "implicit unconscious." The holding environment (Winnicott), containment through making sense of projective identification in the analytic field (Bion), and the therapeutic sense of self through affective attunement (Daniel Stern) are included in the therapist's stance. The aim of therapy is therefore "to collaborate with the patient in containing difficult mental states and the specific object relations that are enacted in the therapeutic encounter" (Stadter 2016, p. 434). Applying Ogden's (1994) thinking about the transference–countertransference matrix, that is, that these are not separate but mutually interpenetrating aspects of an unconscious field, Stadter sees therapeutic change flowing from the therapist's own internal adjustments to the experience of being with the patient. This relates to the use of 'reverie' (Bion) and 'moments of meeting' (Stern). The therapist's internal processing can facilitate change:

> …even when patterns cannot be interpreted in the brief therapy context, the therapist's awareness and internal processing, even when unspoken, can further the therapeutic process.
>
> (Stadter 2016, p. 435)

This echoes the idea that "something happens" (Kraemer 2006) when the therapist takes up a holding or containing stance; it is driven by working collaboratively with the patient towards understanding, and empathic communication. For the patient, being held in mind to detoxify painful and overwhelming feelings "can be a developmental experience, even if brief" (Stadter 2016, p. 435).

Making use of the parameters of brief therapy, Stadter works with time, termination and focus. The latter he conceives as consisting of symptomatic and dynamic aspects. The symptomatic is generally conscious and can be discussed from the start with the patient through engaging with the presenting problems and present suffering. The dynamic focus relates, as with Strupp and Binder, to internal patterns of relationships, and may emerge more slowly in the therapy. It is also possible that a dynamic focus may not be agreed on and the therapy will therefore be more supportive and aim for symptomatic relief rather than seek internal change. This has some affinity with the idea of Lemma et al. (2011) of the Interpersonal-Affective Focus (IPAF) in DIT, though here the aim is to develop the focus through a formulation and share this with the patient, rather like Malan's method, though with different content. Lemma also spells out the steps taken to identify and share the focus, and how it is informed by the counter-transference (ibid; see Chapter 7).

Stadter includes both of Sifneos' approaches to brief therapy; therapies may be simple, or complex, depending on the individual patient. He aims for inclusivity in patient selection (Stadter 2009, pp. 131–132), adapting the focus and aims to suit the individual patient, who is "approached with an attitude of not-knowing and hopeful discovery" (Stadter 2016, p. 435). Bravesmith (2010), drawing on Bion's notion of the 'selected fact' (Bion 1992), similarly emphasises the process of discovery in the focus; it articulates something the patient has not been able to think about previously, and it allows the therapist to take a position of not-knowing.

One of Stadter's case examples, which can be briefly described, illustrates the inclusion of recent thinking about the therapeutic relationship and therapeutic action, and the complex mental health and psychosocial predicaments faced by patients frequently seen now for brief psychodynamic psychotherapy. Diane, a 32-year-old mother of four, had experienced multiple traumas and abuse, and was suicidal, dissociated and fragmented. Additionally, she had been arrested for embezzlement and was both very worried about the outcome of the court proceedings and shamed by her actions. The symptomatic focus was to reduce her depression and suicidal symptoms and attend to the anxiety she felt about the impending court proceedings. The dynamic focus, which emerged more slowly, became articulated as: "how can we understand how a person who is dedicated to her family can suddenly without thinking do things that are so destructive to her and to them?" (Stadter 2009, p. 144). Work on this focus included both examination of themes described as binaries (abuser/abused, rejecting/rejected and depriver/deprived) and exploration of their meaning through her identifications. Stadter allowed his initial thought about the case's difficulty ("what on earth can I do in six months?") to be a concordant identification (Racker 1968) so that Diane's internal world might include a sense of feeling overwhelmed and out of control. The ending demonstrates the fragility of brief therapy. Diane cancelled her last session one hour before the time; Stadter called her, she answered, and the final session was held on the telephone; it was possible to say goodbye. For Diane, this was an experience that was different from previous endings involving feelings of rejecting or being rejected. Reviewing the therapy, it was agreed that considerable work on the focus had been achieved and that further therapy could be helpful. Thus, identifying where Diane could continue in her new location was an important part of the ending process.

Conclusion

The chapter has focused on discussing the similarities and differences between models of brief therapy for adults. Foundational approaches, associated with Malan, Mann, Davanloo and Strupp and Binder were discussed before exploring issues that arise in current brief therapy. Questions of aims, focus, technique, selection of patients and how to handle termination form the key parameters of brief therapy. Current practice suggests that theoretical approaches and theories of therapeutic action strongly influence how the parameters of brief therapy are applied in practice. Recent theoretical developments in long-term therapy influence current practice of brief therapy, and whilst these have not to date been fully discussed in the literature, they open the possibilities for new approaches to psychodynamic brief therapy.

Chapter 3

Development in adolescence and young adulthood

"I would there were no age between ten and three-and-twenty, or that youth would sleep out the rest, for there is nothing in the between but getting wenches with child, wronging the ancientry, stealing, fighting"
                                        Shakespeare, The Winter's Tale (1611/1996)

"to imagine the delicate balance between catastrophic change and brave new world"
                                        Donald Meltzer (1986, p.17)

Adolescence endures across eras, and centuries, and is new with every generation. Shakespeare's shepherd in *The Winter's Tale* captures adults' complaints about adolescents (together with a gender bias that persists); adolescent behaviour causes social anxieties and outrage, and is driven by powerful trends of sexuality, aggression and deviance. The rapidly changing social contexts – for adolescence is quintessentially a psycho-social concept – constantly transform the experience of adolescence, and thus understanding how adolescents work out a sense of identity and take up positions in adult society requires constant revision.

Contemporary adolescence can be thought of as organised around two distinct phases. The transition from childhood to early adolescence, following puberty, is a period of intense growth and far-reaching physical, cognitive, emotional and relational changes. This overlaps with and leads into, in most current societies, a long transition into adulthood, which, though including diverse pathways, is usually extended and lasts for approximately a decade from mid/late teens until at least the mid-twenties. Primarily affected by social changes, this long transition to adulthood severely tests traditional thinking about the adolescent process, particularly the central concept of identity formation. Development in adolescence thus extends into early adulthood; achieving fully adult roles in the social world is often still in process into the third decade. Upheavals in the social world, and radically changed – and changing – contexts for young people mean that theories of adolescent developmental processes lag behind experiences. New patterns of friendship, ways of relating to others and experiences of intimacy and separateness are driven largely by the impact of online and social media; new vulnerabilities especially evidenced by concerns about increasing adolescent mental health problems and new possibilities relating to the body, sexuality and gender create the challenge of how to understand both the enduring aspects of adolescent development, notably the intrapsychic changes that follow puberty, and the impacts of new factors, particularly in the social world. Psychoanalytic thinking has richly theorised early adolescence, but new theorisations are needed that address the psychological experiences of the transition to adulthood in current contexts.

Yet adolescence is also characterised by diversity, socially and culturally, and individual differences. Though time and maturation transform the child from puberty to emerging adulthood, how each individual experiences the time of adolescence depends on a bewildering multitude of factors, and one consequence of this is that there are many different and contradicting theories and accounts of adolescent development. Understanding adolescent development means taking a journey into some of these contesting views, and, perhaps mirroring the confusions of adolescence, coming out at the end of this with an appreciation of the complexities which involve the intermingling of intrapsychic, interpersonal and social experiences; in this sense development is not to be characterised as a simple linear progression through phases from less to more mature, but rather as involving the interactions of different fields. Meltzer (1984) argued that the analogy between physical and mental development is limited when it comes to understanding emotional and relational development; rather it is important to add to this the dimension of field, including for example the movement between different states of mind, and the interconnection between different domains of experience, internal and external, or social. The aim of this chapter is to use this framework to develop a contemporary understanding of the adolescent developmental process that is helpful to and relevant for clinical practice, and which serves as an underpinning reference point for the exploration of psychotherapy with young people.

Adolescent development: a turbulent process?

Psychoanalytic views of adolescence emphasise that it is a turbulent process, and necessarily so. Adolescence is:

> ...a crucial time of inevitable turmoil and confused identity. The emphasis here is on 'crucial', since the undergoing of turmoil and confusion is an important and necessary aspect of the adolescent process.
>
> (Waddell 1998, p. 133)

It is through the experience of turmoil that the adolescent makes the changes that enable him to meet the challenges of becoming more adult. In contrast, usually emanating from academic psychology (Coleman & Hendry 1999) or psychiatry (Rutter et al 1976) is the view that the transition to adulthood is not necessarily characterised by turmoil, particularly for adolescents' relationships with parents; these are "based on close communicative relationships involving a give and take between the needs of both adolescents and parents" (Côté 2014, p. 116). On the surface these are contradictory views, perhaps reflecting incommensurable paradigms (Kuhn 1962), though there is wide acknowledgement that difficult feelings are commonly experienced; Rutter's Isle of Wight study actually pointed out that "inner turmoil…as represented by feelings of misery and self-depreciation is quite frequent" (Rutter et al 1976, p. 35). However, there are many diverse ways that young people and their families experience adolescence; some families – and societies – have greater capacities to integrate the impact of the far-reaching changes of an individual's adolescence than others, and diverse social and cultural contexts significantly affect its meaning. The urgency and importance of the adolescent developmental process is not in doubt; this is a crucial, extremely complex period; different aspects are captured and theorised from many perspectives in different disciplines.

It is perhaps reassuring to think that despite the upheavals and disturbance of adolescence, most young people survive and make the adjustments needed to develop into adulthood:

> Whilst this is a time of turbulence, disturbance and struggle, often of inner uncertainties and chaos, the adolescent's growing discovery of his own sexually maturing body and physical strength, alongside his developing mind and intellect, usually enables him to move from dependence to independence.
>
> (Wise 2000, p. 7)

The force for development and growth that is inherent in adolescence is vital. However, taking a retrospective view can distort the actual experience; Jacobs (1990) thinks that memories of adolescence can be split between idealisation and abjection and that memories of early adolescence are painful:

> …early adolescence…is a time of awkwardness, of disproportions, of frightening sexual maturation, of pimples, and of new and untried feelings. Nothing is set. Nothing is solid. Everything is in flux and change. The aim with early adolescence, is to get past it and then, not to look back. In contrast, late adolescence is idealised, especially as future experiences include disappointments and frustrations.
>
> (Jacobs 1990, p. 108)

André Green identifies the fragility of the moment when the future may have hung in the balance:

> We outgrow adolescence with the idea of having lived through an exalting moment that we will never forget, but, in reality, sometimes when we look back we realise we had a narrow escape.
>
> (Green 1992)

The problem of remembering adolescence, or alternatively of forgetting what it was really like, is that it can also distort adult–adolescent relationships, as adults can defend against the power of adolescent emotionality; either they do not want to look back, as Jacobs suggests, and they back away from being stirred up by contact with adolescents, or they can get carried away both by the sheer exuberance and energy of youth – being "drunk on adolescence" as Brenman Pick (1988) described it – and a mixture of feelings, including envy, loss and perhaps regret, can lead to identifications with adolescent emotionality, and consequent enactments. The impact of adolescent emotionality on parents and other adults in contact with adolescence, including therapists, is important to keep in mind.

Mental health difficulties in adolescence

Concerns about mental health difficulties form a dominant current discourse about adolescence; reports of increasing rates of mental health problems in adolescence, and societal awareness of the importance of reducing the stigma associated with mental health, have brought these issues to the foreground. Mental ill health in childhood and adolescence is now recognised as constituting a severe threat to long-term well-being:

> If untreated, these conditions severely influence children's development, their educational attainments and their potential to live fulfilling and productive lives. Children with mental disorders face major challenges with stigma, isolation and discrimination, as well as lack of access to health care and education facilities, in violation of their fundamental human rights.
>
> (WHO 2017)

Most adult disorders begin in adolescence, up to 75% by the age of 24 (McGorry 2018), though often they can remain undetected until adulthood and not treated. The number of children and young people (4–24 years) reporting mental health difficulties is reported to be rising (Pitchforth et al 2018); this may reflect growing awareness of and less stigma associated with mental health issues (Gunnel et al 2018). Between one in four and one in five adolescents have a recognisable mental disorder in any year (Patel et al 2007). This can be looked at from two directions: the numbers of young people reported as having a mental health disorder are high, but most young people – around four in every five – negotiate adolescence without experiencing mental disorder. Not all adolescents fit the stereotype of being unstable (Graham 2004). The course mental ill-health can take during adolescence also requires binocularity; Patton et al (2014) found that most mental disorders do not persist into adulthood, and though the factors that lead to persistence into adulthood are hard to establish, the strongest predictor of young adult disorders is the duration of mental health disorders in adolescence, and this leads to a strong argument for early intervention:

> The resolution of many adolescent disorders gives reason for optimism that interventions that shorten the duration of episodes could prevent much morbidity later in life.
>
> (Patton et al 2014)

In a similar vein, for self-harm, though up to 28% of young people report an experience of self-harm, (Brunner et al 2014), and up to 50% repeat self-harm (Hawton et al 2012), Moran et al (2012) found that most self-harm resolves by early adulthood. It is crucial therefore to understand which factors lead to experiences of mental ill-health in adolescence, its continuation into adulthood or alternatively its resolution in adolescence. From a clinical perspective, being faced with an adolescent in difficulty means working with an uncertain outcome in terms of the longer-term implications. Understanding the complex developmental processes in adolescence is accordingly crucial.

The experience of puberty

Puberty ushers in changes to the body and mind that are immense and not negotiable. The pace of growth is astonishing; at no other time except in infancy is growth so rapid. Physical changes, the development of characteristics of the adult sexual body, and the vastly increased physical and cognitive capacity are accompanied by powerful feelings. Melanie Klein wrote of "the tempestuous uprush of instincts arising at puberty" (1922, p. 56). We understand this as partly hormonal but also partly as "alterations in psychic balance which come from the way young people feel about themselves" (Anderson 2008, p. 64).

Freud (1905) described puberty as bringing about the individual's final sexual organisation, transforming infantile sexuality into adult, genital form. Crucially, puberty – Freud referred to puberty, not adolescence – revives infantile sexuality and Oedipal conflicts, powerful and intense feelings towards parents, including sexual desires, heterosexual and homosexual. At the same time as experiencing these newly intense feelings, the adolescent must turn away from parents as sexual objects and find new ones for the expression of sexual desires and impulses. The choice of new objects is based on earlier, infantile relationships: "the finding of a sexual object is in fact a refinding of it" (Freud 1905, p. 145). Freud (1914) later described two ways of finding (refinding) an object: the anaclitic method of choosing an object, based on attachment, which is contrasted with the narcissistic model, choosing an object based on the subject's own ego.

The revival of powerful infantile feelings at puberty has been described as recapitulating early experiences. Jones (1922) thought the individual "recapitulates and expands" the first five years; Blos (1967) saw puberty as reworking the separation–individuation struggles of early childhood. The regressive repetition of these experiences created a 'second chance' to work through infantile wishes, desires and relationships. But the young adolescent must contend with the tensions that arise from the reawakening, of infantile impulses and desires in the context of a much stronger body. Whilst this makes it more difficult to contain the impulses, the consequences are that the impulses really can be made reality:

> He can really attack, destroy, rob, murder or commit suicide, and he can really have sexual experiences of a heterosexual or homosexual kind.
>
> (Hoxter 1964, p. 13).

This gives a first hint of the relationship between the developmental process and adolescent difficulties through the enactment of phantasies stirred up by the new situation of puberty. It is a potentially alarming situation:

> …he can enact his genital desires and destructive feelings rather than seek to satisfy those lusts and hatreds merely in phantasy.
>
> (Waddell 1998, pp. 128–129)

The capacity to put impulses and phantasies into action is potentially frightening for the adolescent and his parents. Anderson gives an example of a 14-year-old boy who:

> …had grown eight inches in a year and was now over six feet tall. He had always had quite a temper but before puberty neither he nor his family were terribly worried about this and his family easily helped him to calm down. But now the adults were afraid of him and he in turn felt more anxious.
>
> (Anderson 2008, p. 65)

This vividly shows relationships between adolescent and parents changing through the effects of puberty. The bedrock, in childhood, of the parents' relative strength and the child's relative weakness can contain anxieties, especially about powerful Oedipal impulses. Winnicott, in his epigraphic style, wrote that:

> If in the fantasy of early growth there is contained *death*, then at adolescence there is contained *murder*.
>
> (Winnicott 1971, p. 169)

Winnicott links the activation of Oedipal impulses and phantasies in adolescence with the external reality; adolescence means taking the parent's place; "it really does", he added. He pointed out that the unconscious sense of murder can become evident as a suicidal impulse or attempt. Desire and the capacity to make babies, murderous phantasies and the capacity to kill come together in adolescence and need to be worked through.

Our understanding has been revised by recent studies of the changes in the brain during adolescence; neuroscientific developments initiate the possibility of bringing together several hitherto disparate strands. According to these studies (Blakemore 2018), the turmoil of the pubertal years and the impulsiveness of some adolescent behaviour may have a neural cause. This evidence claims that later development – in the period of puberty particularly but continuing through adolescence – of the brain affects, amongst other things, the cognitive controls needed for mature behaviour; these are therefore underdeveloped in adolescence. Changes to the brain at puberty have an impact on cognition, and affect regulation, learning and memory; the brain shows "greater neural plasticity" (Patton & Viner 2007, p. 1132). Stressful experiences during puberty can affect brain development adversely, increasing vulnerability to psychopathologies;

enrichment of the social and learning environments may be able to reverse the effects of early adverse experiences. It is possible that greater neural plasticity thus provides what Blos (1967) has described as "a second chance" in development in early adolescence.

The adolescent process

Waddell (1998) emphasises that adolescence is a 'process' not a 'state'; a developmental process involves not simply phases, but states of mind, and a dynamic field of emotions, anxieties, defences and ways of relating to self and others, which:

> ...represent an extraordinary range of different ways of processing the mental pain, confusion and conflict which are initially stirred up by the physical changes taking place.
>
> (Waddell 1998, p. 131)

Such changes inevitably introduce a sense of loss; experiencing loss is a significant aspect of the adolescent process, relating primarily to the loss of childhood ways of relating to parents, whilst for parents there is loss of their child; leaving home, it is said, begins at puberty. The recognition of loss and the need for mourning runs through psychoanalytic thinking about adolescence; Anna Freud commented that "some mourning for the objects of the past is inevitable" (Freud 1958, p. 51). Actively engaging with the experience of loss is essential for the adolescent to make progress towards adulthood; this implies an active re-negotiation or re-evaluation of earlier ways of relating, based on the process Freud (1917) described as constituting mourning:

> The ego is required to examine every aspect of the lost object – the lost relationship – to pick up each particular aspect of the relationship, explore it, remember it and face the loss in order to let it go.
>
> (Anderson & Dartington 1998, p. 3)

The process of mourning is difficult and emotionally demanding; whether the adolescent has the capacity to face loss and increasing separateness is crucial:

> All of us grapple with failed mourning to some extent, but for those who arrive at adolescence with serious impairments in their ability to face loss this period can feel like an unbridgeable abyss.
>
> (Anderson 2008, p. 64)

The capacity to face loss is learned through experience, throughout childhood; weaning provides an important prototype. Observations of infants show that there are many ways in which weaning is experienced; it can feel like a passionate Greek tragedy, a disaster or a negotiation, or even a relief. As Salzberger-Wittenberg succinctly describes it, weaning:

> ...puts to the test, like every later loss, the capacity to maintain hope, love and gratitude in spite of frustration and emotional pain.
>
> (2013, p. 44)

In the process of weaning, how the mother and infant together face and recognise the importance of the feelings involved, repeatedly over time, helps work through loss, and reinstate a sense of love and goodness. Thus, patterns from earlier losses and the expectations of how others will interact with her/him have great bearing on how, in adolescence, the loss of childhood relatedness and greater separateness will be experienced. Therefore, experiences of containment from infancy onwards, the adolescent's sense of his own internal resources and the internal and external pressures he faces will all influence the adolescent process. A greater maturity in relationships, self-understanding, harnessing of the power of the energy of the adult sexual body and feeling centred in the body are the outcomes of the process, brought about by the developmental thrust and the individual adolescent's engagement and actively working with the process of loss and change.

However, there are many ways that an adolescent employs defences to avoid the painfulness of mourning, the internal conflicts of the struggle between dependency and separation and the ambivalences that are generated. Ambivalence and the oscillations of mood and attitude are characteristic of the adolescent process. Anna Freud described these contradictions and unpredictabilities:

> ...to fight his impulses and to accept them; to ward them off successfully and to be overrun by them; to love his parents and to hate them; to revolt against them and to be dependent on them; to be deeply ashamed to acknowledge his mother before others and, unexpectedly, to desire heart-to-heart talks with her; to thrive on imitation of and identification with others while searching unceasingly for his own identity; to be more idealistic, artistic, generous, and unselfish than he will ever be again, but also the opposite: self-centred, egoistic, calculating.
>
> (Freud 1958, p. 65)

The adolescents described here seem in fact rather undefended; defences are, as she put it, "strained," and the defences of childhood simply do not work when contending with the power of the adolescent developmental forces. Here the adolescent is passionate and unpredictable, and yet full of feeling, especially of love and hate; this conveys a powerful sense of being alive with the intensity of newness, when "the tide of life is running strongly" (Williams 1978, p. 311).

The unhappy or depressed adolescent might be, as Winnicott put it, "struggling through the doldrums," awaiting the passing of time. Winnicott emphasised the maturational aspect of the developmental process, if it can be protected and nurtured by a facilitating environment. The metaphor of the doldrums captures the adolescent disjuncture of time; the need for an immediate answer to the dilemmas of adolescence – what Winnicott called an emergency situation – sits alongside being trapped in a time warp, where "every minute seems like an eternity" (Vanier 2001, p. 589). In the doldrums, time can seem to be passing so slowly. Winnicott draws attention to the facts of time and death, both of which are essential discoveries of adolescence, including the limitations of the body – including usually its sex – the inevitability of death and the irreversibility of time. Discovering the meaning of death, and with it, one's place in time is a major – and perhaps underrecognised – aspect of development in adolescence.

The many adolescents who experience depression illustrate Freud's (1917) view that there is an overlap between mourning and melancholia; depression can be an outcome when mourning fails, and when the pains of relating to others are overwhelming. New kinds of defences are developed when the pains of loss are – perhaps temporarily – felt to be overwhelming, and through the inability to tolerate the intense conflicts of ambivalence, unpredictability and inconsistency, or not being able to withstand the rapid flow of changing and changeable emotions. Waddell (1998, p. 131) lists these as: getting rid of feelings through projective processes; letting off steam, for example, through delinquency; acting rather than thinking; moving in groups, or gangs, rather than risk being an individual; being ill physically rather than suffering emotionally; splitting good and bad; using substances to become mindless. Defences may hamper or cripple development, and lead to symptom formation, but they can also facilitate the developmental process.

Amongst these frequently used defences, projective processes are extremely common. Whilst projective identifications can be depleting through splitting off and projecting parts of the self into others, they can be facilitating in allowing young people to try on new roles, and to disown – usually temporarily – intensive and overwhelming feelings associated with the process of change; projective identification can be communicative, enabling a receptive other to feel and be affected by what is troubling to the young person. One young adolescent I saw in psychotherapy, Samuel, told me that though he was growing, it was not a problem for him, but he had two friends who did have problems, because for one of them his bones were growing faster than his muscles and ligaments and for the other it was the other way round, that his muscles were growing faster than his bones. One of them was very stiff and the other was very floppy. Here, time seems literally 'out of joint'; this disaster is located, through projection, in a friend. It later became evident that this sense of physical and emotional pain – 'growing pains' – was a good description of Samuel's inner world, and the projection onto the friend made it possible to begin to communicate his distraught sense that his body and mind were in a catastrophic state of disjuncture. Another young man projected onto me a pervasive sense of not liking himself, so that I received this in a disconcerting way as feeling I did not like him; this was probably the only way he could initially communicate this troubling feeling in himself, by making me feel it and then having to work with the discomfort it caused me.

Most adolescents retain a capacity to move between times when projective defences are used, and times when they are more available or negotiable and able to engage in more 'adult' discussions; to "desire heart-to-heart talks", as Anna Freud (1958, p. 65) describes it. That young people can move between these different positions with great speed and without apparent warning puts tremendous pressure on parental figures to move with them. When adolescents use projective processes in this way in their families, they seek and require parents to offer containment through taking in the emotionality as communication. Parents then have to shift gear to have an adult-to-adult conversation. It is easy to get wrong-footed; parenting adolescents is demanding and requires internal flexibility.

On the other hand, adolescents in greater difficulties can get stuck in some roles, whether the delinquent, mindless or projective, and then they are unable to move between life on the outside, in the social world, and life in the family; between times when they have increasing separateness and times when they return to closer, more childlike relationships with parents. Becoming stuck in these ways can result in reaching a developmental impasse or breakdown (Laufer & Laufer 1995). Dartington (1994) referred to the role of 'temporary outsider', where the adolescent's taking up a boundary position enables him to look in two directions, out into the world or back into the family. This requires a degree of both inner stability and flexibility, a capacity to stay in the adolescent process, with its accompanying tasks of mourning childhood ways of relating, re-evaluating relationships with the self and others and gradually becoming more adult. If the adolescent can maintain this boundary position, it leads to the acceptance of greater separateness from parental figures and more adult ways of relating; it can be extremely demanding emotionally. Anderson and Dartington (1998, p. 3) describe this as needing the "inner strength and resources to bear to continue the experience of being out of balance."

When inner resources and limitations in the environment do not sufficiently support the adolescent process, likely outcomes are getting stuck either inside the family, through not growing, or stuck outside, through adopting precocious adult roles. Precocious or premature positioning as an adult bypasses the adolescent developmental process; it can represent a defensive response to anxieties relating to one's own vulnerability and dependency on others. The childhood, dependent relationship with adults is repudiated, replaced by an omnipotent sense of being independent; it is a way therefore of avoiding painful internal conflicts and change, and the process of mourning the loss of childhood. In adolescence, because of its demands emotionally and relationally, depressive pain can easily be experienced as overwhelming; facing the painful affects of guilt, depression and fears of having damaged the object seem often to require capacities much greater than are available to the individual at this point in his development. Growing awareness of the separateness of the other arouses competitiveness and a sense of not being in control of the relationship, which is threatening to the adolescent's omnipotence and narcissism. So an experience of being separate from the parent, and of this not being bearable, and perhaps experienced as abandonment, or being disappointed by the other, can activate a retreat from depressive pain. Defending against the pains and awareness of depressive relatedness leads to the repudiation of the relationship both to dependence on others and to one's own vulnerability, expressed through returning to paranoid schizoid defences including splitting, projection and denial, manic defences or, more violently, defending against depressive anxiety through attacking the source of these feelings – "putting the boot in" (Anderson 1997) – or omniscient intellectuality (Waddell 1998). The question of when overwhelming depressive feelings lead to depression, manic repair or violence directed against the self or others is important, especially in today's contexts of reported high levels of depression, self-harm and suicidal thoughts amongst young people. Rather than aiming to get rid of depression, support in bearing depressive pain and maintaining internal contact with a vulnerable part of the self can help sustain the developmental process: "if the depression can be borne, sustained and worked through there often follows an efflorescence of emotional growth" (Williams 1978, p. 309).

If pseudo-maturity is one way in which adolescents can get stuck when the demands of the adolescent process are too great, being stuck in childhood ways of relating makes a contrasting second pattern. Here it is growth and development which is repudiated, with the aim of retaining childhood dependence on parents and avoiding the pains of separation. Fear of the adult sexual body, and the sense of loss of control that the bodily changes of puberty impart, can be experienced as terrifying; for example, Anderson (2008, p. 67) gives the example of an adolescent who was horrified and disgusted by the growth of pubic hair, which seemed to have a meaning for him that his father's body was being forcefully intruded into him. Another young adolescent, Colin, who was very small for his age of 15 years, in appearance more like a 10-year-old, had difficulties with eating, and with growing. He felt trapped in his smallness, weighing under six stones, not eating and worried about losing his friends as he felt unable to join in their age-appropriate activities. At the same time, he said, "There is a bit of me that is happy to be like this. It is like being in a cell with a heavy door that will take ten years to open." His hopelessness led him to give up and ask for others to undertake his emotional work for him; he implored his therapist to "tell [his parents] to give him his independence."

Changing contexts of adolescence

Adolescence involves the interaction between the internal world and social contexts, and these have changed radically in recent decades, creating new vulnerabilities and opportunities. Notably, the transition to adulthood has been prolonged, a consequence primarily caused by changes at the socio-economic level, the collapse of the traditional youth labour market and the requirement of significantly higher educational qualifications for entry into employment (Côté 2014).

Consequently, young people remain longer financially dependent on parental figures, or they risk becoming marginalised. Though schematic and simplifying of the diversity and complexity of the transition to adulthood, Jones' (2006) characterisation of 'slow track' and 'fast track' routes into adulthood captures the inherent problems. On the 'fast track' route, young people leave education on or before the minimum age and enter the workforce with the risk of poor wages and unemployment. They may have early family formation, teenage pregnancy and higher antisocial behaviour rates. The early attainment of adult independence is likely to mean a premature loss of childhood and social exclusion. The 'fast track' route often includes young people from more disadvantaged backgrounds. The 'slow track' route involves staying on in education, and experiencing repeated semi-independent statuses whilst requiring parental support, and is problematic for those without this support. Many on the 'slow track' do not reach the traditional markers of adulthood – employment, established sexual relationships, parenthood – until much later in the third decade. The traditional process of leaving home has been replaced by, often, a process of partial independence – for example during the university student years – whilst many young people remain living in the parental home. Transitions to adulthood are now variable, diverse, uncertain, fragmented, reversible, piecemeal.

The idea has been mooted (Arnett 2000), and contested (Bynner 2005; Sukarieh & Tannock 2011), that young or emerging adulthood now occupies a new life stage since from the start of the third decade, young people see themselves as less engaged in the adolescent process and more as being on the threshold of making long-term commitments; they move from, in earlier adolescence, being preoccupied with the present moment, the 'now,' to, in emerging adulthood, questions of the future. This view may be contested as not being new, and oversimplifying the adolescent process, or making normative the responses of young people to the impact of their entrapment by socio-economic circumstances. The shift from a time for experimentation – a moratorium in Erikson's (1968) terminology – to a time when engagement with the demands of the external world becomes a present imperative is a more traditional marker of the transition to adulthood; young people either rise to the challenge, with a sense of internal resources that can take them towards adulthood, or they may find it depressing or overwhelming (Waddell 1998, p. 157). The problem in the new contexts is that a deeply contradictory situation is encountered; the young adult may feel emotionally ready to engage with becoming more independent and living more separately from parental figures, and yet the opportunities for this are restricted. Alternatively, he may shelter from having to make developmental progress of this kind and continue to have childlike dependency on parents, not-separating. Additionally, the transition to adulthood, as well as being prolonged, often happens piecemeal, with inevitable confusions and frustrations; some more adult roles – for example, as a student living away from home, or working in paid employment, or having a committed sexual relationship, or becoming a parent – may be taken up, whilst others are not. This is mirrored by the – often illogical – incrementalism of attaining adult rights and responsibilities at different ages.

The question that has been raised and much debated is how these experiences have an impact on identity formation. Arnett (2000) argues that individualised, abstract and even moral criteria drive young people's thinking about their identity as young adults, in contrast to the traditional structural markers of transition. Traditionally, answering questions like "who am I?" and "where am I going?" have marked the establishment of a reflective sense of identity. The idea of having a core identity, based on and rooted in early experiences of internalisation, but also that recognises differences from parental figures, is crucial to the process of identity formation in modernity. However, this view is challenged by notions of identity that flow from the individualisation and reflexivity of society (Giddens 1991; Beck 1992). The problem for young people is to gain entry to an adult world that is fragmented, globalised and rapidly changing; identity in this world needs to be more open, fluid, complex and questioning of traditions; it must be more differentiated and inclusive of many identifications that can change over time and place. It is influenced by and makes use of the vast flow of information through, predominantly, online and social media. There is a choice between keeping in touch with new information and becoming marginalised outside reflexive society; the threat is to "get with it, or miss out" (Johannsson 2007, p. 105). The openness of this approach to identity questions everything; there are few or no givens, including gender and the body. Identity has therefore been described as reflexive, re-inventing and a continuous project of the self (Giddens 1991). The upside is a sense of excitement, new possibilities for rethinking relationships and the questioning or deconstruction of old certainties; the downside is continuous exposure to the fragmentation of the socio-cultural environment and to new risks; anxiety and fear of loss of control are heightened. Risks are ubiquitous in what Beck (1992) called 'risk societies', and require constantly calculating, with decisions based on a spectrum from risk-taking to risk aversion. However, the notion of individualisation in risk societies contains a contradiction; whilst needing to continually make decisions based on assessing risks, choices are in fact limited and affected by social inequalities that are increasing; though seemingly favouring individual agency, structural factors exert a powerful effect and choice and opportunity may be illusory (Bynner 2005); Furlong and Cartmel (2007) have called this "the epistemological fallacy of the individualisation thesis." Individual agency which is limited by structures leads to biographies grounded in different backgrounds of class, place, gender and ethnicity. A crucial implication is that individuals can feel responsible for factors outside their control, leading to confusion, anxiety, distress, and depression. For young people in the transition to adulthood, encountering turbulence in the fluctuating, shifting, rapidly changing and uncertain adult world potentially means encountering confusion, loss which is hard to name and identify, and thus to mourn, and a fear of loss of control (Briggs 2008).

Ethnicity, gender and 'virtuelescence'

Social changes have therefore affected the meaning and process of identity for-mation; rather than one unifying, hegemonic form, differences of ethnicity and gender emphatically show that there are multiple and diverse pathways through the adolescent process and different end points for priorities in adulthood. The struggle to find and establish identity in terms of ethnicity involves the adoles-cent, especially the minority ethnic adolescent, in difficult and exacting processes of developing cohesion of a sense of self within complex and divisive contexts. "Multiple subject positions are juxtaposed, contested, proclaimed and disavowed" (Brah 1996, p. 208); the process of forming a sense of self involves political, social, cultural, interpersonal and intrapsychic processes, often including adapta-tions to new societies and countries, and a complex process of renegotiation and redefining of patterns of relationships, taking account of both traditional and host cultures (Hall 2000). These differences increase the complexity of therapeutic relationships, of understanding how they affect the therapeutic process; a com-plex, ambiguous field is created for therapeutic work (Briggs 2008).

The impact of online and social media creates a new dimension for the ado-lescent process. In one sense, online behaviour simply mirrors the established conflicts of becoming more separate and working through the loss of childhood relatedness, as Graham suggests:

> ...the many ordinary rites of passage of adolescence migrate into the digital domain, and young people are learning and testing themselves in this space.
>
> (Graham 2013, p. 273)

Online and social media have transformed patterns of friendships and relation-ships and experiences of intimacy with and separation from others. As with any significant change process, there are fierce debates about the pros and cons. Online and social media generate a multitude of possibilities; they may create, as Graham eloquently describes:

> ...a modern royal road to unconscious phantasies mated with a vast sea of potential confirmations.
>
> (Graham 2013, p. 279)

Young people can explore the many and pluralist and hybrid social spaces, both online and offline, and they appear to move seamlessly between online and offline relating (Briggs et al 2017). On the other hand, anxieties about the qualities of virtual space have been seen to provide a route to denying the importance of the body, and its limits, and can thus be used defensively as, Lemma argues, online and social media deny corporeality and abolish difference and separate-ness: "painful awareness of the given body and of bodily separateness may be sidestepped" (Lemma 2015b, p. 60), and "it bypasses the need for the psychic work necessary for understanding that inner and outer reality are linked rather than being either equated or split off" (ibid, p. 61); thus the relationship between internal and external reality is altered by virtual space.

The nature of virtual space and how it is used by young people changes the notion of intimacy by moving the boundaries between private and public domains. This is the argument developed by Gozlan (2013) who contrasts the notion of 'extimacy', the process of sharing the intimate with others, as developed from Lacan's work by Tisseron (2011), with her own term 'dis-intimacy', where the adolescent loses ownership of the intimate so that it no longer belongs to him:

> In this moment of pure dis-intimacy, a passage from the intimate to the foreign takes place, gripping the adolescent in loss and solitude.
>
> (Gozlan 2013, p. 16)

Here Gozlan is considering how the adolescent may, in virtual space, lose possession of parts of himself, through sharing with others, and consequently suffer a loss which is difficult, if not impossible, to mourn. The question then is how online and social media are managed by young people. Graham (2013) suggests that being able to do this has become a developmental requirement, and Gozlan (2016) contrasts how more securely attached young people will use the internet for exploration and be able to return to dependence on parents as necessary, maintaining a place on the boundary between family and the outside world, therefore. Others, those less securely attached, seek affirmation and therefore risk rejection online. This may be too schematic a distinction; states of mind also come into this configuration. However, it gets behind the for-and-against binary discussions of social media to begin to identify how its use can either support or undermine the adolescent development process.

Returning to Lemma's consideration of the relationship between online media and the body enables further consideration of a key current issue, the question of identity and gender and sexuality. The cultural shift to more openness about sexuality and gender, and greater recognition and acceptance of different sexualities, transgender and gender-variant people, has created more open discussion, and a greater sense of choice for the process of identity formation. This is of course complex. The acceptance of the adult sexual body, and the reality of that given body, is so central to psychoanalytic thinking about adolescence and identity that the capacity ultimately to modify and change physical sex characteristics opens a new dimension and questions the essence of the identity process. The increasing number of referrals, reported in several countries (Butler et al 2018), for cases of gender dysmorphia reflects both a greater openness of discussion, supported or fuelled, depending on one's position, by social media, and reduction of the stigma of difference. That these issues may be more openly discussed supports the adolescent process; this is the first consideration: that doubts, discomforts, distress and confusion about the body, gender and sexuality can be heard and thought about. There is a side of this which can be used defensively, which Lemma (2015b) addresses through a case example, Paula, whose solution of waiting for sex reassignment surgery also meant avoiding engagement with the developmental process. Di Ceglie (2002) describes the definiteness and concreteness with which some of his patients spoke of being in the wrong body, that is, being a boy but in a girl's body or vice versa. In these cases, confusion and doubt were projected onto others, thus demonstrating closure rather than openness and an absence of symbolisation and 'as if' ways of thinking, and a difficulty therefore in engaging with the adolescent process.

Becoming-a-subject in adolescence

To a certain extent, it is not possible to integrate all the implications of the changing contexts into a theoretical framework for contemporary adolescence and young adulthood; the chasms between competing paradigms are all too apparent in youth studies (Côté 2014). On the other hand, it is imperative that psychotherapy is relevant to the concerns, anxieties and dilemmas of contemporary young people, responds accurately to their experiences and can make sense of their internal and social worlds. What is at stake is the development of internal resources that allow young people to be able to negotiate a pathway into adulthood, separateness and independence, dependence and intimacy, as these unfold for each individual over the extended adolescent period. The process of becoming-a-subject is one approach that can bring together established thinking about adolescence, based on psychoanalytic thinking, as discussed earlier in this chapter, and appreciation of changed and changing social worlds. I will briefly describe the essence of this approach and how it has developed, and then discuss how it can be applied to the process of understanding adolescent and young adult development.

The process of becoming-a-subject (subjectivation) has been developed from Lacan's thinking by Raymond Cahn, Phillippe Gutton and Francois Ladame (Perret-Catipovic & Ladame 1998). Drawing on some classic psychoanalytic accounts of adolescence, and having significant overlaps with these, notably Laufer's work, the process of becoming a subject is conceptualised as involving the adolescent in an internal struggle and a social process, which confers meaning to intrapsychic and intersubjective experiences of change (Ladame 2008, p. 77). The process of becoming a subject involves differentiation, of self from other, inside from outside, new from familiar, and the ownership of one's own thoughts; it requires giving meaning to experiences, symbolisation and reflection and takes place in a 'space' "which is open to interrogation, to the calling into question of the familiar and already known and hence to the possibility of transformation and self-creation", in which "identity may be confronted, enriched or alternatively called into question" (Cahn 1998, p. 150). This notion of a psycho-social space, in which meaning can be conferred through reflection, curiosity, interrogation and feeling has a family resemblance to other social theories, including Bourdieu's concept of habitus; thus, the social and cultural experiences influence and shape internal processes and subjecthood (Briggs & Hingley-Jones 2013). There is correspondence too with Bion's process of container–contained, through which emotional experiences are named and transformed through thinking, and Winnicott's notion of 'holding' that supports the continuity of being and becoming over time (Ogden 2004).

Kennedy (1998) also describes the capacity for reflection and learning from experience, and makes a distinction between being 'subject of' and 'subject to' the forces involved in the internal and social processes; being 'subject of' implies the capacity to appropriate the forces acting in and on the subject, while being 'subject to' means being on the receiving end of internal and external forces that appear to happen *to* the subject. The movement from being 'subject to' and 'subject of' occurs through a reflective process, involving ownership and symbolisation; being 'subject to' leads to repetitions and not understanding cause and effect. Again, there is potential correspondence here between these states and the adolescent process of facing loss and re-evaluating relationships as described by Anderson.

Thus, the adolescent develops characteristic ways of relating to new experiences, primarily in relationships. There may be adolescents who tend to relate newness back to the familiar or already known, whilst others are open to the unknown. Preference for the familiar and known leads to repetitive or mechanical ways of relating, whilst, at the other extreme, a privileging of newness over the familiar can lead to a manic search for excitement. Between these two extremes are oscillating moments of openness and closure. Through ownership – of one's thoughts, drives and the adult sexual body – and symbolisation, freedom from "the power of the other, or the exercise of that power" (Cahn 1998, p. 151) is achieved. The adolescent has to confront the many and powerful obstacles to appropriating his own thoughts, wishes and desires:

> …panic stricken when all is thereby called into question again or even unable to conceive this situation, he may remain inside timeless time, abandoning his psyche and body to the other, devoid of thoughts and wishes of his own, an automaton at the mercy of the other's omnipotence.
>
> (Cahn 1998, p. 159)

Failing to develop the capacity for subjecthood may:

> …lure him/her into a closed ideology or delusion, alienating or imprisoning him/her and distorting his/her world.
>
> (Cahn 1998, p. 159)

Kennedy (2000) argues that the sense of becoming a subject is experienced around times of opening up and closing down, of being present and absent and of appearing and disappearing. Adolescents and young adults are involved in an uncertain and essentially anxious process, of discovering moments of developing their sense of their own subjectivity, in relation to themselves and others. When they are or feel themselves to be 'subject to' experiences from within or outside, that is, from characters in the social world, there results a sense of inauthenticity and frustration. In this sense, becoming a subject admits a more fluid sense of identity formation, combining conscious and unconscious aspects, as a continual project through the entire process of adolescence and the long transition to adulthood. It takes into account different positioning in society, including in relation to ethnicity, gender and other areas of difference, including disability (Briggs & Hingley-Jones 2013), and recognises the multiplicity of pathways through the adolescent process.

Conclusion

This chapter begins with the juxtaposition that adolescence combines some enduring aspects and some that are new to each generation. Over time, psychoanalytic thinking has generated rich accounts of the crucial changes following puberty and these form an invaluable source for understanding development in adolescence. The adolescent process is a powerful and complex process which provides an impetus towards adulthood and is also fragile and easily disrupted; this can lead to adolescent difficulties and disturbance. There is a paradox, expressed by Winnicott, of the urgency of the situation and the need for time to pass; accepting that growth occurs in and over time and being able to do the emotional work to assimilate the impacts of change are the necessary aspects of the developmental process. Unprecedented social changes have transformed, especially, the transition to adulthood and created new contexts for development, including the impacts of diverse ethnicities, different approaches to gender and sexuality and the presence of an online virtual world which is important for many young people. It is important to understand the meaning and implications of these changes for young people; it is suggested that the process of becoming a subject has the potential to help with this.

Chapter 4

Adolescent psychotherapy

"During adolescence, to draw any clear distinction between what might be called mental 'order' and mental 'disorder' is always a challenging and subtle business, defying ready categories or formulations"

(Waddell 2006, p. 33)

I am told that the most popular T-shirt of all…simply reads DEFINITELY MAYBE and as far as adolescents are concerned you cannot get clearer than that.

(Dartington 1998, p. 22)

Introduction

The aim of this chapter is to provide an overview of adolescent psychotherapy and how this addresses the mental health difficulties faced by young people. It looks, first, at how psychotherapy with young people has developed over time starting with classical psychoanalytic sources, notably Anna Freud, Donald Winnicott and Moses Laufer. Second, it explores key tensions and dilemmas in current theory and practice, including consideration of what is distinctive and different when working with young people, with risks and with parents. Current debates include discussion of how psychotherapy with adolescents is being influenced by changes in psychoanalytic theory, practice and technique, especially from the interpersonal and relational perspectives. The need for new approaches to psychotherapy occurs partly through social change; it is important to take account of the effects of social change on adolescence, as discussed in Chapter 3, and how these have an impact on thinking about the developmental process and the development of subjectivity. Finally, consideration of the issue of the duration of therapy paves the way for introducing and situating TAPP as a time-limited therapeutic method that is responsive to young people needing therapeutic help in current contexts.

Classic debates about adolescent psychotherapy: for and against intervention

Though in psychoanalysis frequent references have been made to young people – in Freud's case studies, for example – there has been tension regarding how, or whether, to offer psychotherapeutic treatment to adolescents. There are two voices, Ruggiero (2006, p. 550) suggests, that have:

> ...dotted the development of psychoanalytic theorizing about adolescence in a historical opposition between 'sitting on the fence' (A. Freud, Winnicott, and Meltzer) and being more interventionist (prevalent today).

Being more interventionist is currently more favoured, partly because there is a leaning towards the view that early intervention is needed if adolescent disturbance is not to persist and become adult psychosocial disorder. However, intervention is favoured also because of an increased understanding of how to intervene, and, perhaps paradoxically, because there is less confidence that the developmental process will of itself carry adolescents through turmoil and doldrums into adulthood. Perhaps it is more accurate to say that there is an older view which favours less or non-intervention, and that, currently, intervention is expected.

Anna Freud set the tone for non-intervention, despite her understanding and formulating a view of developmental disturbance that has enduring clinical usefulness for adolescents as well as children (Baruch 2001). She was not in favour of psychoanalytic treatment for adolescents, partly because she felt it was a "hazardous venture from beginning to end" in which the analyst faced "resistances of unusual strength and variety." Because of the nature of adolescent turmoil, it is difficult to differentiate between "adolescent upsets" and "true pathology." Therefore, whilst she would be willing to discuss the problems of adolescents with their parents, she preferred to let the course of time bring its own solutions rather than offer treatment:

> While an adolescent remains inconsistent and unpredictable in his behaviour, he may suffer, but he does not seem to me to be in need of treatment. I think that he should be given time and scope to work out his own solution.
>
> (Freud 1958, p. 65)

Some faith in the developmental process is implied, and that what is needed is time and support, rather than intervention; Freud thus positions adolescents as having the agency to "work out [their] own solution"; in some contexts, however, applying this approach might express a defensive view, based on taking flight from, being dismissive of or not wanting to get too close to the anxieties stirred up by adolescent difficulties and emotionality.

Freud added that the oppositional adolescent who is urged to have therapy by his parents will see the therapist as the parent's agent; rather than offering treatment to the adolescent "it may be his parents who need help and guidance so as to be able to bear with him" (Freud 1958, p. 65). The debate about whether and in what circumstances to work with the adolescent, or the parent, or both, and how to hold the boundary between the parent and the adolescent continue to be live issues, and are discussed further later in this chapter.

Winnicott's belief in the efficacy of the developmental process was expressed in his oft-quoted view that adolescence is a time for living, a problem of existing, solved by the passing of time:

> In fact there exists only one real cure for adolescence: maturation. This and the passage of time do, in the end, result in the emergence of the adult person. The process cannot be hurried up, though indeed it can be broken into and destroyed by clumsy handling; or it can wither up from within when there is psychiatric illness in the individual.
>
> (Winnicott 1963, p. 124)

Since, however, the developmental process could be impaired by intrusions, on the one hand, and the anti-developmental trends within the adolescent, on the other hand, the primary aim, he thought, when working with adolescents is to protect the developmental process. The importance of the facilitating environment runs throughout Winnicott's work, including working with adolescents. Others have criticised his approach for its passivity and reluctance to intervene; Winnicott's formulation of pathological or self-destructive behaviour as signs of health has been described as "indefensible" (Perret-Catipovic & Ladame 1998). Yet Winnicott has a quite contemporary feel when, to use current terminology, he discusses the communicative aspects of adolescent symptoms including suicidal thoughts and behaviour and self-harm (Motz 2009); this provides an impetus to understanding adolescent difficulties as disturbances of the developmental process. However, Winnicott rather provocatively claimed that the adolescent "does not want to be understood" and that "adults should hide among themselves what they come to understand of adolescence" (Winnicott 1963, p. 124); instead, the aim of psychotherapy is to meet the challenge of adolescence, that is, its confrontation with the adult generation. The playing out of Oedipal conflicts in adolescence requires a confrontation between adult experience and maturity, and the immaturity of adolescence, with its "creative thought, new and fresh feeling, ideas for new living" (Winnicott 1971, p. 172); the therapist's duty is to survive, and not abdicate.

Whereas Winnicott positioned himself as awaiting the passage of time, Moses Laufer was on the other side of this divide. For Laufer intervention is necessary when there is a disturbance of the developmental process:

> If the developmental process in adolescence either is seriously interfered with by internalised conflict, or has stopped as the result of a breakdown in functioning, then treatment is not only indicated but urgent.
>
> (Laufer & Laufer 1995, p. 19)

For Laufer, the task of therapeutic intervention is to keep alive the adolescent's sense of having a developmental choice; this leads to acceptance of the adult sexual body, which can then be felt as belonging to him and as separate from the parents. Developmental breakdown occurs when the adolescent surrenders to regressive wishes and surrenders his body to the mother. Therapeutic intervention aims there-fore to "undo the result of the breakdown in the developmental process" (Laufer 1998, p. 121) and to integrate adult genital functioning into the final sexual organi-sation. Even after breakdown of the developmental process, Laufer felt it was pos-sible to restore development to a more progressive trajectory through therapeutic intervention. The urgency, for Laufer, is that the window for change is a small one; failure to intervene whilst the adolescent process is active means that the moment for development, openness and choice has passed. Laufer gives several examples of adolescents enacting, and then becoming stuck with, the implications of these enactments, which, as he described it, meant living out the central masturbation phantasy, rather than integrating the emerging adult sexual body with its drives and phantasies. The constant pressure on the adolescent is to "feel constantly in danger of giving in to what he wants and what he must not allow" (Laufer 1998, p. 119).

Laufer's work has had a deep impact on adolescent psychotherapy, influencing developments in the (mainly) post-Kleinian work of the Tavistock's Adolescent Department and, through Francophone analysts Raymond Cahn and Francois Ladame's formulation of the concept of subjectivation, becoming a subject in adolescence. As discussed in Chapter 3, Anderson and Dartington (1998) saw the adolescent process having, at its heart, the importance and necessity of working through the experiences of loss; intervention thus supports the adolescent, in what is inevitably an emotionally difficult process, especially for those who are more vulnerable or experiencing disturbance.

In the different positions taken with regard to the efficacy of intervention, there are continuities of the original differences between Klein and Anna Freud, and Winnicott's taking an independent position (King & Steiner 1991); Klein's opti-mism about the possibilities and effects of treatment, alacrity for working in depth and establishing a transference relationship with children contrasts Anna Freud's more cautious and more educative approach in this respect. Winnicott often wished to find a minimum necessary intervention; however, each side of the intervention versus non-intervention divide holds an important aspect for working with the devel-opmental process in adolescence; the thrust of development itself, leading towards maturation, tends to be undervalued in current practice. On the other side is the belief in the need to actively work with and address the difficulties that threaten the developmental process, and their behavioural and symptomatic expressions. The dichotomy between intervention and non-intervention resolves therefore into more nuanced questions; namely, which adolescent patients and the problems they bring – or consciously or unconsciously delegate to others to bring on their behalf – can be helped through therapeutic interventions, of which kind, and with what aims?

Engaging young people in psychotherapy

Changes in technique and in how the therapeutic relationship is thought about have led to greater confidence in assessing more young people as suitable for ther-apy. As Catty (2016) comments, the assessment of ego strength and psychological mindedness as crucial factors when assessing suitability for psychotherapy has been largely superseded by the possibility, emerging from Winnicott's work and Bion's thinking about the container–contained relationship, of engaging young people with apparent weak ego strength and with more deprived and depriving personal histories. Thus, changes in how the therapeutic relationship is conceptualised, and alongside this the nature of therapeutic action, open the possibility of providing psychotherapy that is relevant and meaningful for more young people.

These possibilities can be illustrated by Williams' (1997) seminal work on 'double deprivation,' where crippling defences have been developed as a response to an initial deprivation brought about by external circumstances. Williams describes how "the quality of his internal objects…provided him with so little support that he was made an orphan inwardly as well as outwardly" (p. 33). This 14-year-old, Martin, "had developed a talent not only for hardening himself, but *for hardening people around him* and making them deaf to the real nature of his need" (p. 37, emphasis in original). The process Williams describes here involves recognising the precariousness of Martin's internal world, his dread of emotional contact and dependency and how he sought to protect his fragile, idealised internal object through intensely bombarding the therapist with his projections. However, Williams experienced that through the process of projective identification Martin also communicated "a hope that I might bear the impact of his behaviour, and not become a brick wall" (p. 37).

Not all adolescents in difficulties present with such an impoverished internal world, of course, though for many the demands of adolescent development exert terrific pressure; engagement can be a significant challenge with adolescents (Bronstein & Flanders 1998). There are long-standing concerns about difficulties in engaging young people in therapy, especially young adolescents and those who appear to be most in need of therapy (Briggs et al 2015). Though engagement issues are prominent at the beginning, they can continue to be important throughout therapy. Young people have a capacity to surprise; some who seem always about to leave remain, others who seem more settled can suddenly disengage, whilst some young people can present the possibility of leaving at any point in the therapy. At the beginning of a therapeutic relationship, relating anxieties and ambivalences to the developmental process provides the therapist with a starting point for making sense of experiences and interactions and for beginning to understand the adolescent's internal world. Beginning a therapeutic relationship, being one-to-one in a room in this way with an adult, can in itself instil terror in the adolescent, whilst the therapeutic task of sharing and exploring inner thoughts is a significant challenge in itself. Alongside the anxiety and ambivalence of adolescents seeking therapeutic help, therapy can have the effect of adding a new turbulent dimension to adolescence, perhaps exacerbating deep anxieties already stirred up by the experience of the adolescent process (Waddell 2002).

The tensions in adolescence between greater separateness and dependency on adults, and the defences that are being employed to counter intense anxieties stirred up by the adolescent process, are brought directly into the therapeutic relationship. Older adolescents and young adults may have reached a position where this is more manageable, and bring a becoming-more-adult self into therapy, though difficulties and disturbances can leave them defending against feeling small and inadequate. The conflicts and ambivalences about dependency and separateness can be conveyed by some distinctive presentations. Some convey that they do not intend to stay for long: coats, hoodies and hats remain on, attention is focused on phones in hand or earphones in place. Others convey quite a different message, as if they have brought a suitcase with them and intend to stay, and that from the start, the question arises of an inevitable difficulty ahead, of how to separate at the end of therapy, and indeed, each session. There is therefore a polarisation around different ways of contending with the problem of depending on an adult whilst in the process of becoming more separate from and independent of adults. Defending against the pains of the process leads some young people to deny their need for adults, whilst others hold on to childhood ways of relating and forsake development. For some young people, therefore, even a very limited time commitment (in adult terms) can seem entrapping, and a 50-minute session an eternity, whilst for others a hint of an ending can seem like abandonment; for some, it may be both. Since adolescent relatedness is highly linked to ambivalence and action, with both these kinds of adolescent positioning it is important to assess actions as much as words; often, this amounts to watching where young people's feet take them and what they move towards and away from. Combining the two – feet and words – can give a good picture of the quality of ambivalence the young person is contending with.

It is perhaps evident that as these expressions of anxiety and ambivalence are so important in the process of engaging young people in therapy, it is imperative that the therapist recognises and speaks to these as soon as possible, and in a way that reaches out to the young person. There are different approaches; Baruch (2001) recommends that therapists should provide a structure for taking responsibility for the direction of the session and for not leaving the young person sitting in silence. If not wishing to be so overtly structured, the therapist can have a sense of structure in her mind. On the other hand, for some young people, directly addressing deep anxieties which include infantile roots and future fears may provide relief and a sense of feeling understood; this then heightens engagement and interest in the process of therapy. When therapists make these interventions, they may not get a response, or, if they do, the response may be akin to "sitting on the fence." However, young people often do respond to a therapist who is wondering what it was like to come to the appointment, and what it is like talking to her, and this can increase the quality of engagement (Briggs et al 2015). These interventions can also elicit discussion of some common anxieties at the start of therapy, including uncertainty about the nature of the therapeutic process and anxieties aroused by the clinical or therapeutic setting. The therapeutic task in engagement is therefore to aim to increase the young person's sense of being an active participant, partly through explanation and clarification, and partly through containing anxieties.

Seeking therapy, however reluctantly, does represent a move, on the side of life, towards self-understanding and relief and discovering "whether the fear of change is greater than the bid for relief and for emotional freedom" (Waddell 2002, p. 146). A significant aspect of adolescent communication is through projective identification:

> Adolescents, who often have difficulty in expressing their emotional turmoil in words, frequently fall into this category as the intensity of the problem exceeds their representational capacities.
>
> (Ruggiero 2006, p. 537)

As suggested by the example above of Williams' work, if the therapist can bear and work with this quality of emotionality, it can form an important route towards engagement and understanding. It is, however, a difficult task, requiring

> ...freeing the clinical mind of preconceptions in order properly to engage with the actual troubled young person in the room, at the time. Perhaps at no other point in a clinician's relationship with a patient is the capacity for 'negative capability' (Keats 1817: 43) more hard to achieve or more severely tested.
>
> (Waddell 2002, p. 367)

A further dimension to consider here is the socio-cultural context of the therapy; working across cultures, including often working across languages too, increases the complexities for hearing emotionality in the context of the young person's relationships, and for the therapist's conscious and unconscious preconceptions. Working across cultures is, of course, a very frequent occurrence in contemporary practice. As noted in Chapter 3, ethnic diversity shows there are different pathways through the adolescent developmental process and different end positions. The intercultural therapeutic context creates the potential for not understanding and for ambiguity. The therapist has to move between the internal and the socio-cultural domains to understand meaning in context, to explore how embodied differences in the participants, young person and therapist, relate to internal processes. The paradox is that the cultural context confers meaning, whilst unconscious processes do cross cultural boundaries; as Thomas observed, "the unconscious does not distinguish between colour as far as the perpetrators of pain are concerned" (1992, p. 138).

Assessment

Engagement and assessment of young people are crucially interlinked and simultaneous; the combination forms a therapeutic intervention in its own right. This is particularly so if the model used is of repeated assessment sessions, as developed in the Tavistock Clinic's Adolescent Department. This model offers advantages to both the clinician and the adolescent patient; for the adolescent patient, it provides an opportunity to learn from experience about the therapeutic process, to get used, to an extent, to the regularity of appointments and to reach a view, based on this experience, of what continuing in therapy would be like. As summarised by Waddell (2002, p. 146), it:

> ...offers the troubled person an opportunity to engage in a thinking process; to explore the degree of motivation in seeking help; the impact of beginning to look at private or hidden things; the capacity to sustain the scrutiny, to bear the possible discoveries and to risk the change.

For the therapist too, the repeated assessment sessions, usually consisting of four meetings at weekly intervals, provide opportunities to see how the young person responds to these challenges, to obtain a more rounded view than is given by a one-off meeting and to obtain a sense of how he processes the content of the sessions. It is striking how often an adolescent will present differently in the second session from the first one, either in his presentation, how he relates or the content that he brings; perhaps anxiety is less, perhaps the first session has an immediate impact and something changes, whether developmentally or defensively, and perhaps the disparate sense of identity in adolescence is seen in the presentation of a different aspect of the self. Waddell (2002) comments that what is discovered is how the adolescent learns when thinking about emotional experiences: is he able to think between sessions, and bring new material to subsequent sessions based on this thinking, or is this too difficult an emotional task, and are the contents ejected, denied, or 'dumped'? It is important to attend to the impact of the gaps between sessions, each having the meaning of a separation:

> ...to see whether it is possible to hold on to trains of thought and emotional links over periods of separation to foster a relationship with a therapist which could be a thinking one and not merely a dumping one.
>
> (p. 153)

The four sessions provide the opportunity for discussing and testing the motivation to accept an offer of therapy, and to explore ambivalence, which is quite often expressed through actions such as missing sessions or parts of them. To offer therapy in the third session, for example, provides the chance to review this in the fourth, allowing any mixed feelings to surface and be explored. Although four sessions may seem generous for this purpose, so much has to be thought about, and communications can be so ambiguous, that the time can seem very tight; it can feel like quite a scamper.

The assessment process over repeated sessions in a sense offers a response to Anna Freud's concerns about assessing and treating adolescents as a result of their inconsistencies and unpredictabilities, and a way of considering the pros and cons of offering treatment to someone who does not self-evidently meet the usual criteria for psychotherapy, were it an adult patient, for example, being assessed; it takes account of the specific qualities of adolescent communication, and the challenges these represent:

> ...certain ways of acting, projecting, or communicating that are present in adolescents (especially in the most disturbed ones) are configured almost as a unique 'language'—a way to express their conflict and/or desire that we must learn to decipher.
>
> (Zac de Filc 2005, p. 461)

She adds:

> It would be risky to see this behaviour necessarily as a negative reaction to the treatment. On the contrary, sometimes these very ways express a desperate desire to get help that finds no other means to manifest itself.
>
> (Zac de Filc 2005, p. 461)

There is continuity here with Winnicott's thinking, and, in current practice, resonance with working with problems such as self-harming and eating difficulties.

The assessment of Annie, aged 16, contributes an example of how the therapist tries to decipher the young person's combination of verbal, embodied and acted communications, and attempts to find ways in which these can be thought and talked about. The assessment is beset with missed appointments and lateness, and yet Annie gave a sense of desperately needing to make contact with the therapist, but painfully being impeded in her ability to do so. Mondrzak (2012) writes about a young man who lived on his own time, which did not coincide with the therapist's, including when sessions should start or finish. On the other hand, Annie seems to feel she has to live on other people's time but cannot manage this successfully:

> Annie did not attend the first two appointment times that were offered; first she said she misread the date on the appointment letter, and the second appointment coincided with an exam she was taking. She came on her own and was 15 minutes early for the third time offered, and said she was desperate to get here, since though she had felt better a few months ago, things were now worse; she was down and had suicidal feelings. She appeared tightly wrapped in layers of clothing and her long hair covered much of her face. Annie mentioned a sequence of mistakes, and losses that she felt couldn't be put right; she had misread the questions in an exam, and she had lost her phone and her purse. Annie was tearful and said that she felt she should manage herself better, not lose things. In her counter-transference, the therapist felt that it was very difficult to get close to Annie, despite the ways she had been open in the session.

The sense was of a lot to try and think about, and not much space for thinking; Annie was clearly in pain, experiencing loss and being anxious about herself and her future. The therapist felt that her responses to Annie were inadequate but to say more could be premature without knowing more about the qualities of Annie's defences and internal objects. The Laufers have stated the importance of the assessment process for adolescents, that in some situations "assessment errors at this age are fraught with serious consequences" (Laufer & Laufer 1984, in Ruggiero 2006, p. 540). This, of course, heightens the anxiety for the therapist and tends towards erring on the side of caution. Having the opportunity for repeated assessment sessions at least provides the opportunity of seeing how this might develop and obtaining a more rounded picture. With Annie, her worry about herself and her fear of failure became live in the assessment sessions:

> Subsequently, the assessment included Annie's lateness and a missed session (the third), alongside her defensiveness when the therapist raised issues Annie found sensitive; in these moments Annie seemed to retreat even deeper into her many layers of clothing. Annie was genuinely frustrated with being late, saying that she wanted to come and she really wanted therapy but despite wanting to arrive on time she had not been able to. She talked about the traffic and buses being late; it seemed she was subject to things that just happened to her, that were beyond her control. She spoke again about fearing failure in her exams and ruining her chances for the future. The therapist sensed, and wondered aloud, if she was worried perhaps about 'failing' in her therapy. Annie responded initially by saying no, she was just late, but then back-tracked and said that might be the case, and said again she was worried about herself and repeated her fears for the future.

Assessment for psychotherapy needs to consider a whole panoply of factors: early experiences in childhood and current relationships, the impact of life events and how current difficulties, problem behaviours and symptoms relate to these. Rather than history-taking, the aim is to arrive at an assessment of core relatedness in the context of the adolescent process:

> …an examination of the quality of internal containment is crucial and can be arrived at by exploring the quality of the young person's relationships both to themselves and to others.
>
> (Anderson 2002, p. 167)

In some assessments, it is vital to ask questions, including about risks, though these may be difficult to ask, and to follow through discussion about key events; in others, the overall picture is put together through reflections on the sessions, discussions with colleagues and supervision. Running through this is indeed a tension between 'history-taking' and a process of working within the emerging therapeutic relationship. The tension is experienced by the therapist as being able to feel what can be asked and talked about in any moment, and between making interventions that further engagement or those that give priority to important content in the young person's account and concerns, and concerns about the young person. Into this category can be placed discussion of risks.

Assessing risks

Risks usually fall into categories of suicide and self-harming behaviour, violence towards others, breakdown and psychosis, as well as child protection/safeguarding risks, which include risks of abuse in the family, by physical, emotional and sexual abuse and neglect, and from peers and adults outside the family, including child sexual exploitation and bullying. These risks appear very often in therapeutic work with young people; rates of self-harm (including suicide attempts) have been reported as very high amongst young people (see Chapter 3), whilst social vulnerability, including abuse, inside the family and the wider community are also frequently present and contribute significantly to young people's vulnerability to mental health difficulties and their complex presentations in mental health services (Cottrell & Kraam 2005; Briggs et al 2015). Assessing these risks is always an uncertain and often an anxious process, involving predictions of future behaviour and its outcomes. Though accounts of practice, including some case studies (e.g. de Rementeria 2017; della Rosa 2016), describe the processes of continual risk assessment, this aspect of working with young people is under-theorised; risk assessment has become a predominant theme when working with young people, and its practice raises important questions of epistemology, that is to say, of how risks can be assessed, and therapeutic strategy.

Therapists' anxieties raised by the apprehension of risks in adolescent patients, and often under the pressure of organisational demands and fears, can split therapeutic work and risk assessment. This is particularly evident when applying research which has identified risk factors; risk assessment is mistakenly attributed objective, impartial or neutral status, and whilst this may seem reassuring, it overlooks the problem that risk assessment occurs in an uncertain field of possibilities rather than provides definitive answers (Briggs 2010b). For example, though an episode of self-harm is the strongest risk factor for repetition and, ultimately, suicide completion, in most studies the percentage of people who have multiple episodes of self-harm is around 50%. Risk assessments undertaken on the basis of asking a set of questions based on risk factors lead to false positives and false negatives when applied to individuals in clinical contexts. Thus clinical guidance recommends not using risk assessment tools to predict future behaviour (NICE 2011; Quinlivan et al 2017).

To be valid, the application of risk assessment needs to occur within rather than outside theoretical frameworks. It can be helpful to talk directly about suicide, for example by asking a young person direct questions about whether he feels suicidal, or violent towards others, or if he has a suicide plan; being able to be open and straightforward contributes to containing the young person, and counteracts the myth that talking about risks is dangerous (WHO 2014). Drawing on research and knowledge about risks when used reflectively, including discussing different perspectives with colleagues, creates a triangular space for the therapist (Britton 1989). For example, de Rementeria (2017, p. 69) describes working in partnership with a colleague to link risk assessments with the therapeutic process for a young woman who had repeatedly attempted suicide:

> She saw her care coordinator for weekly formal risk assessments and without these it would have been hard for me to keep faith with an analytic stance.

This is quite different from assuming that asking direct questions will lead to objective knowledge, or, alternatively, from positioning the young person as knowing the extent of their risk themselves. This reverses the container–contained relationship by making the young person responsible for judging risks. Risks, too, have an unconscious dimension; conscious suicidal motivation changes over time and is not a good predictor of behaviour, whilst the meaning and motivation behind each act may differ considerably from one incident to the next (NICE 2011). Unconscious motivations, phantasies and dynamics underpin behaviours and feelings that are suicidal and violent towards others. Psychoanalytic understanding of suicide provides a framework for understanding suicidal relatedness, which can be used in conjunction and dialogue with knowledge from risk factors (Briggs et al 2008). In adolescence, risks are closely related to the developmental process; Ladame (2008) works from the premise that suicidal behaviour, representing an attack on an internal parental object, will be repeated unless the unconscious motivation is understood, because the attempt has a traumatising effect, rupturing development.

Clinical guidance supports the idea that risks are best assessed in a reflective space; NICE (2011) recommends undertaking a collaborative and integrated psychosocial assessment of needs and risks to understand and engage people who self-harm and to initiate a therapeutic relationship. The clinical direction then changes from seeking certainty, through risk assessment, to establishing what provides sufficient containment for each case (Briggs 2010b). Maintaining a therapeutic relationship and providing a space to think is often key to assessing and reducing fluctuating risks, which increase if therapeutic contact is lost. At the same time, it is difficult to convey the intensity of the anxiety and sense of threat that is experienced by therapists when working with actively suicidal young people, and how they are pushed and pulled in the counter-transference; ensuring the therapist has sufficient containment themselves is a primary consideration.

Risk forms a ubiquitous discourse in contemporary therapeutic practice, and indeed, as discussed in Chapter 3, in contemporary risk societies; risks therefore originate from several sources: from adolescent behaviour, societal discourses, organisational pressures and the nature of the therapeutic encounter. It is important to consider the range of ways that risk manifests so that therapists can be aware of the different sources of risk, and also how risk is embedded at various levels of thinking. From a societal perspective, adolescents have been seen, or constructed, as having a propensity for "risk-taking behaviour." This term is used within social and psychological theories in different ways. It can indicate views that all young people are "presented as either actively deviant or passively at risk and sometimes both simultaneously" (Griffin 1997), views that are often attributed differently to gender, race and class distinctions. In part, this represents the societal generation of negative images of adolescents that can distort interactions between adults and adolescents and create "folk devils and moral panics" (Cohen 2002), and which can be pervasive. As Bradley (2017) recently pointed out, discussing Hoxter's (1964) classic paper on adolescence, the conflict between adolescents and adults enacting Oedipal rivalries features adolescents' physical capacities to put phantasies into action, whilst "the fury generated within the adult population is that it was rendered impotent, forced to watch passively" (p. 109). As we have seen in Chapter 3, the propensity to act, including in risk-laden ways, comes about through the impact of pubertal changes, whilst the encounter with adolescent emotionality can have a forceful impact on adults. Some young people are more vulnerable: "Singly or more usually in combination, at risk behaviours and adverse circumstances increase the vulnerability of young people to psychosocial disorders" (Baruch 2001).

A constant process of decision-making is always present in psychotherapy, taking more or fewer risks with interventions; for example: "Making transference interpretations felt like a risky step, as these generated a lot of anxieties for [the patient] and me" (della Rosa 2016, p. 176). Bion (1970) commented on the strength of feeling that "derives from risk of change of the psyche" (p. 99). Young people take risks in therapy, facing their difficulties and risking being stirred up by the process and destabilised, and thus engage the respect of therapists for their courage; de Rementeria (2017) comments, on her feeling for an adolescent patient, that "I have immense respect for the extraordinary courage it took to risk it all to do this work" (p. 81); this evokes Winnicott's (1958) idea that "the true self may at last be able to take the risks involved in its starting to experience living" (p. 297).

Diagnosis, complexity and the developmental process

Whilst recognition of symptoms is important for early intervention and the reduction of mental health difficulties that can persist into adulthood (see Chapter 3), there are particular problems associated with the instability of diagnoses in adolescence. Many mental health difficulties including depression and self-destructive behaviour as well as anti-social or conduct disorders may be transient and specific to the turbulence of the adolescent developmental process. Waddell (2006) and Flynn and Skogstad (2006) both discuss how young people, even with an apparently severe or established pattern of destructive relatedness to the self, can turn away from the pathology, with the:

> …swiftness with which what seem to be deeply entrenched narcissistic structures may be modified or modulated in response to even quite small internal or external changes.
>
> (Waddell 2006, p. 23)

Or alternatively apparently small factors can equally lead to "narcissistic states near psychotic in their intensity" (ibid). Instability of diagnoses does not mean they should not be used; the question is how and with what contextualisation. Assessment aims to distinguish between temporary adolescent developmental issues and deeper longer-term patterns of internal object relatedness, often established through adverse environmental circumstances, to identify the 'plasticity' of adolescence and the capacity for change: the availability for bearing the pain of new experiences, on the one hand, and patterns of repetition and closure, on the other. Diagnoses distinguish the different kinds of characteristic adolescent problems; differentiating between diagnoses and behavioural categories, and relative levels of severity, can help to focus interventions and lead to elaborations of meaning for each individual. Working with a thoughtful process of diagnosis is crucial where there are concerns about developmental breakdown and the possibilities of psychosis.

Ruggiero (2006) points out that diagnoses can also be used in ways that parallel risk assessments when dealing with anxieties, including treating diagnoses as 'objective' rather than providing a specific perspective:

> Haste thus replaces the capacity to tolerate anxiety and uncertainty, which is what is specifically asked of adolescents by the particular existential phase they are moving through. The result can be a diagnosis that closes instead of opens the discourse, and thus risks crystallizing adolescents' symptoms and colluding with their need (often shared by parents) to defensively find a negative identity to grab on to, with the expert's endorsement.

(p. 541)

Young people can be terrified of, or seek and feel reassured by, diagnoses. Especially for young people who have endured long-standing problems, making sense of their difficulties and excluding some other possibilities that might be more frightening can be reassuring. As with risks, working with diagnoses can take place in a thoughtful, triangular space, combining, for example, psychotherapy with psychiatric monitoring and the use of medication to provide the young person with some relief from very troubling or overwhelming states of mind to thus support therapy; or it can be used defensively, as an antidote to thinking. Working with and understanding symptoms and their meanings for the individual within the developmental process can be contrasted with the wish to get rid of symptoms, which concretises and avoids meaning.

Evidence-based practice has generated a particular problem for thinking about adolescence through the tendency for research to focus on single issues, especially depression, in order to simplify the research task. This has created a gap between the world of evidence and that of practice (Cottrell & Kraam 2005, p. 115). Young people's 'troubling predicaments' include mental health difficulties that often do not fit neatly into a single category, and which fluctuate, alongside social vulnerabilities. When diagnoses are made in order to focus on symptom reduction, and the difficulties young people face are reductively trimmed to a single issue, it is hard to hold onto and keep in mind the possibilities of growth through the developmental process; bearing complexity and uncertainty are then necessary aspects of the therapeutic process.

Involving and working with parents

Surprisingly little has been written about involving parents of adolescents in their therapy, despite the recognition, tracing back to Anna Freud's writing, of how this has an important impact on the therapy. This may reflect that, as Schmidt Neven (2016) comments, parents are often marginalised in their children's treatment; her approach aims to bring parents to the centre of therapy by including a systemic perspective and there is, of course, an extensive literature for family work and family therapy. Catty et al (2016) discuss working with parents within the model of Short-Term Psychoanalytic Psychotherapy for adolescents with depression.

Trevatt (2005) discusses how a Parents' Consultation Service works with parents troubled about their adolescents. This takes the perspective of exploring how parents experience the process of their adolescent's development. Parents may be troubled, anxious, angry, confused and in pain about their adolescents, and required, like the adolescents, to mourn and re-evaluate (Briggs 2008); parents' early childhood and adolescent experiences are revived through parenting their adolescents. Parents of young people in difficulties may be, and often are, vulnerable and have troubles of their own. Parenting adolescents is inevitably demanding; adolescents will at times need to use parents to be recipients of projections but at others they will be more separate and independent; parents need the internal flexibility to move between responding to moments when there is a need for containment and times to allow the adolescent to be more separate. As recipients of projections, parents can experience being left with feelings:

> Sometimes it feels as though all the unwanted feelings, hopelessness, incompetence, and fear on the one hand and responsibility and worry without power on the other.
>
> (Anderson 2002, p. 166)

There are many ways of characterising parenting adolescents; in one of these Dartington (1998, p. 21) describes the way parents have to adapt to what she calls the adolescent's "language of approximation," an indeterminate, ambiguous dialogue that keeps all decisions open and avoids any commitment: "a multi-cultural-user-friendly pidgin in which there are limitless possibilities to express desire without commitment. It is a language of identity-in-flux."

The lack of discussion of involving parents in adolescent psychotherapy might stem from its difficulty, practically and conceptually. Parents may be worked with alongside the young person or met with periodically for meetings to review the therapy, or, in the case of young adults, not seen at all. Meeting with parents can have the purpose of working on the parents' difficulties in parenting, or it can aim primarily to support the adolescent's therapy, to maintain engagement and prevent the parent from withdrawing the young person. 'Parent work' is not individual or couple therapy, though parents may subsequently seek or be referred for psychotherapy. A key purpose of parent work is to support and protect the space for individual therapy; ideally, when resources permit, work with parents is best handled by a colleague of the therapist seeing the young person, so that she is able to maintain focus on the adolescent's therapy. The nature of appropriate parent involvement depends to a great extent on the young person's age, or more accurately, his positioning in the adolescent developmental process. Whilst young people in early adolescence could expect parents to be actively involved in the practical, emotional and relational aspects of the therapy, older adolescents and young adults are more likely to approach therapy more independently. The relationship between parents and adolescents lies on a spectrum from enmeshed, in which the process of separating is avoided, to disengaged. In the latter are included absent parents, relationships with whom feature prominently in young people's narratives in therapy; where parents and adolescents are more enmeshed, joint rather than individual assessment may be indicated initially.

Therapists can be pulled towards trying to engage an adolescent who does not wish for treatment because an adult involved with him is demanding that "something is done." Sometimes, the first thing that is known about an adolescent in pain or difficulty is that another – an adult or perhaps a peer – is angry or anxious. Pain, anxiety and anger may be held by parents, perhaps projected onto them by the adolescent. The question of who holds the pain or anxiety, on behalf of whom, is an important assessment question (Bird 1989). Working with parents of young people can be effective when the adolescent finds it hard to engage in therapy (Trevatt 2005). Recognising the importance of the boundary between adolescents and parents, and the emotional experience of this for both, is an important consideration for the therapeutic frame or setting. Boundary issues always need discussion and negotiation, including where parents are experienced as absent or intrusive.

Transference, counter-transference and the analytic attitude

Developments in theory and technique have transformed how psychotherapy with young people is approached in current practice. Developments in thinking about transference and counter-transference are crucial here. The transference–counter-transference relationship is now widely understood to refer to a relational field of current emotions, states of mind and relatedness that reflect internalised relationships and are externalised into the 'here and now' of the therapeutic relationship (Lemma 2015a). Rather than historical reconstruction and giving insight, the shift to a more process-led approach (White 2007) puts emphasis on ideas about events that take place in the therapeutic session, in the field between therapist and patient.

There are, of course, differences between the various relational approaches; they do have in common the implication for therapeutic practice, which Donnel Stern (2013) describes as "experience-near understanding."

Working in the transference implies allowing all the patient's communications to have potential transferential meaning (Ferro 2004; Joseph 1989). The aim of psychotherapy is then to symbolise unformulated or unmentalised experiences, bringing about narrative transformations through the internalisation of the therapist's capacity for reverie, which leads to growth and repair of the mind (Stern 2013, p. 633), or through the co-creation of an analytic third, the recognition of each other (therapist and patient) where "the shared third, the dialogue, creates mental space for thinking and an internal conversation with the other" (Benjamin 2004, p. 22). An implication is that transference and counter-transference are not separate entities but an intersubjective field between therapist and patient (Ogden 1994), a matrix in which, notably through projective identification, the therapist and patient share an intersubjective field. Bion's thinking about the container–contained relationship is an influential example of how transference and counter-transference intermingle, so to speak, and the therapist's 'reverie' accesses the meaning of the patient's communications by projective identifications.

The application to adolescent psychotherapy of a relational, growth-focused approach is implicit in recent case studies and other accounts that aim to bring together the concept of growth and development with this approach. Waddell's (2006) discussion of reverie and negative capability when working to understand and repair destructiveness, and Jackson's (2017) exploration of the sexual and erotic aspects of the therapeutic relationship, both exemplify this relational approach when working with young people and the focus on the therapist's self-reflective process. Jackson reflects on the shifts in his thinking and feeling, about:

> ...how to draw the defining lines between what is safe and containing as opposed to something that might be rationalised as safe and containing but which is essentially evasive and defensive on the part of the therapist.
>
> (p. 12)

These reflections are important for the process of making real emotional contact with young people to understand, promote and contain development; the aim is to increase their capacity to think about feelings and to symbolise, to develop meaning and sustain emotions as bearable. Developing and sustaining an observational approach, drawing on infant observation (Bick 2002), forms a basis for the therapist's stance in working in this way with young people (Briggs 2018).

Adolescent psychotherapy in contemporary contexts

The developmental perspective makes adolescent psychotherapy different and distinctive; engaging with the central concept of the adolescent developmental process underpins therapeutic action. The therapist has to position herself to be receptive to ambiguous communications and the delicacies, contradictions and paradoxes in the therapeutic relationship whilst the young person is struggling with developmental issues of dependence and independence, realising greater separateness from parental figures, developing new forms of intimacy that follow from acquiring the new adult sexual body and being in the process of developing a more adult subjectivity; this develops through fluctuations between states of mind and in time. Paradigmatic is the question of dependency: how can a young person, who has a fragile sense of his own independence, allow himself to be dependent on a therapist and bear the ensuing confusion? On the other side is an equally difficult question – what does the therapist need to know about and what can be kept private? This tension about dependency creates an important dilemma in psychotherapy with adolescents and necessitates adaptations to the therapeutic method. The therapist's adaptations are to the adolescent's fragile sense of gathering within himself a sense of separateness from parental figures, his aloneness in the world and the responsibility for his own thoughts and actions.

In current contexts for practice the importance of the developmental process can be lost sight of or overridden by other considerations, including anxious responses to manage risks or symptom management; the consequence is that the essence of adolescent psychotherapy is also lost to sight, and, to paraphrase James Mann, the young person in difficulties is then the loser. Current practice shows that it is possible to bridge the earlier division between intervention and non-intervention in adolescent psychotherapy, to respect the importance of the passing of time and the maturational processes, whilst also intervening to support the developmental process and reduce the effects of developmental disturbance.

There are still few accounts of psychotherapy with young people that recognise the changing nature of the social context especially for later adolescence and young adulthood. The complex, extended routes into adulthood, the frequent lack of structure that young people experience, the tensions that arise from individualised decision making, as discussed in Chapter 3, have an impact on the therapy that is needed. The psychosocial conflicts in which young people feel themselves absorbed require recognition and understanding in psychotherapy. When and how they feel themselves subject to or subject of experiences is influenced by the complex field of past experiences, experiences of adolescent development and current contexts and the meanings these hold.

Finally, we return to the issue of duration; most accounts of adolescent psychotherapy assume an open-ended duration, whilst in practice much psychotherapy is relatively short-term. Responses to the increasing numbers of young people requiring therapeutic treatment, and to the wide range of situations and difficulties they present in diverse socio-cultural contexts, require different therapeutic approaches and modalities. Yet as noted in Chapter 2, it is only recently that time-limited models of psychotherapy have begun to develop. Therapeutic structure is an important aspect of the therapy; time-limited approaches can provide a structure that facilitates the young person's engagement in therapy. Even short-term therapy can be experienced as entrapping, whilst for others, any hint of a thought of an ending can be experienced as an abandonment or an affront to the develop-ing but vulnerable becoming-more-adult self. In current contexts, the demands for shorter-term therapy require that these are meaningful and reach the emotional, developmental needs of young people. Time-limited and longer-term psychother-apy can be complementary; they have different aims and suit different people at different points in time.

Conclusions

From earlier debates about the pros and cons of intervention to current preoccupa-tions with risks, adolescent psychotherapy presents some significant challenges. Working with the adolescent developmental process underpins psychotherapy, whilst the therapist's orientation towards the developmental perspective requires openness to the ambiguity of meaning of communications. Recent psychoanalytic thinking about the therapeutic relationship enhances thinking about therapeutic interactions and about being challenged to explore preconceptions, especially, perhaps, when addressing sensitive issues including sex, sexuality and ethnicity. Focusing on the developmental process and the therapist's stance in facilitating engagement, recognition and understanding in the therapeutic process leads to the conclusion that adolescent psychotherapy requires distinctive skills, knowledge and training.

Part II

Practice

Chapter 5

TAPP

Rationale and overview

Introduction

In this chapter, the principles and an overview of the practice of TAPP are introduced, to be elaborated on in the chapters that follow. The aims, rationale and therapeutic priorities of TAPP are described to show how the approach is used to help young people with mental health difficulties and to create opportunities for their growth and development. This overview of TAPP relates to the conceptual framework discussed in Part I to locate TAPP in the practice of brief psychotherapy, adolescent psychotherapy and an understanding of the adolescent developmental process in contemporary social contexts.

The advantages and disadvantages of manualisation of therapies have been widely debated; Lemma et al (2011) provide a detailed discussion. For psychodynamic practice, it is important that manuals provide practice guidance without restricting the clinician's judgement of the clinical task in each case. In the approach taken with TAPP, the guidance is less about providing prescriptions and more about orienting the practitioner towards the relevant underpinning frameworks and principles. However, to be clinically effective, there are some key points in the process that require the principles of TAPP, which have been grounded now in extensive clinical experience, to be adhered to, especially with regard to engagement of young people in therapy, working with the developmental focus and working within the time limit. There are two advantages of providing guidance for practitioners that are important here. First, the distinctive features of TAPP can be described to provide practitioners with an understanding of how to optimise the approach. From this, practitioners will be able to apply the approach in their own contexts and settings. Second, guidance provides researchers with a protocol for designing studies to test the effectiveness of the method.

Rationale

Time-Limited Psychodynamic Psychotherapy, or TAPP, is for adolescents and young adults in the age range of 14–25. The age range is approximate; the main consideration is whether it makes sense to relate the young person's difficulties to problems and disturbances of the adolescent developmental process. In the younger age range, the young person will need to be sufficiently engaged in the adolescent developmental process to be able to undertake individual psychotherapy. Young adults at the upper end of the age range will continue to be in the process of the transition to adulthood, reflecting this extended transition in current social contexts. TAPP has been undertaken by some individuals younger than 14 and older than 25. It draws on the practice of time-limited psychotherapy, as discussed in Chapter 2, and is a model that is distinctive and designed solely for young people. TAPP formulates that problem behaviours, states of mind, feelings and symptoms can be understood as disturbances in the adolescent developmental process; this makes them amenable to treatment and provides a powerful framework for therapeutic intervention.

The organising principle for TAPP is the view that through the therapeutic focus on a significant area of developmental difficulty and/or disturbance, for a time-limited period, the young person can recover the capacity to meet developmental challenges and/or have this capacity strengthened. This focus involves attention placed on and intervention with maladaptive, stuck, regressive or anti-developmental aspects of the self and the aim is to strengthen developmentally supporting and sustaining aspects of the self. TAPP formulates that resolution of problems occurs through a focussed exploration of the meaning of the patient's difficulties and symptoms within the process of adolescent development and change. This process is defined, as discussed in Chapter 3, as the emotional, relational and cognitive changes that follow puberty, necessitating the re-evaluation of relationships to self and others, including relating to the adult sexual body; the process continues through the development of subjecthood ('becoming a subject') leading to the taking up of adult roles.

Therapists using TAPP work with a developmentally based focus. Thus, consistent with most time-limited psychotherapies, as discussed in Chapter 2, the aim of psychotherapy is limited to this focus, which is established collaboratively between the young person and therapist for each therapy. The aim, therefore, is not to completely work through all difficulties, nor to claim to resolve all difficulties in 20 sessions, but rather to provide the conditions whereby the young person's own resources, and those in his environment, harness the power of the developmental process so that growth and development continue after the end of TAPP.

Aims

TAPP aims to meet the needs of young people experiencing a wide range of disturbances and difficulties, through providing a focussed therapeutic intervention which ameliorates the aspects of developmental processes that act against and/or restrict growth and development whilst supporting aspects that promote growth and development. There are several ways in which this overarching aim can be met in the process of time-limited psychotherapy. The aims of TAPP are always formulated referencing age-appropriate developmental levels; patients of different developmental levels experience and articulate their problems and needs in different ways. Therapeutic aims always take account of the young person's social and cultural contexts, and differences of gender, sexuality and abilities. The aims of TAPP include one or more of the following:

- Reducing distress and the symptoms of mental health difficulties whilst increasing the awareness of distress and its sources
- Encouraging and enabling greater reflective capacity regarding relatedness to self and others
- Increasing the young person's capacity to take responsibility for his own emotions, thoughts and bodily based desires rather than projecting these into others
- Becoming more aware and recognising of needs and vulnerabilities, and being able to identify and understand the needs of others
- Becoming more able to manage, name and make sense of powerful and potentially overwhelming emotional experiences and strengthen the capacity for regulating emotions, impulses and desires
- Through empathic connection with the therapist, promoting the development of more coherent narratives of self and relatedness to others as a young person in transition from childhood to adulthood in personal, social and cultural contexts
- Understanding internal experiences in connection with external, social contexts, i.e. in relation to parents and family members, education and employment and peers; and obtaining a greater capacity to negotiate and sustain relatedness to others in any of these contexts
- Recognising characteristic defences that restrict or impede development and developing greater flexibility of responses to stressful or anxiety-provoking and demanding situations

Structure

TAPP is an individual psychotherapy for adolescents, with an overall structure of 21 sessions, composed of three phases. The initial phase of assessment and engagement has four sessions at weekly intervals, leading to the formulation of a developmental focus agreed on between the young person and the therapist. Therapy consists of 16 sessions, also once weekly, working on the developmental focus, and this is followed by a post-treatment review six to eight weeks after the end of therapy. Work with parents and other professionals can be facilitated alongside the TAPP. The time limit provides an active structure that, when worked with purposefully, enhances the therapeutic process. This process requires having reflective, supportive spaces available for the therapist as an essential part of the TAPP structure.

As was discussed in Chapter 4, having repeated sessions in the initial assessment and engagement phase has been shown to be important when working with young people. The choice of 16 sessions for the length of therapy requires explanation. In developing the original model of brief therapy in the Brief Therapy Workshop in the Tavistock Clinic's Adolescent Department, the duration was chosen initially as it was used in other, earlier models of brief therapy, and was also currently applied, including in other therapeutic modalities. As practice experience has developed, this duration has been found to be long enough to sufficiently engage the young person, work therapeutically on the focus and to allow time for working with the ending and the process of separation involved. There are some examples of TAPP practice where the number of sessions has been varied, either reduced or extended, and some of these have been successful.

The assessment and engagement phase

The extended assessment phase is based on the approach developed in the Tavistock Clinic's Adolescent Department, as described in Chapter 4; this has a family resemblance to the idea of trial interpretation in adult brief therapy (Malan 1976; Stadter 2009) and to Davanloo's notion of a trial therapy (Malan & Coughlin Della Silva 2006). The assessment aims through repeated meetings to provide the young person with an experience of the therapeutic process and to actively engage with him in identifying the focus for therapy. It also provides a very brief intervention and an opportunity to not continue in therapy, for both therapist and young person. Providing opportunities for the young person to learn, from experience, what it means to take part in a therapeutic relationship in TAPP through repeated sessions in the assessment phase is one of the adolescent-centred features of TAPP. The therapist's stance facilitates understanding the young person's narrative, preoccupations and concerns and how he expresses his conflicts and distress. The emphasis is on engaging the young person in the therapeutic process and enhancing his active participation. The focus and duration of therapy are discussed as relating to the young person's preoccupations and relating to events in the social world that are important for him. Thus, the aim is to actively engage the young person in the contracting process and to work to develop his active participation.

Strategies

Articulating strategies is a way of helping the therapist identify therapeutic priorities and focus on what she needs to consider and work with, as well as, by omission usually, identify what is not part of the intervention and less likely to be part of TAPP. Strategies are detailed in the chapters on assessment (Chapter 6) and therapeutic priorities (Chapter 8). In general terms, the strategies for the therapist working with TAPP are to:

- Work within a psychodynamic framework
- Work in depth with unconscious processes and hence with transference and counter-transference

- Maintain an analytic and observational stance that promotes holding and containment of emotions and exploration of the young person's inner world
- Link the internal and external worlds of the young person, through applying a psychosocial approach
- Identify and work therapeutically with a developmental focus
- Work within the structure of TAPP, including the time boundaries for each session (usually 50 minutes) and the time limit, for the duration of the therapy, and to explore, hold and contain the young person's experiences of time
- Work with the emotionality of the ending
- Review continually through the therapy and in the post-treatment review the young person's development and future therapeutic needs

Therapeutic priorities, method and stance

The therapeutic priorities in TAPP are to work psychodynamically, to identify and work with the developmental focus to promote change and growth, to work in depth, including with the transference and counter-transference, and to work with time limits. The therapist will also work with a psychosocial understanding of the young person rooted in his internal, interpersonal and social worlds. The therapist will aim to develop a therapeutic stance that supports the containment of emotional experiences and facilitates exploration of the young person's internal world.

Though summarising briefly what is core to psychoanalytic practice from the wealth of psychoanalytic theory is, to an extent, hazardous, some initial and probably widely agreed on statements can be tried. Psychoanalytic practice focuses on the impact of earlier experiences on current development and functioning, alongside taking account of inborn characteristics and personality. It emphasises the internal and external processes and experiences that shape mental functioning, and that therefore inform perceptions of self and other. Anxiety and other emotions, if felt to be too much for the individual, or his ego, to hold, lead to the formation of defences which are not conscious. Unconscious processes of projection and introjection underpin relatedness, and transference is central in organising relatedness to others, on the basis that experiences are transferred from one relationship to another in place and time.

As is consistent with its emphasis on the relational and the developmental, TAPP is positioned within current relational and object relations approaches to psychodynamic psychotherapy. This means that in addition to the above core concepts, TAPP understands internal development in terms of the patterns of relatedness with significant others that are internalised. Through the processes of projection and introjection, and communication through projective identification, the therapist's counter-transference can be informative of aspects of the young person's state of mind. The therapeutic relationship consists of meaning-creating processes, and development of symbolic capacity, including the capacity to think about emotional experiences that are shared in the therapy. Therapeutic aims, in this approach, involve developing the capacity to sustain feelings rather than discharging them through action and projective processes, increasing awareness of distress and its origins in past and present experiences and transforming narratives both through holding and containing difficult and overwhelming experiences and through shared understanding in the therapeutic relationship. However, as advocated by Stadter (2009), and consistent with the conclusions reached in Chapter 2, the application of these core concepts need to be adapted to meet the therapeutic needs of individual young people and the strategies that are required in each case.

TAPP applies the concept of 'therapeutic stance' as introduced into brief therapy by Strupp and Binder (1984); this includes not only techniques but also the therapist's values, beliefs and attitudes. The therapeutic stance in TAPP aims to enhance the capacity to work with these key psychoanalytic and relational processes. It consists of taking an analytic attitude and establishing a therapeutic frame or setting. The therapeutic frame in TAPP is based on a clear and rigorous analytic structure of regular sessions of usually 50 minutes at weekly intervals, at the same time and in the same place each week. Maintaining the frame is vital in order to provide the means for recognising and attending to unconscious processes, in the young person and the therapist, and to provide the young person with a sense of the therapist's reliability. It is important to think reflectively about occasions when the structure is breached or altered. This includes noticing how both therapist and young person observe the structure, or not. Lateness, missed sessions and the impact of breaks in the therapy, whether planned, as in the case of holidays, or unplanned, for example, through illness or unexpected absences, always have impacts and meaning. In TAPP, working with the structure is a powerful way of working towards therapeutic change. This is particularly true with regard to working with the time limit, and the powerful feelings that are involved in the experience of separation and loss in the process of ending the therapy.

The concept of the analytic attitude has been subject to diverse interpretations; there are debates over this relating to the different positions taken *vis-à-vis* Freud's formulations of the concepts of analytic neutrality, free-floating attention and free association. Chapter 2 outlined the different positions taken towards the applications of these principles in brief therapy: earlier models of brief therapy challenged these principles, whilst more recent approaches, particularly from the relational perspective, at least partly reinstated them. The key debate is whether the therapist eschews the principles described by Freud as constituting the analytic attitude in favour of a more direct and active approach. In TAPP the essential features of the analytic attitude are that a therapeutic stance is developed in which the therapist is open and available to the emotionality in the therapeutic session, both in the patient and in herself. The process with the young person requires that the therapist is available for emotional experiences, applying Bion's (1962) concept of reverie, in which the therapist allows a space in her mind for receiving, digesting and thinking about emotional communications from the patient. In brief therapy this provides what Laor (2001) has called an 'active containment,' allowing the discovery of unconscious aspects of relatedness, as discussed in Chapter 1. This entails taking an observational stance, as described in Chapter 3, and the capacity to suspend judgement, in order to allow for uncertainty, ambiguity and the apprehension of the new and unknown. Thus, the therapist adopts a stance which provides the possibilities for containing emotional experiences, and for making emotional contact with the young person's conscious and unconscious communications and explorations of their internal and social worlds. This requires in effect that the stance does use free-floating attention, which as we saw in Chapter 2 is not incompatible with a time-limited approach, and that the therapist's responses are informed by this process and by the counter-transference, therefore, rather than any injunctions to be more direct and more interventionist. The therapist is not required to be more active working in TAPP than in longer-term therapy, but rather to be responsive to the young person, to stay with the emotions in the room, to not hurry and to respond to developmental changes in the young person.

This does not imply that the therapist's stance is timeless. The therapist combines free-floating attention with working therapeutically with the structure of TAPP, including the time limit. Stadter's (2009) distinction between "time near," or clock time, and "time far," which holds the sense of timelessness is helpful in thinking about how the therapist works in both these dimensions; combining these in the therapist's stance provides a good metaphor for the way that the therapist, in her mind and through how she intervenes, moves between an awareness of the external reality of the passing of time and a suspension of this in the process of working in the room with unconscious processes. Another analogy that fits here is that the therapist needs to work within herself with both the maternal, for example, reverie, and the paternal, for example the attention to boundaries and structure. Working with the counter-transference is therefore a crucial aspect of the therapeutic stance in TAPP. The therapist reflects on her emotional experiences in the room with the young person, to access what may impede her understanding of the young person, and also uses her thoughts and feelings to inform her of the young person's state of mind communicated through projective identification.

Working with time limits

Working with time limits is a therapeutic priority in TAPP. The time-limited duration of therapy provides an active structure that has an impact on the therapeutic relationship; the meaning of the time limit at any point in the therapy infuses the therapeutic relationship and requires the therapist's active attention. This is particularly so at key points; the transition from assessment to therapy, and the ending. The sense of an ending and impending loss and separation runs through the therapy, at times less near the surface than others, but in the last few sessions of the therapy, it is unavoidable, bringing an intensity to the relationship. The mid-point of therapy is also often a key moment regarding how the young person relates to time, initiating the feeling of being nearer the end than the beginning.

How the young person experiences the time limit, and the passing of time in the therapy, relates closely to his experience of adolescence and the transition to becoming more adult; recognising this in the transference and working with it provides an important opportunity for change and growth. Mann's (1973) view is true for TAPP that the powerful feelings of the ending affect the therapist as well as the young person and can exert tremendous pressure on the therapist, including her capacity to hold onto the time frame. In TAPP, the post-treatment review session, as well as providing an opportunity to review the therapy, is part of the therapeutic structure; the presence of the review six to eight weeks after the termination of the therapy holds a sense of continuity and contains some of the feelings about ending. For example, the therapist can focus on the processes involved in bringing to an end the regular weekly therapy, whilst pointing to the review as offering an opportunity to reflect together and to think some more about future plans.

Reflective process

For the therapist, TAPP can be an intense therapeutic experience; there is a lot to think about and hold in mind, meaning that maintaining therapeutic sensitivity and judgment under the pressure of powerful emotions and complex, often ambiguous communication is a demanding task. Reflective spaces that support the therapist are essential for undertaking TAPP effectively.

The development of the TAPP model of time-limited psychotherapy in the Tavistock Clinic's Adolescent Department employed a workshop structure – the Brief Therapy Workshop – following the method Malan had used earlier for the development of brief therapy for adults (see Chapter 2). The weekly meetings of the adolescent Brief Therapy Workshop provided a reflective space for therapists, both staff and trainees, working with these cases, and a space in which reflection on the model and learning from it could take place. The practice in the workshop was similar to that used by other Tavistock clinical groups, and for infant observation, consisting of therapists reading a detailed written process account of a therapy session; in the discussion which followed, the therapist supplemented the written account of the session with additional thoughts and feelings recalled from within the session. The workshop provided a triangular space for sharing therapeutic responsibility which allowed the therapist to be free to work with the relationship with the young person. This was particularly helpful when therapists were new to the process.

The core learning from the workshop transfers to other settings. In current practice in all settings, it is recognised that support for the therapist is vital. Therapists new to the model use the reflective seminar process as the central part of learning how to work with TAPP, and experienced therapists find the process helpful in working with the intensities and complexities of time-limited therapy with young people. Therefore, a reflective space which contains the elements of the Tavistock workshop is an important component of TAPP. A number of approaches have been developed, including group, peer and individual supervision, and seminars that replicate aspects of the workshop; these have been found to be more containing when available weekly, and this is now an essential part of the training for TAPP practitioners.

Chapter 6

The assessment and engagement process

Introduction

This chapter explores the initial assessment and engagement phase of TAPP. The assessment phase in TAPP follows the distinctive pattern of assessment for psychotherapy for young people, as discussed in Chapter 4; it consists usually of four sessions of 50 minutes held at weekly intervals. This is adapted for the purposes of assessing for time-limited psychotherapy, through identifying, discussing and agreeing on the developmental focus, and offering and agreeing on the duration of therapy. Since there are distinctive processes of engagement and assessment when working with young people, these are discussed in this chapter, and related to the theoretical framework discussed in Part I. The following chapter, Chapter 7, will discuss in detail how to identify the developmental focus and the negotiation and agreement of the time limit.

Aims of the engagement and assessment phase

The assessment process prioritises learning from experience; the young person is given an opportunity to learn from experience what psychodynamic psychotherapy involves, the feelings that may be stirred up by therapy and the way the therapist relates to him: how she listens, explores and provides a containing space. For the therapist, the assessment model provides an opportunity to understand, through repeated observations across the four sessions, the young person's ways of relating and the meaning of his difficulties, and to reach a conclusion about whether time-limited psychotherapy is suitable. The therapist is oriented towards noticing the young person's ambivalences and confusions, and his anxieties about entering into a therapeutic relationship. The aim is therefore to engage the young person in actively thinking about how psychotherapy can support and enhance his development and reduce the difficulties that interfere with and threaten his development; it helps him gain a flavour of what would be involved for him, practically and emotionally, in being a participant in a therapeutic process.

The aims of assessment are therefore to identify the nature of the strengths and resources of the young person and to understand the nature of his difficulties and disturbances. In the assessment process, the therapist engages with a range of material and perspectives and explores the qualities of the young person's internal containment and his relationships with self and others. The therapist will wish to understand the young person's earlier childhood experiences, how the transition to adolescence was experienced and thus the changes that have occurred following puberty; current relationships, the impact of life events and current difficulties, problem behaviours and symptoms can be understood within this holistic approach to the patient. The aim of understanding the relationship between the problems, symptoms and distress presented by the young person, as well as disturbances of the developmental process, is a key organising principle for the assessment.

The therapist therefore aims to undertake an assessment for psychotherapy over the four weekly meetings of the assessment phase. Additionally, she will identify and assess factors for and against time-limited therapy, and thus reach a decision about the young person's suitability for TAPP. Formulating and articulating a developmental focus for the therapy should lead to discussing and agreeing on this collaboratively with the young person. The assessment phase is thus concluded by the sharing of and agreement on a plan and focus for therapy.

The aims in the assessment phase can be summarised as:

• Engagement of the young person in a therapeutic process
• Providing an initial experience of the therapeutic process
• Identifying how psychotherapy can support and enhance the young person's development
• Undertaking a psychodynamic assessment of the young person's strengths/resources and difficulties/disturbances and arriving at a view of his suitability for therapy
• Assessment of factors for and against time-limited therapy
• Identifying, discussing and agreeing on a developmental focus for the time-limited therapy

Strategies for the assessment and engagement phase

In the initial assessment and engagement phase the key activity of the therapist, which underpins all others, is to address and empathically explore the young person's emotional experience of taking part in these sessions. The therapist takes up an analytic observational therapeutic stance (see Chapters 4 and 5) to facilitate noticing details in the young person's presentation, both verbal and non-verbal, and to provide the basis for accessing unconscious processes. The therapist's free-floating attention and her reflections on her own thoughts and emotional experiences are important for achieving openness to the emotional communications in the sessions. During the assessment the therapist, operating from this stance, will aim, as appropriate at the time, to explore and empathically name and contain anxieties the young person experiences in the process of attending the assessment sessions.

The therapist will take responsibility for the structure of therapy, and provide information about the therapeutic process, clarifying the duration and frequency of the sessions; for example, the purpose of offering four sessions will be shared and thought about. These clarifications will be contextualised by reference to the setting in which the assessment is taking place; naturally, this will vary in different settings, whether a mental health service, primary care, educational or private practice.

The therapist will identify and explore the young person's fears, hopes and expectations of therapy and his feelings about coming to therapy and being in the room with the therapist. The therapist will aim to tune into the young person's capacity to make and maintain emotional contact, and the capacity to bear and think about emotions. Seeking to understand these can lead to exploration of current and past experiences, the qualities of the patient's accounts of his development through adolescence, his relationships and the kinds of difficulty and symptoms being experienced. This will need to take into account age, social and cultural contexts, familial and interpersonal contexts and aspirations in key domains: familial, peer, educational/employment and intimate/sexual/love relations.

The therapist will seek to make appropriate initial interpretations based on their understanding of the emerging therapeutic relationship. Included are transference interpretations aimed at addressing experiences in the room, to assess and further develop emerging themes, to deepen the understanding of the young person's relationships and difficulties and to link experiences in the therapy with their current and past relationships in the psychodynamic triangle (Malan 1979/1995; see Chapter 2).

In TAPP the aim of these interventions is also to work towards identifying a meaningful developmental focus for the therapy. The therapist will have in mind, and ask questions or seek clarifications about, the young person's narrative of themselves and significant others, including parents, family members, peers, boyfriend/girlfriend, teachers, employers. She will explore the qualities of relatedness, emotionality and object relatedness of these narratives and the qualities of significant life experiences. This will lead to reflecting on emerging thoughts about a developmentally based focus for time-limited therapy together with initial articulations of the key developmental issues. Over the course of the assessment, this leads to the formulation of the developmental focus, and discussing and agreeing on the aims of therapy with the young person.

It is expected that the process will involve a rich but complex and probably emotionally intense experience for the therapist, and a key strategy will be to ensure that supervision or a reflective peer group is available to support the therapist's thinking, particularly about the qualities of emotionality and relatedness between the young person and therapist, thus fine-tuning the therapist's orientation to the young person.

Strategies in the assessment phase can be summarised as:

- Taking up an observational therapeutic stance to notice details, facilitating openness to and reflection of emotional communications and facilitating engagement
- Exploring fears, hopes and expectations of therapy and containing anxieties experienced in the process of attending the initial sessions
- Structuring the assessment sessions and providing information about and clarifications of the therapeutic process and the thinking of the therapist about the process
- Focusing on the qualities of relatedness, emotionality and object relatedness of the young person's narratives
- Making initial interpretations based on the emerging therapeutic relationship
- Identifying the quality of the patient's experience of the adolescent development process
- Formulating the developmental focus
- Discussing and agreeing with the patient on the formulation, aims and goals of therapy
- Making use of peer support and supervision to enhance therapeutic sensitivity

The first assessment session

Beginning the first assessment session can be thought of as marking a transition across the boundary into the therapeutic setting (Bird 1986). The therapist manages the communications prior to the session; there will have been some preliminary contacts with the young person, his parents or carers and/or with professionals making the referral. Practical procedures naturally vary according to the setting; there are also differences for younger adolescents and older adolescents and young adults. More parental involvement is expected with younger adolescents and they are likely to be directly involved before the first meeting with the therapist; this may differ for psychotherapists working on-site in educational settings. Before the first session there need to be discussions about the suitability or appropriateness of seeing the young person with a view to starting therapy; in some settings, especially mental health services, there will be a detailed referral process. It is important to have a sense of whether the young person wishes to attend, or if the motivation stems more from parents or professionals.

For younger adolescents, preparatory communications with parents can include asking what the young person's thoughts are about attending, and indeed if he knows about the plan. It has to be decided whether to offer an appointment for the young person alone, or a meeting with him and his parents, or to suggest an initial meeting with the parents. This is a delicate area to negotiate, and is ideally handled by a team, if resources permit, so that one member of the team can undertake the preliminary work with the parents, and be available for subsequent meetings, whilst the therapist who will work with the adolescent aims to keep this space solely for him, uncontaminated, so to speak, by direct contact with the views and projections of others. Working with parents is considered further later in this chapter, where the considerations discussed in Chapter 4 are developed. For older adolescents, it is expected that they will make contact with the therapist directly, supported as necessary by parental figures, to accept the initial appointment. Involved in these considerations is the key principle that adolescent psychotherapy in general and TAPP specifically require the young person to be engaged in the adolescent process and to assess to what extent that they are able to bring themselves into their therapy under their own steam, or, more accurately and concretely, on their own feet.

Establishing emotional contact, and through this gaining an initial understanding of the reasons the young person is seeking therapeutic help, can be complex, anxious and highly demanding of both participants. The therapist's state of preparation for the first session is in fact assisted by a certain amount of anxiety; Bion (1970), aphoristically, said that there should be two frightened people in the room, or, if not, how could anything new be learned or recognised? The therapist has to be prepared to tolerate a certain amount of anxiety arising from not-knowing, whilst attempting to find a way of communicating that she is interested in and wishes to understand the young person's anxieties, hopes and expectations. Both the young person and the therapist will have some preconceptions of the other, a pre-transference (Salzberger-Wittenberg 1970; Thomas 1992).

The transition across the boundary into assessment usually requires some management, which is aided by adopting an observational and reflective stance; the therapist aims to notice both what happens at this point, and how she feels in the moment. How to think about and make appropriate plans for involving the parent in the therapy, and, on the other hand, for maintaining a boundary for the adolescent's therapy, which does not include the parent, are important initial considerations.

It might be necessary to negotiate with a parent in the waiting room about who the session is for; it can be useful to note who has arrived for the appointment with the young person, or whether he has arrived on his own, and how they appear in the waiting room. Are they sitting close together or far apart? Do they seem relaxed in each other's company, or do they seem anxious, or is there some tension? How does the young person then come into the room, with reluctance or with apparent confidence? The therapist at this point is usually keen to get into the consulting room to get started, and exchanges at the point of transition across the boundary can increase anxiety. The range of experiences, in short, can be very great. For example, Annabel, a 15-year-old, walked very slowly behind the therapist from the waiting room to the consulting room, her feet dragging; the journey seemed interminable, as the therapist slowed down to her pace. Jerry, 16, confounded his therapist's preconceptions; from prior discussions about him, she expected him to be a very anxious, thin young man and was surprised to find a large boy smiling at her and jumping to his feet to head out of the room, almost leading her. These moments can give an immediate sense of the young person's relationships, his feelings about coming for therapy, how he contends with anxiety and his positioning in the adolescent process. Diana, who was 17 at the time of her first session, came accompanied by her boyfriend, who waited for her. In contrast, the therapist observed a negotiation between Jim, who was nearly 18, and his mother, who came with him to the first meeting. In the waiting room they sat separately, both on their phones; when the therapist arrived, the mother asked Jim whether she should wait or leave, to which Jim replied that she could leave. The mother asked if she should return at the end of the session and Jim said he would walk home. All these different examples give the therapist an immediate feel for the young person, his relationships and initial feelings about therapy, which can be thought about as the assessment continues.

The young person's preconceptions often require some exploration once the session begins, with the aim of providing containment for anxieties about starting therapy. Wondering aloud with the young person about how he experiences the setting, thoughts he may have about coming to the session and, later, how he now feels in relation to these are important strategies in the first session. Of course, the young person may defend against these anxieties in a number of ways: brashness and omnipotence, shyness and not speaking or alternatively talking seamlessly, filling the space so there is little chance for the therapist to speak or even to think. The therapist will begin to notice splits between words and actions, how actions can communicate states of mind; – where adolescents' feet take them – and how – can be very informative, – and how anxieties and tensions are communicated through the body.

Taking an observational stance continues to be important to note how the young person presents, and his ways of talking and relating. For example, Annabel, whose slow walk to her first session was initially striking, communicates immediately a sense of her fragility, as the therapist recorded:

> Once in the room she gave the impression of tying herself in knots as her arms cross and uncross. I asked her if she would like to tell me something about herself and I notice I have softened my voice and I felt that any loudness could send her scurrying from the room.
>
> (Briggs et al 2006, p. 325)

Being aware of adolescent emotionality and responding to it is crucial to the engagement process, yet it is difficult to make informed responses at the beginning, when so little information is available; adapting one's tone and pace is one way of tuning in to a sense of the emotionality in these communications whilst reflecting on the quality of early counter-transference experiences. As discussed in Chapter 4, working with young people involves adaptations of the therapeutic method; in the initial stages, these include, for example, not leaving the patient in silence, and being ready to provide information about the process.

Establishing the frame

The therapeutic frame, or setting, is extremely important in TAPP; the essential aspects are the provision of regular, weekly sessions at the same time each week and in the same place. This rigorous frame is necessary to provide containment and to facilitate understanding the adolescent patient's experiences of emotional contact and separation. How the young person responds to the frame is a fruitful source of information about the therapeutic relationship and the young person's internal world, if it can be reflected upon and linked with other material and the therapist's counter-transference:

> Annie's struggle with arriving in time for her sessions was described in Chapter 4; she missed or cancelled three appointments and was late for two; she vividly conveyed an intense struggle involved in attending, feeling both 'desperate' to arrive and held back by apparently powerful forces, which she appeared subject to. Though she was reluctant to take up the therapist's suggestion of thinking about the emotional meaning involved, an understanding of this conflict as relating to fears of rejection and a wish for acceptance emerged, and could be related to issues in her current and past relationships.

Annie did recognise the time frame and her conflicts about it. In other cases, the therapist may feel pushed or pulled by the adolescent testing the frame:

> Harry, a 17-year-old, arrived 20 minutes late for his first session; he apologised lightly and explained that his mother had been late in leaving to bring him to the appointment. He asked if there could be a later time as his mother has difficulty with this time. Harry appeared much younger than his age, shy, compliant, reliant on his mother and evoking maternal responses in the therapist, who then found that unwittingly and uncharacteristically she had run over time at the end of the session. She reflected after the session that Harry had exerted a powerful effect on her and the therapeutic frame.

Alongside reflecting on these experiences, and aiming to understand any ambivalences the young person has about attending, a priority in the first session is to explain the framework of the session, simply and directly: that the sessions normally last for 50 minutes, that usually there are four meetings at weekly intervals and that the aim is to provide opportunities to think and discuss how the therapist (or service) can be of help and whether and how the young person wishes to decide to have therapy. The therapist makes a judgement, however, about how much of this to discuss and when based on what may be most helpful to the individual young person; some may take flight from the idea of four sessions without some preparation having taken place. For example, James, 15, appeared initially very hesitant about starting an assessment and the therapist decided that offering one session after the initial meeting would be more acceptable than four. The aim is to provide sufficient information to best facilitate engagement in the primary task, which is the elucidation of the young person's narrative of himself, so as to provide an initial understanding of the developmental disturbances that can become the focus for treatment.

Beginning the telling of and listening to the young person's narrative

Central to the approach of TAPP is the focus on finding, providing, maintaining and sustaining a therapeutic space in which the young person can relate to the therapist. Sensitive and containing responses to the anxieties of the new adolescent patient and sufficient explanation of the framework/setting should enable the young person to begin an account of himself, in his own words, either unsolicited or following a straightforward prompt such as "would you like to tell me something about yourself?" If this does not occur and the young person remains silent or questioning of the therapeutic process, these obstacles need to be recognised sympathetically and discussed; the therapist may wish to comment that the young person finds beginning difficult, and then to explain that her wish is to find out something of the patient's life and concerns, but that this appears not to be easy for him, and the therapist will be prepared to stay with the anxieties or difficulties that are experienced in getting going. Comments on the newness of the situation, or similar statements, may be helpful at this point.

Once the young person does begin to talk about themselves, the therapist notices both the content and the way it is communicated. Although this simplifies the different ways young people can present their stories, and the emotional flavour of these, narratives can be described as belonging to one of the following categories:

- Reflective, elaborated and detailed and appearing to be communicated with relatedness to the therapist
- Short, abbreviated and brief, 'factual' rather than emotionally alive and waiting for the therapist to provide a lead and structure about what is said
- Long, involved, perhaps self-absorbed, entangled and not particularly related to the therapist as an involved participant in the telling of the narrative

The therapist focuses on the emotional experience of receiving these communications, distinguishing between the following:

- Are they emotionally engaging with fluctuating intensity of feeling, evoking perhaps sympathetic engagement with the young person's experiences?
- Do they seem to be short of, or light on, emotional content invoking a sense of not feeling engaged or concerned?
- Do they transmit intense feelings to the therapist, evoking perhaps annoyance with the young person or others in his life, or filling up the therapist with feelings in ways that suggest projective identification?

Additionally, the therapist may become aware of and attentive to the sense of time in the young person's narrative and how he uses the time-frame of the session. There may be a sense in which the young person is able to make use of or work within the time limit of the session, being aware of how time is passing. On the other hand, the duration of the session may seem to be taxing to the young person and being in the room for 50 minutes can feel like a feat of endurance. Other young people can seem to be in a timeless state and surprised when the end of the session arrives. Attending to these qualities helps to begin to get a sense of whether the young person can stay in the therapeutic process:

> Ben, 14, seemed to be compelled to recount at length traumatic and difficult episodes in his life, as though talking to a familiar person rather than to someone he had known for a few minutes. Though this suggested that he was quite desperately seeking someone who could listen to him, his therapist, whilst attending carefully to this, commented on the relational context between them, that this was their first meeting. Nevertheless, at the end of the session, the therapist wondered if Ben had said so much that he may not be able to return for the following session.
>
> Hester, in contrast, told her story in vivid detail but conveyed a sense that it was well-rehearsed. 21 years old, she appeared small, neat and wrapped in a large coat; she held her appointment letter tightly in her hand as if she feared losing it. She made apologies for being late, saying she had got lost, and quipping that though she was doing a geography degree it did not help her much with map-reading. She then gave a detailed account of her childhood and the complicated and conflictual relationship of her parents. Though the content was gripping, it was also distancing and the therapist had the sense she was listening to a news report. Hester's attempt at humour and the journalistic style of her narrative appeared to have the aim of both informing the therapist and distracting her from the immediacy of what it was like for Hester, at that moment, to be in the room with the therapist.

These emerging narratives communicate a flavour of the experience of beginning the therapeutic relationship and a transference relationship; they make reference to relationships, past and present, and the young person's feelings about which of the array of age-related tasks in the social world preoccupy him. How he feels about these, including issues relating to the changing body and sexuality, to difference and cultural contexts, to parents, siblings and peers, to experiences in education including feelings about exams, to pressures to attain and to future choices, may all be mentioned and described or suggested. As the young person talks about these, the therapist will pay attention particularly to:

- Qualities of flexibility and negotiability on the one hand, and more rigid or confused and undifferentiated, mutually projective qualities on the other hand
- Expressions of tension and anxiety; the therapist will aim to assess how the young person appears to characteristically address change and conflict, with

the objective of making initial formulations or hypotheses about these, for testing and deepening through further contact

- The ways that relationships are described, whether they are experienced flexibly and with complexity or in simple 'black and white' terms
- Whether the young person appears entangled in relationships with parental figures and in other relationships or more able to think and experience self separately from these, and/or whether there is a sense of denigrating, degrading, downplaying the importance of or mocking dependency on and vulnerability to parental figures
- How the young person feels about being alone, and how he can think about being an individual in relation to groups
- The presence of deeper anxieties about self and in relationships, for example including fears of rejection, of madness, of being blamed and punished, of hurting or being hurt

The therapist's role in the first session

In the first assessment session, the therapist's role is to facilitate sustaining the young person's capacity to communicate about himself and to respond to the quality of communication. Optimally, a reflective discussion is sought, in which the therapist can respond in ways that demonstrate the value of being able to think about and reflect on experiences, and the therapist will aim to distinguish between this more reflective mode of mental functioning and those modes which are evacuating of experience through projective processes or are hostile towards or dismissive of relating to others. The therapist may begin to make interpretations to note the emotionality of these communications within the context of wishing to understand the young person and his anxieties.

In summary, the therapist's role in the initial session includes:

- Deciding how to respond to questions, explicit and implicit, that the young person has about the process and framework
- Sustaining the young person's attempts to begin his narrative through empathic listening and prompting
- Commenting on and interpreting the way the young person communicates, with an emphasis on promoting reflective thinking
- Noticing and recognising anxieties about being in a therapeutic relationship, and the qualities of emotionality in the session

Additionally, and perhaps most usually towards the end of the first session, the therapist will make some comments which summarise, clarify or give feedback about key aspects of the process so far, placing these in the context of thinking about how to proceed. The therapist then makes an offer of meeting again the following week or reminding the patient of the offer of meeting up to four times in order to think together and decide about therapy. She will ask the young person if he wants to say anything about how he has experienced the session. The session ends with an agreed-upon time for the next session and the therapist's clear statement of commitment to that time, whether or not the young person is ambivalent about returning.

Interpretations and initial formulations

Taking an observational approach and listening to the young person's emerging narrative involves the therapist in a continuous process of making formulations. These are likely to include thoughts about how the young person is experiencing the initial process of engagement and particularly thoughts about how he is relating to the therapist. Early strong evidence of transference, positive or negative, may be observed or heard and the therapist may consider commenting or working with these. Counter-transference thoughts and feelings will guide the therapist's attention; strong feelings evoked in the therapist, or ways in which the therapist finds herself being pressured to act – for example, Martha's therapist extending the session time – will be particularly noted.

The therapist has to steer a course between intervening too little or too much. To make interpretations that may be premature can put the engagement process at risk; to not interpret, especially with some patients, can reduce the capacity to offer an effective containment. If by the end of the first session the therapist has an initial formulation relating to an aspect of the adolescent developmental process, this can be put tentatively to the young person. Formulations may be stated in more complex ways, drawing on some of the material presented in the session, including life experiences or thoughts and feelings the young person has mentioned, to identify a focus for thinking and discussion in future sessions. Sometimes patients give a warning about fears or difficulties they may have about being in therapy. These "cautionary tales" (Lemma et al 2011) are usually thought of as being unconscious, though in adolescence they may be near the surface; one 14-year-old girl said, with total clarity, "it's no good, it won't work, I won't change." In the example of Annie described earlier, her expectation of others in relationships was linked to her expectations of therapy; the therapist aimed to communicate noticing and thinking about what Annie has said, and to provide a holding comment that provided a sense of continuity and of going on thinking:

> Annie talked towards the end of her session about needing to manage herself better, about losing things and feeling that others often disappointed her. The therapist commented that she wondered if Annie was raising here some important thoughts of what she might expect from her therapy, and perhaps this was something they could discuss further together.

Although the emphasis in this discussion has been placed on recognising the anxieties that young people may bring to the first assessment session, and the therapist's role in containing these, it should not be overlooked that the drive and energy of adolescence may also be present and have an impact on the therapist's counter-transference through playful, imaginative or passionate associations. The therapist may be impressed by the adolescent's spirit and ideals, by the passions in their relationships, by their being happy, sad, wistful or troubled, and by their humour. Their capacities to take risks in the service of their development, in their relationships or aspirations and their capacities for irony may be glimpsed. Recognising these is the first step for the therapist; trying out some initial comments may bring into view another side of the adolescent and deepen the contact in the therapeutic relationship; manic defences and getting "swept away" by these powerful trends has to be guarded against (Brenman Pick 1988).

Risks

Assessing risks is a continual process (see Chapter 4). In the first assessment session, lack of knowledge about the young person makes this an uncertain and potentially anxious process. The therapist will think about and reflect on emerging risks and make decisions about whether to focus on these in the session. When a young person mentions an episode of self-harm or thoughts of suicide, or episodes of violence towards others, these may be explored directly with the aim of understanding whether self-destructive actions seem likely, and to what extent. In cases where these seem imminent the therapist will assess if talking about the feelings, and their triggers, together with the offer to think together through the following assessment sessions, contains the immediacy; if this appears not to be the case, appropriate action to provide safety will need to be taken, in accordance with the practices in the therapist's organisation.

The therapist's priorities will be to assess risks in this way and to establish a containing framework for the young person, which includes working with other professionals on a team, particularly in mental health services, like psychiatrists, nurses and social workers; in the case of therapists working alone, through establishing a virtual team. Ensuring the patient's safety is the prime objective, and this should not preclude aiming to understand the conscious and unconscious meaning of the risks. To an extent it is more straightforward to work with risks that are explicit and talked about; the feeling that there *may* be risks, frequently experienced in the initial meetings, can increase uncertainty and require reflection to avoid both over- and under-reaction. Young people tend to feel more able to disclose risky behaviours, by or towards themselves, as the therapy progresses and with greater containment. It is stressed that continuing with the assessment, with additional support from colleagues as necessary, is in most cases the best way to proceed, as this will lead to better knowledge of the young person and the risks he presents. Offering a firm and clear therapeutic structure is an important way of managing risks. In many cases, the process of reflection after the session is vital, in which the therapist, alone or with colleagues, can review the detail of the session and think through the appropriate responses.

The reflective process

The availability of a reflective space, as described in Chapter 5, is essential for working with young people using TAPP. The reflective process, in a small group, individual supervision or peer consultation, aims to support the therapist and helps provide optimum sensitivity to the patient and openness to the emotionality in the therapeutic relationship. Counter-transference experiences form an important and illuminating aspect of these reflections. After the first session, the reflective process will focus on the experiences of the session: how the young person presented, challenges that appeared, risks, tentative formulations and what may be important in the following sessions. These are inevitably tentative at this stage since one of the thoughts that will occur is the question of how the young person will present in the next session; often this is different from in the first session, and being prepared to be surprised is a helpful state of mind when working with young people.

Involving parents in the assessment

Parent and carer involvement in the assessment depends on the age of the young person and his positioning within the adolescent process. Older adolescents and young adults are more likely to attend therapy independently of parental figures, though the nature of the extended transition to adulthood may mean that parents, who often continue to be needed for practical and financial support, are involved in the early stages of therapy. Parental involvement is expected for younger adolescents; it is helpful to have a meeting with parents during the assessment which explores their thoughts and feelings about the adolescent's difficulties. Parent work may be necessary, both to support the adolescent's therapy and to work on parenting issues. It is possible that an outcome of the assessment is that parent work is agreed on, with or without therapy for the young person. Risks also need to be attended to, including parental mental health and safeguarding or child protection issues. It is by far preferable to have someone other than the adolescent's therapist conduct meetings with parents, in order to protect the therapeutic space from contaminating or intrusive factors. Resources may not permit this; the therapist may be the only person available to see the adolescent and the parent, in which case the therapist has to make the compromises that least threaten the integrity of the adolescent's therapy. In practice, again especially with younger adolescents, therapists have found it can be manageable and facilitative to have some involvement of the parent at the beginning; this can include an initial discussion with one or both parents and the young person to explain the setting and to address any questions. If TAPP is offered to the young person at the end of the assessment, a discussion with the parents can then be scheduled between the end of the assessment and the beginning of treatment. Plans for further contact can be made at this point. If it is identified that parent work or individual or couple therapy is indicated, this can be discussed and referred within the service, or to an available therapist.

The second to fourth assessment sessions

During the rest of the assessment, the second to fourth sessions, the interconnected tasks of engagement of the young person in a therapeutic process and assessment of suitability for psychotherapy continue. The aim is to arrive, by the end of the process, at a formulation and an offer of treatment based on this. In the course of the four sessions, the young person will experience a brief therapeutic engagement; changes that occur inform the assessment and require evaluation in their own right. In TAPP the formulation of a developmental focus is a crucial aspect of the assessment phase, and this is considered in detail in the following chapter, along with discussion of the process of offering and contracting for time-limited therapy. To an extent, it is artificial to separate these elements. Whilst recognising this limitation of so dividing the assessment tasks, this chapter concludes by discussing some key themes in the assessment process as it unfurls over the four sessions.

The therapist's role, the therapeutic methods and the processes established in the first session continue to be appropriate for the subsequent assessment sessions. One new element is that the second session provides the first opportunity to assess how the young person relates experiences since the last session. Thus, the therapist will focus on observing and asking about the thoughts the young person has about, and has had since, the last session. This information is used to assess the qualities of the young person's capacity to think about emotional experiences and how these experiences are kept in mind. A crucial distinction which may come into view at this point, and which can be elaborated over the subsequent sessions of the assessment phase, is whether the young person is equipped to think about experiences, or whether these are evacuated or dismissed; as discussed in Chapter 4, Waddell (2002) contrasts the capacity to hold emotional experiences in mind with ejecting, denying or dumping these when thinking is too difficult, painful or overwhelming. It will be assessed therefore how these different patterns of relating and learning are present in the assessment: are the tendencies towards thinking, or dumping, more circumscribed, linked to a particular emotion or relationship, or are they more global? Do they seem to be more severe, therefore, or less so? These are complicated assessments since the anxieties of starting a new relationship may heighten or distort understanding; the intensities of the therapeutic experience may have the effect of bringing these features into clearer focus, along the principle, described by Freud (1933), of the metaphor of the dropped crystal breaking along apparently invisible lines of structural weakness. On the other hand, the initial presentation of the young person may be not entirely characteristic and hence distorting. Repeated observations over time, throughout the four sessions, are important therefore to identify pattern and disjuncture, to obtain an overall view that balances different ways of relating and learning.

Thus, it is important that the therapist ask about what thoughts the young person has about, and has had since, the last session, whilst observing continuities and differences. In the second and subsequent sessions, the young person may convey either, on the one hand, having not thought at all about the previous session and even having dubious recall about what happened, or, on the other hand, that he has been thinking about the previous session, and that it has affected him emotionally, perhaps quite deeply. This may be expressed explicitly as reflections on an aspect of the previous session(s), leading perhaps to questions about how therapy will help with concerns. Or the sense of being affected by the previous session may be observed, and felt, more in the way the young person relates to the therapist, including the feelings that are evoked in the therapist's counter-transference. A characteristic response is that young people feel exposed and anxious by getting into contact with an emotion or perspective that surprises or disturbs them. This can lead to difficulties in attending subsequent sessions or to the therapist having concerns that this will occur; the examples of Annie, Chapter 4 and above, and Ben, above, illustrate these respectively.

When they do return, young people may bring new material that indicates internal work that is taking place, or they can defend against a repetition of this experience. Waddell (2002) gives the example of a patient, Sarah, aged 19, who in her first assessment session had begun to look in some depth, including in her dreams, at new and unconscious aspects of herself, ending the session with the statement, "I've never thought about things in this way before" (Waddell 2002, p. 148). Therapists may be moved by the courage young people show in looking at themselves in a new way and bearing the discomfort in doing so, or equally concerned by or anxious about where this will take the young person in his internal world and by the way actions may be precipitated. Assessment is therefore about coming to and holding a view about how therapy may unfold, balancing the potential for exploration with the need for the holding and containment of anxieties and how these may be managed in the therapy. Much of this depends on how the young person views being helped by a therapist in this process; whether it is welcomed or treated with suspicion – usually a bit of both is present – and how this links to the adolescent tensions about becoming more separate, and yet having feelings of depending on others.

Following this exploration of the processes in assessment for TAPP, it is now crucial to integrate these with discussion of collaboratively formulating the developmental focus with the young person and negotiation of the duration of therapy; these issues will be discussed in the next chapter.

Chapter 7

Making the treatment offer
The developmental focus

Introduction

The assessment and engagement phase in TAPP culminates in an offer of therapy, which is arrived at through following four interconnected processes: making a psychodynamic formulation, forming and sharing a developmental focus, negotiating an offer of treatment and contracting for therapy. These involve the therapist reaching a decision about the suitability of time-limited psychotherapy and the young person agreeing. The key parameters for brief therapy – aims, focus, suitability and termination – are worked with in TAPP, drawing upon models of brief therapy, as discussed in Chapter 2. How TAPP aligns with these models of brief therapy and adapts them to work with young people will be discussed in this chapter.

Offering therapy: the process

Working within the four-session model for the initial phase of assessment and engagement, the therapist follows a clear sequence to initiate the transition to therapy. The offer of therapy is primarily a process which requires discussion, negotiation and containment of the emotional experiences involved. Initial thinking about the young person's suitability for TAPP takes place in the first two assessment sessions, and in the reflections on those sessions, ideally with supervisory or peer support. The crucial point around which everything else revolves is that in the third session, the therapist will make a firm offer of therapy, and its duration, together with beginning a discussion about the developmental focus. In this third session, the therapist will listen to the initial response to this offer from the young person, and she will make a clear commitment to discussing it further in the following and final assessment session. The young person is invited to think it over and to bring their thoughts back to the next session. In the fourth assessment meeting the therapist will ask the young person if they have thought more about the offer of treatment, and through further discussion, the developmental focus for the treatment and the timescales are defined and agreed on.

This sequence is a core aspect of the TAPP structure; it optimises the young person's active contribution to the aims and purpose of therapy and to exploring their commitment. It has been found crucial to make the offer of therapy in the third session so that the young person has time to think about and then discuss their responses in the fourth session. Thus there is space to think about and review any ambivalence about starting therapy, as well as questions that arise for the young person over the week between the third and fourth sessions. It increases the possibility of collaboratively reaching an agreement that has taken into account the feelings involved, and can address the meaning for the young person of making a commitment to therapy. Not making the offer during the third session deprives both therapist and young person of the opportunity for reflection, discussion and negotiation. Unresolved issues about the agreement on therapy can carry over and be played out at the start of the treatment sessions, including a scenario where the young person enacts their ambivalence by not attending or disengaging. Of course, feelings of doubt and ambivalence are always present in therapy, but the therapist's commitment to discuss, and not to hurry or be hurried into, a decision provides the opportunity to work with some of the most important and immediate thoughts and feelings. It also demonstrates the therapist communicating the importance of the idea of agreeing on treatment collaboratively, recognising that the young person's thoughts and feelings are important and that they may have mixed feelings. Engaging the young person in this process of constructing a therapeutic frame in terms of duration, aims and focus means it is held in a containing process.

How the young person responds to the offer of therapy of course varies. They may have a thoughtful response which creates the opportunity of a genuine negotiation, or, alternatively, they might be eager to accept, in a way which appears to need no discussion, or which pre-empts it. They may show passive deference to the therapist's authority and knowledge. At this point, some ambivalence frequently emerges, expressed through words and actions, or contradictions; for example, the young person says they agree to weekly therapy but does not have the availability to attend regularly, or they say they may prefer to meet less frequently, or only at times they feel they need to come. They may express the wish for a form of help that will not involve effort and work, perhaps in the form of an instant prescription which can be taken away and ingested. They may use what Dartington (1998) called "the language of approximation," through which they remain sitting on the fence. Facing the reality of commitment to a therapeutic relationship can have a considerable emotional effect on the young person; some responses at this point can surprise the therapist, given the processes in the assessment to date. For example, it has been known that young people, who hitherto have expressed the sense that their problems are so overwhelming for them that they fear they may never change, or will need therapy for a very long time, now suggest that things are suddenly much better and that therapy, particularly of such a duration, is no longer necessary. Fears of entrapment or abandonment may be raised at this point. These issues can be worked with in the fourth assessment session and often provide further understanding of the young person's internal world and how they are relating to the adolescent developmental process. In adolescent psychotherapy, ambiguities and ambivalence are thought about as needing to be held within the interpersonal, relational processes of the therapeutic relationship, including its transferential aspects.

Offering therapy: the content

The offer of TAPP which is thus made in the third assessment session and confirmed after discussion in the fourth session consists of, first, an offer of time-limited therapy, and, second, exploring and agreeing on the aim of therapy in terms of the developmental focus. In brief therapy, as discussed in Chapter 2, there are diverse views about how to define the time limit and the duration of therapy. Usually, either a specific number of sessions is agreed on, or as Malan (1976) advocated, a date for the final session. The duration of time-limited therapy can either be strictly adhered to, as in Mann's (1973) approach, or, like Strupp and Binder (1984), it can be applied more flexibly, including allowing additional sessions. In TAPP the time limit is discussed by stating the number of sessions – usually 16 – alongside relating the duration of therapy to events that are meaningful for the young person. In other words, the therapist will say that the therapy will continue up to and end at a particular time and name the event(s) that is (are) taking place in the young person's social world at that time. The purpose of this is to locate the duration of therapy in the context of the young person's social world and of their own immediate future. Therefore, in TAPP the priority in setting the time limit is that it is related to a meaningful event in the young person's life. This is usually one of the key markers of adolescent transition, such as exams, school holidays or the end of school years before university or employment. For some young people, family events may also provide a meaningful time scale, such as moving, taking holidays and so forth. In some cases, if the young person is having a geographical move, an end date may be imposed on the therapy. Service transitions also provide a clear time limit in some cases, most commonly the transition from child and adolescent to adult services. The therapist will therefore aim to discuss the duration of therapy as taking place over the period of time that will be linked to a named event in the young person's life.

The time scale identified is then calibrated to the number of sessions available; the usual duration of TAPP is 16 treatment sessions followed by a post-treatment review which takes place six to eight weeks after the final treatment session. The therapist will therefore propose to the young person that therapy will consist of this number of sessions. The therapist will need to do some work with her calendar to make calculations as to where the number of sessions – 16 plus the 6 to 8 weeks for the review – fits with the identified event in the young person's life marking the ending. Though to an extent complicated, the process offers the reward of relating meaningfully to the young person's sense of themselves in their life and in time; both the end date and the number of sessions are important components of the TAPP structure.

Once calculated and discussed, the number of sessions is adhered to, following Mann's approach rather than Strupp and Binder's. In this respect, TAPP accords with Mann's view that the time limit provides the opportunity for working with a process of separation within the therapeutic relationship; this is discussed further below as a part of the developmental focus. The total number of sessions includes missed sessions, so if the young person does not attend a session this is usually counted towards the total number of sessions available. However, unlike Malan, who felt the process of discussing the meaning of missed sessions was a nuisance, in TAPP this is an important aspect of the therapeutic process with young people, to understand the meaning, to give value of the number of sessions and to work with time. In making the offer of therapy, the therapist may be able to say that if the young person misses a session this counts towards the total, whereas if the therapist misses a session, this will be replaced.

Talking about the timescale and in particular the date for termination can often lead to an increase in the young person's anxiety; the external reality – that the therapy will happen and is finite in time – has resonance with the young person's development in their social world, in which forthcoming events and landmarks, both feared and desired, are anticipated. How the young person responds to the offer of therapy refers to their sense of time; for young people, therapy with the duration of around five months consisting of 16 sessions can seem to be an entrapping, endless space, or a brief and insubstantial moment that immediately ushers in anxieties about ending and separating. There is usually a link between reactions like these, at both ends of a spectrum: between how the young person is experiencing the adolescent process and their positioning as a subject within this. Thus the structure for TAPP in general, and the time limit, in particular, links to the adolescent process and the individual's passage through it; this has therapeutic importance if it can be recognised and thought about. TAPP follows in this respect Mann's (1973) thinking about the importance of separation and loss being worked with within the therapeutic relationship, and of linking this to experiences in current and past relationships.

The developmental focus

Accompanying the discussion of time limits in the process of making a treatment offer is discussion of the aims of therapy and its focus. As in all brief therapy, establishing the focus is a complex process involving several key elements. As discussed in Chapter 2, there are different approaches to the development of a focus, ranging from the therapist formulating and presenting the focus (Malan and Mann) to more interactive and collaborative methods (Strupp and Binder, and Stadter). In TAPP, the formulation of the focus is interdependent and jointly, though often unequally, constructed; therefore, it has more in common with Strupp and Binder's method than with Malan's or Davanloo's. In practice, there are some variations on how the focus is formulated and discussed.

In TAPP, the concept of focus in time-limited therapy has been adapted to working with young people; it is constructed and expressed as a developmental focus, and, as has been described in Chapter 5, the developmental focus is the distinctive and decisive concept in TAPP. Identifying and articulating the developmental focus collaboratively with the young person is frequently the aspect of TAPP that practitioners find most difficult when new to the approach; it does involve some complex thinking and reflecting, and can be difficult to introduce into the sessions with the young person. It is, however, crucial, and becomes a powerful and facilitative process, once, with experience, the therapist has integrated the various aspects into her practice. Therefore it is helpful to consider each of the elements and to explore how these are then combined to form a sequence in the interactions with young people.

The developmental focus is formed through, first, reflecting on how the young person has presented themselves in the assessment, taking account therefore of their version of themselves. It is based on and responsive to the young person's concerns and difficulties, including symptoms they presents and their preoccupations in the social world, including relationships and the immediate future transitions and challenges (for example exams, changing school, etc.) Second, it is based on the formulation that the therapist reaches about how their difficulties relate to their internal world; the therapist, through reflection, including in supervision and/or the seminar group supporting the process, will:

- Make a psychodynamic formulation of the young person's object relations and defences, their narrative of themselves, their thinking style, their capacity to bear emotional experiences and the ways they defend against emotional experiences that feel overwhelming
- Make formulations of the young person's experience of the adolescent developmental process, including where it may be stuck or appears anti-developmental, or where it is lacking in internal or external resources to support them with its emotional demands

There is a tension in psychotherapy between the idea of making a formulation during the assessment phase that summarises the individual's core internal conflicts, and that of continual assessment over time gained through deepened understanding. In Chapter 2 we saw how Balint, for example, strived to achieve a formulation that would concisely put into words the patient's inner conflict to effectively guide the brief therapy; Hinshelwood's (1995) notion of finding the point of maximum pain expresses a similar aim. In contrast, Malan thought that the formulation would crystallise over time. Psychodynamic formulations aim to state the relationship between the patient's symptoms or difficulties, their inner world and their object relatedness and defences as understood at a point in time; making a formulation is couched within the limits of what is known. It can also be viewed as a working hypothesis that will be tested, refined and reformulated over time (Lemma et al 2011). We have seen how in assessing young people, the process of formulation is further complicated by the qualities of adolescence, including ambivalence, ambiguity and different presentations over time, as well as by the process of internal change that is taking place in the adolescent developmental process. In Chapter 4, the example of Annie showed how the assessment provided rather limited information of this young woman's internal world, yet, through reflecting on the developing relationship with the therapist, some striking and emotionally laden ideas about her emerged, notably about an internal conflict between being accepted or rejected which appeared to suggest the quality of an important object relationship. This example raises the question of how much information is needed to make a formulation for therapy; as discussed in Chapter 6, the repeated assessment sessions help to understand how the young person experiences the therapeutic relationship, leading to formulations about the capacity to think about emotional experiences, the characteristic ways the young person appears to defend against this and their relative rigidity or flexibility.

It is important when making formulations for TAPP that as good as possible a view of these factors is linked to an appreciation of the young person's experiences of and in the adolescent developmental process. This involves considering how difficulties and symptoms relate to disturbances of the developmental process: for instance, how feelings about harming the self or having difficulties with eating signal disturbances in relating to the new and developing adult sexual body, or how fears of one's own violence and aggression may relate to the new sense of physical strength or capacity to act and to the relative power of the adolescent to the adult, compared with in childhood; in other words, considering how these relate to Oedipal conflicts whilst difficulties with managing strong feelings may relate to experiences of containment in the adolescent present and the infant past. The sense of the adolescent's capacity to harness their capacities and be a subject of their experiences contrasts with the passivity of feeling subject to what happens to him; their responses to adverse circumstances in their environment indicate the toll that adverse experiences may exact on development. Central themes that are very important for formulating the developmental focus are the tension between separateness and intimacy that flows from the process of becoming more separate from parental figures, the loss and mourning of childhood ways of relating and the finding of new, more adult ways of relating intimately to others, including sexually. The relationship between underlying disturbances in object relatedness and the impact on these of the adolescent process underpin the making of a psychodynamic formulation that can be used to identify a developmental focus. Once a formulation has been made, the challenge is how to communicate this to the young person when articulating the developmental focus with them.

Integrating the developmental focus in the therapeutic process

There is usually, perhaps inevitably, a gap between the formulations of the young person and the therapist, reflecting the differences between them in their roles and experiences, including working with unconscious processes. It is rarely the case that an exposition of the therapist's psychodynamic formulation is given in its entirety to the young person; this would most likely be indigestible and probably not therapeutic, especially for a young person in distress and anxious about what their difficulties mean. Therapists need to work out what is important to say and include in the articulation of the developmental focus, and how to speak to this; there can be a problem of understating as well as overstating, as the young person will usually want to hear what the therapist thinks, even though that may be a process complicated by anxieties, including whether the therapist will confirm their worst fears of themselves (Lemma 2015a). Discussion of the developmental focus needs to be located within a holding and containing process, and within the therapeutic relationship as it has developed thus far. The principle for making interpretations, of closely observing the patient's response and then working with that response, applies.

It is preferable, in fact, when making a formulation, to start not from the therapist's formulations but from the young person's accounts of themselves, paying close attention to the words he uses and the examples they provide about themselves, their relationships and their hopes, fears and aspirations; and to use their descriptions of their problems and symptoms, alongside what has become named in the therapeutic relationship. This approach increases the possibilities of discussing the focus together and of further developing engagement in the therapeutic relationship. The therapist has to hold, within herself, the tension between the aims of establishing the developmental focus and of working with the young person's preoccupations. A case example illustrates how the process of discussing the developmental focus can be integrated into the therapeutic process of the session. This is the assessment of a younger adolescent, Jenny, aged 14:

Case example: Jenny

Jenny's view of herself was that she feels bad; her parents recently separated, and she lives with her mother and spends time with her father. The therapist's formulation after the first three sessions was that Jenny has some bitter feelings, reflecting the current adverse circumstances in her family. She may be dealing with the pains of adolescence by adopting an already grown-up adult way of being and relating. Underlying this were some difficult episodes in her earlier childhood, which have so far been briefly glimpsed, that suggest that her parents may not have been emotionally available for her; she may have felt neglected by them and may have felt responsible for her feelings and others'. Jenny's expectation of others in relationships was, in her words, that she "doesn't like to be told 'later' then nothing happens." Jenny's symptoms of depression appeared to relate to losses, in the present and past, that were difficult to bear and mourn, and which were complicated and further stirred up by her early adolescence. Jenny had shown some reluctance to engage in therapy, but during the assessment, she seemed increasingly interested in the process, whilst also being quite guarded as though protecting herself from becoming too deeply involved; moments of being involved were followed by withdrawal. In thinking about the transference and counter-transference the therapist felt she might become a tantalising object who then disappoints.

The developmental focus was tentatively formulated by the third session as helping Jenny to bear the pains and disappointments of her current predicament whilst she was beginning her adolescence with the changes these pains and disappointments were bringing to her relationships with others, including her peers. There seemed, in fact, to be little space for her adolescence. At the end of the third assessment session, the therapist offered time-limited therapy of 16 sessions that would take Jenny to Christmas, which she felt would be a difficult time in her family. The therapist said that the focus could be on thinking about what made her feel bad and low, whilst going through her own changes and development as well as the changes that were happening around her in her family. Jenny listened, and seemed interested, but did not comment, and the therapist said they can think about this together in the next session.

In the fourth assessment session, the therapist said they should discuss if they would continue, and wondered what Jenny thought now about this; Jenny replied quietly and hesitantly that it might be good. The therapist reminded her of the proposed duration of therapy and the end date, and Jenny immediately said, "That's short." The therapist reflected that Jenny felt this was a short time, and Jenny returned to talking about the worries she had about her parents with which she had begun the session. The therapist, wanting to soften the sense of an abrupt ending, said there would be a review after the end of therapy to see where things were then, and added that she was aware of some difficult things in Jenny's life and that these would probably continue beyond the therapy. But Jenny said that she hoped she would feel better in herself soon, and that was something they could work on together. Jenny said she did feel better, except that she didn't feel as good as her peers. The therapist asked her to say more, and Jenny said that she felt her peers could do things, whilst what she did never came out right. She gave an example of a project in her school work and added that she should be able to do this by now. The therapist wondered to herself if this related to the "short time" she had been offered in therapy, and perhaps a feeling she should be able to not need therapy, but said, directly referencing the developmental focus, that it was as though Jenny felt she had to be an adult already, that there was no space to make mistakes or to learn. Jenny responded with an emphatic "yeah," and then talked about having to learn to be more independent from her mother. The therapist asked her if she thought this was because she was growing and changing, and Jenny replied that she had to do this now, and it was hard. The therapist agreed that it was hard when she had to think about what was going on around her as well as her own changes. Jenny looked sad but interested and said she did want to continue.

The key point for this discussion is that the therapist must use judgement in how – and to what extent – to discuss the developmental focus, in each case taking account of the young person's age, the quality of therapeutic relatedness thus far and the formulation of their strengths and internal resources for thinking about themselves in this way. Alongside this, the case example shows the therapist working with the issue of agreeing on the focus within the therapeutic process; she listens closely to Jenny's responses and follows them, for example the comments about not being able to succeed, and relates to them within the therapeutic relationship.

In some cases, the developmental focus may be stated more minimally and in others more fully. Stadter's (2009) distinction between the symptomatic and dynamic focus can be applied here; a minimal discussion of the developmental focus might include the wish – using as near as possible the young person's own terms – to relieve distressing symptoms together with a statement that locates these in the adolescent process. These may simply refer to the young person being in a process of growing and changing, or being concerned with a transition in the social world with reference to a particular event, a current set of relationships or a current task and how these may affect him. There will be opportunities to develop the discussion and understanding of the focus as therapy proceeds, and in all cases, it is deepened and refined with better understanding. In some cases, the therapist's sense of the young person's inner world may lead to a formulation of the focus stemming from the understanding of these inner relationships. The aim, whether the focus is minimally or more fully elaborated, is to locate the process in time, to place emphasis on becoming (future time), on the process of loss and change (where the young person has come from) in past time and in present preoccupations.

Difficulties in reaching a focus: miracle cures and prescriptions

In contrast to the example of Jenny, in some cases the process of establishing the developmental focus can meet obstacles for young people anxious about themselves, the therapeutic process or their own capacity to change and grow. The idea of working together in a relationship might seem too much; instead of the interaction of the container–contained the young person relates by wanting to be given something, or for change to happen without undertaking emotional work; the relationship is perceived, to use Benjamin's (1988) phrase, as "doer and done to." In these situations, the therapeutic process is replaced by a wish for miracle cures or prescriptions. Therapists may be able to anticipate this in the assessment process, by recognising the young person's passivity or difficulties in learning through experience and giving information about the way the therapeutic process works, or by commenting on the importance of the young person being the subject of their own therapy. If there is a strong trend throughout the assessment of not engaging in the therapeutic process, and of seeking miracle cures and prescriptions, the question of suitability for therapy will need to be addressed, and, if offering therapy, it would need to be part of the formulation and focus. If, on the other hand, discussion of the time limit and developmental focus stirs up anxieties about committing to therapy or about being able to change, this needs to be prioritised in the fourth session. The case of Aretha, discussed below, provides an example of one way of working with the wish for prescriptions; the aim is to find a path that addresses the conflict between active and passive, or between "yes and no" (Anthony 1975):

Case example: Aretha

Aretha became tearful early in her first session when describing her states of panic, and said she knew she needed help but did not see how therapy would help; she had seen a counsellor before who she said had been "rude and stupid." The therapist said it may be difficult to feel so upset with someone she has only known for a few minutes, and Aretha nodded in agreement. The therapist added that she would like to get to know more about Aretha, and suggested she say something about herself. Aretha said, no, she wanted the therapist to ask questions. The therapist said Aretha has expressed doubts about how therapy can help and so we need to think about this together, and commented on their different perspectives; Aretha wanted the therapist to ask questions and the therapist wished to hear Aretha's own version of things. Aretha then did talk about her family, relationships with her parents, her education and hopes for the future. She felt her father, whom she described as "stupid," was unreliable and often rude to her. Her girlfriend had recently ended the relationship with her, which, though Aretha said it had not been a serious relationship, provoked the crisis that led her, on her mother's advice, to seek therapy. She was worried she would not be able to go to university in a few months' time and said she needed to "get rid of these stupid feelings by then." She had finished her exams and was taking a year out, but felt unable to make use of it.

Aretha is clearly distressed and troubled, and she is anxious about the transition to university, which is a familiar theme for young people starting therapy at this age. She presents a time scale, linked to going to university, which may indicate time-limited therapy but which needs to be considered within the assessment overall. Aretha is troubled in her relationships, and distressed, and risks need to be attended to. Aretha's narrative is interspersed with phrases that convey a wish to violently eject unbearable feelings; feeling hurt in relationships appears to elicit these responses. She conveys her fear of being in a therapeutic relationship through a "cautionary tale" (Lemma et al 2011) of her scepticism about how therapy can help. Her description of her father as unreliable, and the previous counsellor as "rude and stupid," suggests a relationship pattern that may be replicated in her therapy; she seems to experience her father as quite attacking of her. The therapist therefore has to tread carefully to not also be experienced as "rude and stupid." Aretha's experience of feeling upset in her first meeting with the therapist also requires attention. When Aretha asks the therapist to ask her questions, she (the therapist) finds a way between the dilemma of 'yes' and 'no' (Anthony 1975) through expressing the different perspectives of each; this appears to sufficiently contain Aretha at the time.

In her second assessment session, Aretha appeared to be quite different, as is often the case with young people beginning a therapeutic relationship. She seemed more held together, less floppy and more "muscular" (Bick 1968). It was evident she was responding to her experience of the first session; she said she was making a conscious effort not to "cry about everything." She had also decided to find work during her gap year and had started an office job, which she was enjoying. There appeared to be simultaneously an attempt to actively get hold of her development, by starting work, and a defensive manoeuvre to not feel embarrassment and shame in her therapist's presence. The therapist asked more about when Aretha felt distressed, and Aretha gave examples in which she made rather impulsive decisions involving travel and then got into a panic when out of contact with others, in particular her mother. The therapist asked her, introducing a sense of irony, if she often makes big decisions like this. Aretha responded to the irony, laughed, and said that big decisions weren't a problem, it was the little things that upset her. The therapist ended the session by saying that it does seem that difficult feelings arise when she feels separated from people that are important to her and that this is something to think more about.

> Aretha, dressed smartly, looking older and quite powerful, started the third session by saying the therapist had said last time that she had a problem with separation, and if so, this was a very serious problem to have. It seemed that the concern about separation was the therapist's idea, not Aretha's. Perhaps this was hinting at a deeper fear about herself and what the therapist was thinking of her; the therapist wondered to herself if this might become a "stupid" thing she had said, but commented that Aretha had kept her session in her mind. Aretha replied that she expected the therapist to ask her what she had been thinking, so she had anticipated this question. She added that she had been thinking about her therapy during the week and had been quite looking forward to this session. The session ended with a discussion of whether she would like to have therapy and for how long, and Aretha reasserted her wish to sort all this out before she went to university, and the therapist offered her time-limited therapy, of 16 weekly sessions, up to the time she would make the transition to university. She added that though understandably Aretha wanted to sort it all out, it was important that they thought together about what to focus on and what could be reasonably addressed in the time available.

The therapist formulated the idea that, when separated from her mother, Aretha feels herself in the presence of an attacking paternal figure which brings about panic. There are sudden shifts in Aretha's state of mind and some gaps in the way she thinks about these. Aretha is engaging in the therapeutic relationship; despite the restricted ways in which she relates to the therapist, it is possible to explore to a certain extent how she experiences relationships and emotions, and she is able to respond to irony. Her therapy is in her mind between sessions, suggesting quite a strong attachment, and a positive transference which she speaks to. Whether time-limited therapy is appropriate is not clear; the time limit is imposed by Aretha, and her wish to sort everything out suggests a miracle cure; negotiating a focus will not be easy. However, the structure of TAPP offers an opportunity to contain some of Aretha's states of mind and thus create a possibility for greater thoughtfulness; focussing on this could be a strategy for working with the developmental issue of accomplishing greater separateness from her mother, without feeling attacked from within and hence paralysed in her development. This would necessitate containment of her intense anxieties, and working towards Aretha recognising transitions as a process rather than a series of decisions which are asserted suddenly and without thinking about pros and cons and their potential emotional consequences.

> At the start of the fourth session, there was a palpable feeling of discomfort in the room; Aretha was quite slumped and seemed to be more like she had been in the first meeting. Aretha said that, as this is the last assessment session, she wondered what would be different and whether this was the "diagnostic bit"? The therapist said she wondered what thoughts Aretha had, and Aretha said she wanted to know what the therapist thought. This appeared to be said with spirit, and not, apparently, with hostility. As in the first session, the therapist stated the difference between them; Aretha's position was that she wanted the therapist to "diagnose" and the therapist wanted to know her thoughts since they had last met. Aretha was then tearful, talking about the difficult time she had had over the past week: at the weekend, she had gone to stay with a friend, but then had felt in a panic and wanted to get back to her mother. She said these stupid feelings were ruining her life. This was discussed in some detail, before the therapist returned to the issue of discussing plans and decisions for therapy, asking if Aretha had thought more about the offer of therapy. Aretha repeated she wanted to get rid of these feelings and had to do so before she went to university. The therapist said that it is important to think about these, about how and why she has these feelings and about how to see if together they could find ways of helping her feel less overwhelmed by them and more able to develop in herself. Aretha listened, before saying she would "give it a go." The therapist added that it can be difficult, when feeling so overwhelmed and at the mercy of strong feelings like these, to think there is a way out, to which Aretha agreed.

Aretha's hopes for her therapy, driven partly by her desperation and being so overwhelmed, tend towards the wish for a prescription or miracle cure. It has been possible to find a way of negotiating this, by recognising rather than challenging Aretha's perspective but also stating some clear objectives for the therapy. There is a process of collaborative discussion of the focus, of Aretha being able to manage the emotional experience of being separate from others, and of understanding more about the internal processes that contribute to these states. Introducing the realistic possibility of working together towards this ensures that the therapist does not collude with the wish for a miracle cure. The process suggested by the focus is one of containing Aretha's strong and overwhelming feelings as well as aiming to develop some insight. The formulation that, when separated from her mother, Aretha feels herself in the presence of an attacking paternal figure is a hypothesis that the therapist can think further about, elaborate or discard in the light of the understanding that develops in the course of the therapy to which Aretha has agreed.

Working collaboratively to agree on a focus

The key steps to working with the focus can be summarised as:

- Thinking and reflecting, including in a supervision/seminar group, about psychodynamic and developmental formulations throughout the assessment and refining these as the assessment progresses
- Noting and carefully observing the young person's terminology and the ways they describe predicaments
- Noting the gap between the young person's view and the therapist's, and finding ways to link these and/or articulate the gap within the therapeutic relationship
- Making an initial formulation of how to state a developmental focus for the therapy; considering how simple or elaborate a focus to propose and discuss
- Stating the focus in these terms and carefully noting the young person's response and responding/elaborating as appropriate, thus working with this within the therapeutic process
- Reaching a conclusion of what has been shared and agreed on, noting and commenting as appropriate on any limitations or areas not agreed on

Suitability and selection of patients

The assessment of suitability for brief therapy is one of the key parameters for brief therapy and is linked with the aims, techniques or strategies and focus of the therapy. In brief therapy, when assessing suitability, emphasis has been placed on the patient's motivation (Malan 1976), the capacity to establish the unconscious therapeutic alliance (Davanloo 1980) and the ability to withstand the pains of separation in the ending (Mann 1973). Based on criteria for suitability, models of brief therapy are more exclusive or more inclusive in their selection of patients; more exclusive models have stressed that ego strength is a criterion for brief therapy. Changes in psychotherapy theory and technique have had an impact on criteria for suitability. As discussed in Chapter 2, Bion's model of container–contained and developments in interpersonal and relational approaches have widened the possibilities for greater inclusiveness in selection for brief therapy. The process of therapy is, as Stadter describes, a process of discovery, where the aim is "to collaborate with the patient in containing difficult mental states and the specific object relations that are enacted in the therapeutic encounter" (Stadter 2016, p. 434). Suitability for adolescent psychotherapy in general has similarly become more inclusive, as has been discussed in Chapter 4, with considerable emphasis placed on engaging and sustaining young people in therapy.

There are, however, criteria for suitability for brief therapy that even allow for these trends towards greater inclusivity. The case examples and earlier discussions show the careful consideration of suitability in the process of assessment. The therapist aims to establish whether the young person can engage in weekly psychotherapy, testing this through the repeated sessions of the assessment process. This enables the therapist to see if the young person is able to manage the inevitable stirring up of feelings in a therapeutic relationship without resorting too much to action, especially of a destructive nature, or of being regressively overwhelmed. How the young person relates to the therapist over the four sessions and, as in the example of Aretha, whether a way can be found to work together provide important information about suitability.

In all brief therapy, a key question when assessing suitability is the extent to which it can be anticipated that the patient is able to manage the pains of separating at the end of therapy. In TAPP this is usually thought about in the context of the adolescent developmental process, in which experiences of becoming more separate are inevitable, and have different impacts on young people; this occupies a spectrum between those who turn away from committing to closeness in relationships, and those who experience all separations as unbearable abandonments. TAPP aims to work with these experiences, of course, rather than see them as criteria for not engaging in therapy. It can in some assessments become a serious consideration that the young person will either not engage in therapy for the full duration of 16 sessions, or that the ending will be likely to prove such a painful experience that it would seem better to find a longer-term alternative. During assessment, exploring previous experiences of endings helps to make these formulations. However, it should be borne in mind that TAPP provides for these young people a different experience of an ending, in which there is thinking about and containing of the emotional experiences. Thus the experience of ending in TAPP can work with, and to an extent work through, the young person's difficulties about separating from others; having a different experience in therapy is what Alexander and French (1946) had in mind when they coined the term "corrective emotional experience," which in this context might be used to mean working with the transference–counter-transference matrix to understand and make sense for the patient of the feelings that ending therapy arouses. The anticipation of difficult feelings about endings can be appropriately softened, as seen in the example of Jenny, by discussing the ending as part of a process; the idea of reviewing is integral to TAPP. The post-treatment review provides a space to reflect on the experience and to think about what is needed in the future. For some young people, a reasonable outcome of TAPP is that, having overcome fears of being trapped or overwhelmed by a therapeutic relationship, they may wish to continue with a longer-term or open-ended therapy. The softening of the meaning of ending should not be confused with weakness in maintaining the frame. In TAPP additional sessions are not added to the therapy, as this can lead to a loss of integrity and credibility for the therapist and the process; as Mann (1973) suggested, the patient would be the loser. In summary, TAPP is thought to be suitable for most young people; aims, focus and techniques are adapted to suit the young person, so that with some young people there is more emphasis on containing difficult states of mind, and in others, a more exploratory approach is taken. All of this is discussed in detail in the following chapters.

There is a pragmatic context; considerations of suitability for TAPP have changed over time, through the experience of its application in different settings. There is a significant difference between a multidisciplinary team in a mental health service, with expertise in a range of therapies and resources available for brief and long-term methods, and a psychotherapist working, often alone, in primary care or an educational setting, or in private practice. Constraints in mental health services have led to the greater deployment of time-limited approaches. This has led to the inclusion of a wider range of young people being offered TAPP; successful therapies have been conducted with young people with complex difficulties, on the point of transition between child and adult services and with young people with learning disabilities. This leads to adaptation of the aims and approach, whilst maintaining the integrity of the TAPP model. Ideally, there is a complementarity between TAPP and longer-term therapies. It is important to avoid deciding between TAPP and longer-term therapies based on the idea that the therapist feels the young person needs more time than is provided by TAPP. This both reduces longer-term therapy to a question of duration and underestimates the quality of change that can be achieved in TAPP. Longer-term therapy and TAPP should have different aims, strategies and methods.

Considerations of suitability for TAPP may take account of the following:

- Has the young person demonstrated, during the assessment, a capacity to engage in a therapeutic relationship?
- Is there a sense that the experience of ending therapy will be manageable, or are there strong contraindications?
- Is there evidence, as experienced by many adolescents in contemporary social contexts, of considerable fragmentation in their social worlds, and/or is this subject to change? Is this experienced as being vulnerable to change and disintegration, or confusion? The lack of an external dependable structure supporting adolescent development is a strong indicator for time-limited therapy, as providing a structured intervention.
- Is there an external constraint that it would be unreasonable or inadvisable to challenge, such as a geographical move or a point of transition (e.g. exams, change of school/institution), and where recognition of the importance of this event is necessary for the integrity of the treatment? In these cases, time-limited therapy is indicated.

- Is there evidence of the young person's narrative being organised around a traumatic event, or significant life event for which the treatment priority is a time-limited and focused intervention?
- Is the young person's narrative such that a significant factor is the fear of being trapped in a relationship from which there appears to be no way of escaping? If so, time-limited therapy is strongly indicated.
- Has the young person recently experienced another course of treatment in any modality of therapy and approaches this therapy with some anxiety and caution about how helpful it will be? Time-limited therapy is indicated in these conditions in order to offer opportunities for reflection and negotiation.

Chapter 8

Therapeutic priorities in the treatment phase

Introduction

This chapter begins discussion of the treatment phase of TAPP, continued in the following three chapters. In this chapter, aims and strategies are described, and emphasis is placed on discussing how therapists develop and sustain a therapeutic stance that facilitates working with the young person. The emphasis on working in depth is discussed, particularly focusing on working with and in the transference and counter-transference; these are explored in detail and links are made to recent psychoanalytic thinking. The crucial point guiding these discussions is how therapeutic method and strategies are employed in TAPP to promote dynamic internal change and augment developmental growth.

Beginnings, middles and endings

TAPP is not formulated programmatically; the therapist aims to ensure that the priorities for TAPP are followed throughout the treatment phase and that these are related to the needs of the individual young person. However, although schematic, relating important characteristics of treatment to the beginning, middle and ending periods of the therapy provides a framework for thinking. The schematic nature of this structure does have to be borne in mind; the distinction of beginning, middle and end is a simplification, as there can be significant overlaps, notably where ending issues are present in the beginning or, with some young people who find engagement a challenge, where the beginning can continue throughout the therapy.

Beginning

The therapist enables the patient to make the transition from assessment to focussed, time-limited treatment; this means exploring the meaning of beginning therapy for the patient, which can be experienced in several ways. For some young people – and therapists – the transition from assessment to therapy can feel almost seamless, especially if – as is optimal – the therapist who undertook the assessment continues with the treatment, and if there is no gap between ending assessment and beginning the treatment sessions. It can be important to name the transition to prevent it from being hidden from sight; sometimes the transition is observed or felt through almost subtle shifts in the way the young person relates to the therapist, whilst the young person's experience can also be more powerfully communicated and experienced, including, for example, through his non-appearance. This can be surprising for the therapist especially when the young person has appeared to be accepting of the therapy and overtly keen to begin.

As discussed in Chapter 6, the assessment process allows time and attention for the expression of ambivalences about starting therapy; however, ambivalence about engaging in therapy is not always fully contained by this process and can carry over into treatment. The beginning phase of treatment continues, therefore, to hold an important sense of continuing to work with the young person's engagement in therapy. Alongside this, the reality of the time scale may be felt by the young person, either as a pressing immediacy or alternatively as a long period of time stretching unimaginably ahead. In either sense, the meaning of time for the adolescent comes to the forefront and requires acknowledgement, exploration or containment. Young people may begin the treatment saying that after the assessment they feel better and now do not feel the need for 16 sessions; others may take the opposite view, that they think, for example, that nothing will change in 16 sessions and in effect that longer is needed. It can be helpful in some cases to restate, reflect on, further elaborate and refine the developmental focus, and to relate this to the timescale. It is helpful to bear in mind that in time-limited therapy, the beginning means also the beginning of the ending; issues of termination may be present, though often not on the surface; the therapist will decide if it is helpful to name these.

It can be helpful to state that the therapeutic process continues, as in the assessment and engagement phase, with the young person free to say whatever is on his mind. The therapist has to find a pathway between working with the developmental focus, and thus how to stay focussed, whilst allowing the patient freedom to say whatever comes to mind. It is important that the therapist is alert to the emergence of new understandings of the young person; new clinical material may significantly affect the assessment and hence the focus. The therapist will need to continually attend to fluctuating risks.

Middle sessions

Gradually, as in any therapy, ways of communicating and the content of sessions become established uniquely for the patient–therapist dyad. In the middle sessions, the therapy is characterised by cooperative work on the developmental focus. However, with some young people, it can seem that the 'middle' never arrives – and then is gone as the ending looms. The therapist's role includes working with the TAPP structure, keeping in mind the number of sessions that have been used and remain, and integrating this factor into interventions. The therapist aims to work at an appropriate pace, concentrating on detail, on working to increase depth of understanding, particularly through techniques of containment, and on working within the transference and managing her own anxieties about the pressures of time to not hurry or procrastinate.

Ending sessions

As the end of therapy approaches, it is a practical requirement that the therapist makes the ending of the therapy a priority for discussion; the complex and multi-layered processes of ending therapy are discussed in detail in Chapter 10. In the ending phase, the therapist will initiate thinking about the perceptions of gains, changes and areas that appear not to be changing. Planning for the future includes discussing further treatments as appropriate. However, the central process of the ending phase is to link the experience and meaning of ending, separating from the therapist and the therapist's separation from the adolescent patient to the work that has been undertaken and to the developmental focus. As will be discussed in detail later (in Chapter 10), the replication of the individual's developmental issues in the dynamics of the therapeutic relationship and the therapist's handling of this form a powerful process of change and growth. Ending is usually in the forefront in the last three to four sessions, though ending and separation are present throughout TAPP, based on the time-limited contract which means the ending is agreed on at the outset.

Strategies in the treatment phase

The therapist's strategies in the treatment phase overlap and are consistent with those articulated for the assessment and engagement phase (see Chapter 5). Of primary importance is maintaining a psychodynamic therapeutic stance which is oriented towards adolescence. This involves taking an observational, self-reflective approach in order to notice detail and to process the experience of being with the individual young person. The orientation to adolescence implies actively recognising and taking account of the young person's positioning between childhood and adulthood. The therapist will aim to be receptive to unconscious processes in the interactions with the young person, including how these become evident in the transference and counter-transference. The therapist stays aware of and makes use of the structures of the time-limited therapy: the time-limit, the number of sessions used and still available, the young person's attendance within the weekly 50-minute structure, absences and planned breaks and so on. Working with the structure includes working with the agreed on developmental focus and this can be referred to, discussed, reconsidered and refined. Relating emotional experiences to the therapeutic structure is an important and often fruitful strategy in TAPP. The therapist will apply appropriate psychodynamic techniques and processes to facilitate growth and change and to attend to emotionality; holding and containment; exploratory interventions that aim to deepen the work; and interpretation of present relatedness, including within the therapeutic relationship and past experiences to elicit richer, more nuanced and more rounded personal narratives. The therapist will review and appraise risks, ensure the appropriateness of links with parents, family members and other professionals and see that there is sufficient support for the process through supervision and/or a peer or seminar group.

The therapeutic stance in the treatment phase

As discussed in earlier chapters, in TAPP the term 'therapeutic stance' is preferred to indicate the therapist's positioning and approach to the distinctive task of adolescent psychotherapy. The capacity of the therapist to attain the optimum therapeutic stance with the young person, overall, in each session and at different points in the session requires considerable resources, flexibility and attunement.

In the treatment phase, the aim is to continue to maintain a therapeutic stance that facilitates containment of anxieties, to make emotional contact with the young person's conscious and unconscious communications and to explore his internal and social words. This requires that the therapist is positioned to experience the emotionality in the room, and to have space in her mind to listen to and reflect upon these experiences. The observational and reflective stance is emotionally demanding and, when working with adolescents, complicated by ambiguities. The therapist aims to move flexibly between the young person's accounts of their social worlds and relationships, the infant, child and emerging adult aspects they bring, and between times when they are seeking containment of anxieties and times when they are more exploratory, when moments of emerging subjectivity open up new possibilities and ways of relating to self and others. It is a demanding task that requires constant decision-making and active tracking of changes, sometimes minute by minute, in the young person's verbal and embodied communications. At times, young people present a disjunction between words and actions, and demonstrate this in relation to the therapeutic frame through absences, lateness or by wanting to leave early or stay after the end of the session.

The therapist is helped in maintaining the therapeutic stance in TAPP through the structure of the model and the rigour of the setting: the regularity of weekly sessions, ideally at the same time and in the same place, the 50-minute sessions and, perhaps most importantly, the set number of sessions of the treatment, usually 16. Working with the time limits has dynamic potential and is a key feature of the therapist's interventions. Attention paid to how the young person – and therapist – experiences the passing of time of the therapy, as well as the feelings and thoughts this generates, can be a particularly fertile way of understanding what is happening in the therapeutic process. The duration of TAPP – 16 weeks – means that there is usually one planned break in the course of the treatment; the way the young person experiences this and other breaks needs attention and management; how they are experienced yields important information, especially about the young person's reactions to separation, and this may anticipate how they will experience ending the therapy.

Unlike some models of brief therapy, the therapist does not adopt a more active approach than in longer-term therapy. The stance involves the therapist's free-floating attention; the pace of the therapist's interventions is governed by the clinical material and the orientation to adolescence. It is not usually helpful, for example, to leave the adolescence in a prolonged silence and the therapist may want to ask what the young person's thoughts are, or to comment on a difficulty in expressing his thoughts. The therapist is very active internally; she employs an active, attentive and empathic manner to facilitate engagement with the adolescent patient, orienting herself to his states of mind and aiming to occupy a position from which she can both reach out to and contain anxieties arising from his needs for emotional support from more-adult others, whilst refraining from intrusive or infantilising interventions that may have a crushing effect on his aspirant independence and separateness. In practice, this means providing a space to think and move responsively between the patient's more adult or more child-like states as they occur within the sessions. The therapist aims therefore to not become identified by the patient as solely expecting or relating to adult-like states nor solely as a parental figure of a child–patient. Thus, the therapist aims to take upon herself some of the 'in-between-ness' of the young person's developmental process and to occupy a state which permits contradictions, doubt, uncertainties and more 'knowing' or understanding and reflective states – between 'yes' and 'no' (Anthony 1975). The therapist aims to tolerate, and to enable the young person to also tolerate, the propensity to be up and down, excited, passionate, depressed and the extremes of being at times helplessly overwhelmed and, in contrast, irritatingly omnipotent.

Transference and counter-transference

White succinctly expresses the importance of transference and counter-transference:

> As the crucible of the analytic relationship, the transference-countertransference matrix is where the subject's unconscious conflicts and psychopathology come alive in a powerful two-person drama.

(White 2007, p. 133)

Working in the transference in TAPP is crucial for bringing about dynamic change to disturbances in the developmental process, and hence developing the individual's sense of emerging adult subjectivity. As with all adolescent psychotherapy, the dimension of the adolescent developmental process is a key factor in the transference–counter-transference relationship; the developmental struggles, blocks and disturbances gather meaning in the transference–counter-transference relationship. Working *in* the transference is different from working *with* the transference. This distinction reflects the development of how transference is conceptualised; in current thinking, the transference–counter-transference relationship is where current emotions, states of mind and relatedness reflect internalised relationships, which are externalised into the "here and now" of the therapeutic relationship (Lemma 2015a). The transference relationship consists of the benign, hopeful and loving feelings and phantasies – the positive transference – along-side more disgruntled, hateful and hostile feelings and phantasies – the nega-tive transference. The qualities of internalised relationships experienced in the transference may also be thought of as including maternal and paternal aspects, relating to aspects of internalised relatedness to parental figures and to functions of parenting: nurturing, feeding, holding, thinking about and setting limits and boundaries and addressing realities and separateness. Thinking about 'functions' enables a degree of separation for the therapist from her actual gender. The gender of the therapist is important to the adolescent patient, but the transference contains aspects of relatedness to both maternal and paternal figures. Thus, though the cur-rent emphasis on working in the transference is present-oriented, links to the past and to early development are crucially alive and active, permeating relatedness to the therapist in the present.

Initially thought of as evidencing a problem in the therapist – and requiring more analysis, a view still valid and important – counter-transference has come to be seen as a source of information about the patient's unconscious and as part of the intersubjective field between therapist and patient (Ogden 1994). The idea that transference and counter-transference are separate entities has thus been revised to be considered a 'matrix' as, for example, through projective identification the therapist and patient share an intersubjective field. Bion's thinking about the container–contained relationship is an influential example of how transference and counter-transference intermingle, and the therapist's 'reverie' accesses the meaning of the patient's communications through projective identifications. To make sense of the transference, especially to be able to follow the minute-by-minute changes of states of mind (Klein 1952) the therapist needs to observe these details. This is where the supervision process can be especially helpful in process-ing experiences; counter-transference as a source of information can be misused if the therapist's own contributions are not carefully considered.

Progressive and regressive transference

Meltzer commented on the paradox of regression when working with adolescents;

> One of the paradoxes of adolescence is that the adolescent believes that what makes them advance towards the adult world is in fact regressive, whereas what turns them once more into a child is actually what makes them an adult.
>
> (Meltzer 1978, p. 7)

This can be taken to mean that facing the intensity of feelings of dependence, espe-cially in early adolescence, is necessary for growth (Mondrzak 2012). Therefore, regressive forms of transference are inevitable in adolescent psychotherapy, and hence in TAPP, in the sense that in adolescence the developmental process revives infantile conflicts and relatedness. This is a necessary part of development; we saw in discussing assessment (Chapter 4, Chapter 6) that the experience of therapy can add a new turbulent dimension to adolescence, perhaps exacerbating deep anxieties already stirred up by the experience of the adolescent process (Waddell 2002). It is important to think about this, to take into account risks that may be part of this turbulence, and provide necessary support through containing the emotionality involved.

When the time limit of TAPP appears to be linked to a sense of loss and to something ending or being taken away, the consequent loss of love, fear of separateness and fear of surviving alone are felt vividly in the therapy, creating an awareness of a sense of weaning, interplay with early states of mind and unconscious aspects that are revived in the therapy. Holding these and working with them is important for containing anxieties and risks, and for facilitating understanding and growth. Fostering regression would be inappropriate in a time-limited therapy. It is important to accept and work with, but not encourage manifestations of, regression. For example, John, aged 15, came into some sessions clutching a milk drink in a takeaway cup. The therapist noticed that he brought the drink, and tracked how this linked to states of mind in the therapy; a more pseudo-mature state of mind accompanied not bringing the drink, more dependent relatedness with bringing the drink. In one session, he drank from the cup in a way that powerfully evoked scooping out and draining, evoking an early infantile feeding relationship. The therapist could think about how other material in the session, or in the structure of TAPP, might connect with this quality in a feeding relationship. Ferro's (2015) idea of unsaturated interpretations, where the therapist picks up the narrative theme and develops it with the patient without directly speaking about how it relates to herself, as would happen with a full, or saturated, transference interpretation, is a way of conceptualising how the therapist may work with this kind of material in the room, with the aim of developing and transforming meaning. When working with young people with clinical material of this kind, saturated interpretations can raise anxiety and self-consciousness and close down the possibilities of understanding: "Interpretation, before becoming classical transference interpretations, must often go on a long journey" (Ferro 2015, p. 139), through unsaturated interpretations of the young person's narrative and its relation to the transference.

Ferro's emphasis on the work of narrative transformations is an example of recent thinking about the transference–counter-transference relationship that has begun to emphasise the progressive potentialities of the transference–counter-transference relationship (White 2007). The transformative potential of the analytic relationship means new possibilities for growth and subjectivity can emerge in psychotherapy with adolescents. This is particularly pertinent as the aim of therapy is to harness the transformative potential of the developmental process. The "intersubjective analytic third" (Ogden 1994), the process of subjectivation (Cahn 1998) and the transformations in container–contained relationships are different ways a similar preoccupation with progressive aspects of the transference have been conceptualised. The oscillations between different states of mind and the way these are felt and perceived in the counter-transference can be thought about as a theatre in which the struggles of development are taking place; the young person 'uses' the therapist in moments in which a new sense of awareness emerges: awareness of having one's own thoughts, of authenticity and of the benefits of showing courage or aggression in the therapeutic relationship. Being involved in the transference–counter-transference relationship in experiences of oscillations between paranoid schizoid and depressive relatedness is one important way in which the sense of growing separateness and ownership of the developmental process takes place.

This view of the transference relationship helps the therapist keep open in her mind the possibility of growth, the importance of feeling dependent and defences against this, even when the therapy and development appear stuck and repetitive. There is a need to keep open the possibilities of change through relating to ambiguities and observing the minute-by-minute fluctuations in the sessions. Defence and development often seem to be closely connected; the therapist needs to tolerate the defence – for example, the adolescent moving away from emotional contact, perhaps trying out being more separate – and to work with the ambiguities in order to be able to not miss the developmental possibilities. These frequently appear first as small details in the session, accompanied by feeling states in the therapeutic relationship. An example taken from a session towards the end of a TAPP illustrates the young person taking a new position of some ownership of the process of separation, through an emerging sense of being the subject of his development.

Case example: Joshua

Joshua, now 19, was approaching the end of his TAPP, in which he had made considerable progress in being able to recognise and think about his feelings. He began his 13th treatment session by telling the therapist he had a dream that he had failed his exams; it was just the same as last year. The therapist tried to ask him for some more details about the dream, but he was reluctant and the therapist felt that if she pursued the subject Joshua would retreat. Joshua did add with an aggrieved tone that his mother had wished him luck with his exams but he knew she did not mean it because she really did not want him to leave home. The therapist said that Joshua had started the session feeling anxious and he did seem to feel he had a lot to handle at the moment, including how to think about leaving home and the end of his therapy. Joshua said he was in the same situation as last year, that nothing was different. The therapist said it was true that his dream referred to failing exams, and that Joshua felt drawn to similarities with last year, but that it was also possible to think about some differences in him now. He asked what the therapist meant and she said that Joshua seemed for example much more aware of his feelings now, though this awareness puts an additional pressure and burden upon him. He was thoughtful for a moment and then said that he did feel he was different and that he was more aware of his failings. The therapist paused, wondering whether to draw attention to the implicit idea that feelings were synonymous with failings. Instead, she said that Joshua did seem to be worried that in the future he would fail in his attempts to manage this burden of bearing his own feelings himself after his therapy ended. There was a pause and Joshua tensed. He said he was going to change the subject. He wanted to know (strongly emphasised) what would happen in the future. Would he be able to come to see the therapist? He wanted to prepare himself.

Joshua, struggling with anxieties about separating, fluctuates between a more thoughtful and symbolic way of relating, on the one hand, and one in which there is a blurring of boundaries between himself and others, more projective ways of relating, accompanied by persecutory anxieties and grievances, on the other hand. The therapist experienced having choices of how to respond: should she push Joshua to say more about the dream? Or to draw attention to the negative, the sense of failure? It would be easy to be nudged into a critical position, into a power relationship, with Joshua positioned as passive. Joshua's challenge gave him, at this moment, a more active presence in contesting the therapist's knowledge and demanding this knowledge was shared for him to use.

The transference–counter-transference field is complicated in working with young people who differ in age, gender and ethnicity. Psychotherapy with young people always involves an intergenerational factor; gender and sexuality are crucial to the development of subjectivity in adolescence, whilst in intercultural therapy, the differences between therapist and young person can create another layer of uncertainty. Often the three – age, gender and ethnicity – are intertwined, increasing confusion about how to understand communications. These differences can be difficult to talk about; they are not straightforward and carry unconscious meanings. Thinking about the transference can be complicated by how different levels of experience cross over; it can be challenging to find a way of talking to young people's conflicts in their social and internal worlds. For example, Amira, 16, depressed, unable to study or participate in class, was caught in a conflict between different identifications; she wanted to study, and she identified with a traditional view of her culture, but on the other hand she felt stuck in her peer group of similar young women and wanted to access another group of peers who were into going out, parties and relationships. This was further complicated by her fury with her father for, on the one hand, preventing her from having a social life and, on the other hand, being deferential towards the host culture. This conflict was replicated in the therapy when the therapist was also subject to Amira's anger, projected onto her, when she did not solve the problem of how to bridge the divide between her two, apparently incompatible wishes. Her complaints that the therapist did not understand her in these terms, and that she represented a culture that she hated was the cause of her problems, was complicated by her not feeling understood by her mother. Differences of age and culture between Amira and her therapist were palpably felt as exerting a powerful presence that had to be recognised and thought about.

Sexual and erotic transferences present distinctive difficulties for the therapist in working with young people. In effect, erotic transferences can be extremely disturbing and hard to work with, often stirring up disconcerting feelings in the therapist. Jackson (2017) has recently provided a detailed account of the effects of erotic transferences on the therapist, and describes the dilemma for the therapist as a no-win; if the issue is addressed it can be experienced as intrusive, and if ignored as rejecting. The therapist has to work out in the counter-transference what is safe and helpful, and distinguish between a genuinely containing response and one which defensively finds a path that feels safer and less disturbing for the therapist. The adolescent process of relating to the new, adult sexual body is suffused with anxieties and fantasies (Lemma 2015b, see Chapter 3). The intergenerational nature of adolescent psychotherapy and the confusional states that accompany the process of relating to the body in adolescence can lead to miscommunication, or cross communications, between the infantile and the adult parts of the adolescent's sexuality; the sexual body in adolescence can be an obstacle to closeness to parental figures, involving loss, as well as a way of seeking closeness and recognition and of powerfully affecting the other. Jackson (2017) vividly describes the excruciating process of being confronted with a young woman's sexuality. In a different way, a young man, Samuel, aged 15, was tentatively beginning to talk about identifying as homosexual; whilst sitting in silence in his sessions, he cracked his fingers loudly conveying something he was doing to the therapist. The aggression and challenge left the therapist feeling impotent and disturbed. Eventually, it became possible to talk about Daniel's anxieties that his homosexual desires would fill all relationships, and he would have no control over them.

Counter-transference

In TAPP, working with counter-transference experiences, feelings and thoughts is crucial and central; reflection in supervision or a group setting has the important role of enabling the therapist to retain optimum positioning, work with and make sense of feelings and thoughts, relate to the developmental focus and maintain the sense of time in the time-limited therapy. There is often a great deal of anxiety to manage. The therapist has to overcome and eschew the temptation to become caught up with an anxiety to work quickly and cover breadth. Instead, the aim is to work in depth, repeatedly returning to the focus to explore it in greater depth and thus to understand its meaning for development. It is important to not lose patience in the face of recurring difficulties, which can be accompanied at times by intense emotions and the risks of unhelpful and possibly self-destructive actions. Equally, it is also vital to have the capacity to notice change and growth, although this can emerge ambiguously, suggesting either development or defensiveness, or both.

In TAPP, working in the counter-transference involves having lots of material of different kinds to hold in mind, in a field of uncertainty and often with a sense of ambiguity. These contents can be thought about at different levels. First, there is the need to think about one's own feelings, thoughts and experiences, especially those which may interfere with making emotional contact with the patient, and hence with understanding and empathising. It is important to recognise and reflect upon the therapist's own experience of adolescence, and especially adolescent sexuality, to prevent these from becoming problematic. Second, the therapist undertakes the complex emotional work of thinking about how what she is thinking and feeling is influenced by the patient's projective identifications and how this may inform her understanding of the patient's unconscious. Then there is the question of how to work with this in the session. This is not simply about technique – though technique is part of the story – but also about having a feel for what is happening in the intersubjective field between patient and therapist, for one's own states of mind and reactions, for what can be said helpfully at the time in the session and for what may be better to hold in mind. The role of supervision and reflective discussion is important in providing time and space to identify what might be happening at different levels and how to think about this.

One situation to illustrate is the difficulty that arises when the therapist feels that the discomfort is about oneself; perhaps not feeling oneself or not understanding, or making interventions about which she feels self-critical at the time or afterwards. The experience for the therapist can be confusing: whose feelings are these? The temptation to ascribe all therapist feelings to the patient's projective identification should be resisted; however, if by careful reflective scrutiny an idea about an unconscious communication that has been projected onto the therapist can be identified this can be very helpful for the therapeutic process. The therapist may feel something similar to the patient's feeling and thus be able to identify with it: a "concordant identification" in Racker's (1968) terminology. However, this supposes to an extent the patient's awareness of the feelings in question. More likely is that the therapist is experiencing a projection onto her with which she identifies, of something which has not yet been thought about and is not conscious for the patient; following Bion's thinking, the therapist's process of reverie is needed to transform the original feeling which does not have the symbolic content (beta element) into one which is thought about (alpha element).

A therapist finds herself becoming uncharacteristically forgetful of what has been discussed in sessions with Emma, 17 years old. A sense of not quite seeing was given a concrete form when the therapist thought she saw Emma across a crowd of people in a shopping mall; both she and Emma seemed to look at but not quite recognise each other; this episode had a dreamlike quality. Being disconcerted the therapist spent some time reflecting on her feelings and experiences with Emma, who then talked in her therapy about not being able to connect with her friends and feeling separate from them, about feelings she has for her boyfriend not being reciprocated and about others seeming to be uninterested in her. She added that her boyfriend does listen to her and whereas he remembers what she says, she is forgetful.

Emma thus begins to speak about things the therapist felt, about a relationship in which someone is forgetful, not recognising and not connecting. This is (at least) bidirectional: was it Emma's comment on how she experienced her therapist which matched the therapist's self-appraisal, or was the therapist in receipt of ways that Emma experiences herself in her relationships with the therapist and others? Or both? The therapist's reflective process opened up the possibility of hearing what appeared to be an important theme in Emma's relationships, over time and in a way that neither prematurely jumped to conclusions nor returned the therapist's discomfort to the patient before it had been thought about. The therapist's reflective work in the counter-transference changed something in her approach to this young person's therapy; as discussed in Chapter 2, internal processing can facilitate change.

Joseph (1989) described how patients unconsciously "try to get us to act out with them" (p. 157). There are many ways that therapists experience this 'nudge' from the patient's transference to act in the counter-transference. In TAPP, and adolescent psychotherapy generally, this can include getting caught up with young people's aspirations, their anxieties, for example about exams, risks of various kinds or pressures to pull the therapist out of her role, all of which threaten the boundaries and the setting. Brenman Pick (1988) described how the power of the adolescent process can "sweep away" the therapist either by the excitement – "getting drunk on adolescence" – or by constructing defences against the power of the impulses; counter-transferences filled with these specifically adolescent characteristics can 'nudge' the therapist towards enactments, towards being seduced by the energy or defending against it or towards being simply anxious about the adolescent's capacity for action. This complicates the reality-based activities of assessing risks and maintaining the therapeutic setting. With adolescents in TAPP much can happen on the boundaries, at the start or end of sessions. The way a young person comes into the therapy, lateness, non-attendance – how easy it can be to be pulled into going over time, and how difficult to end a session; alternatively, there is the challenge of the young person saying they will or need to leave a session early. Relationships with parents also complicate the counter-transference; the negative transference can become located in one of the parents, and the therapist can feel pulled into being annoyed with the parent on the adolescent's behalf. Parents may also be recruited by adolescents to express things they would rather not say themselves; they may also be intrusive and not able to resist trying to enter the adolescent's therapy space. Parental anxieties are best held by parent work (see Chapter 4), but this is not always possible if resources are not available and if the parent is reluctant to attend. In this way and others, in TAPP the immediacy of the transference–counter-transference relationship is often experienced as relating to the structure of therapy – the setting – to time and time limits and to the developmental focus.

Thinking in the transference: making transference interpretations

In TAPP one of the most important aspects of the therapist's stance is thinking in the transference; there are several ways in which the therapist can use this thinking in working with the young person. Interpretation is one important and powerful intervention. Whether or not the therapist's thinking in the transference is interpreted to the patient is a matter of judgment in each case and moment within the therapy. This judgement depends on many factors: the purpose of interpretation, a sense of how it will be received, when and what exactly to interpret and how and whether other techniques or methods are preferable. The therapist can also decide whether to use unsaturated or more saturated transference interpretations. Understanding of the patient, and how they experience interpretations, is also a crucial factor; whether an interpretation might increase anxiety in an unhelpful way, and how the young person defends against this, needs to be considered; interpretations should address both anxiety and defence. In TAPP it is also important to consider how interventions relate to the focus. A thoughtful observational stance and a reflective approach in the counter-transference should guide what kind of intervention is offered at any particular moment in time. Interpretations need to be seen as one of the interventions available to the therapist, and as fitting within an overall containing approach to the patient. In TAPP, and probably with all time-limited therapies, the overall experience is that much, probably most, of what is experienced and thought about is not interpreted. In TAPP, transference interpretations may be used often in some cases, and in others rarely or not at all. Maintaining an overall containing approach means taking in, digesting and thinking about what can be put back to the patient, in a digestible and helpful form, at any point in time.

Interpretations in TAPP, when they are offered, are most usually of the kind Lemma (2015a) describes as "restricted," in comparison to full interpretations that link aspects of the transference relationship to the patient's early object relationships. Restricted interpretations reflect that not much is known about the patient in the early stages of treatment and thus interpretations may need to be tentative. Subsequently, links between the present transference relationship and the patient's past life – and most importantly his internal object relationships – can be made with more confidence. In time-limited therapy, there is inevitably a limit as to how much progression there is over time in terms of the kind of interpretations that can be made. Initially, therefore, transference interpretations may take the form of simply stating that a feeling or aspect of relatedness is present in the room, or it can draw attention to a feeling being expressed in relation to the patient's current relationships that may also be present in the therapy.

Tentative interpretations in the initial stages of therapy can show the young person that the therapist is interested in the feelings that are in the therapeutic relationship and are couched in terms that are open and permitting further discussion; the therapist does not seek the patient's agreement but will follow carefully the patient's response. Frequently the interpretation will be met with a non-committal 'maybe,' or a denial. Persisting with interpretations that receive denials is not usually helpful. On the other hand, seeking affirmation of the correctness of the interpretation from the patient is unlikely to progress the therapy; interpretations can – at least – make explicit something that has not been said, and with young people there is often a sense of a struggle about whose mind can see, know and comment on what. A fledgeling sense of growing separateness can be crushed by an insistence on the therapist's part that she, the adult in the room, has the power-knowledge. On the other hand, the therapist does not abdicate responsibilities by deferring inappropriately to the young person. It is important when interpretations are made to carefully attend to the way the young person responds, verbally and non-verbally, and to follow closely any changes in the material being presented after the interpretation and the states of mind that accompany this, noticing and often commenting on changes in the quality of the emotional contact the patient makes with the therapist.

With adolescents, there is always a decision to be made about whether to stay with the external, social world and the relationships they are describing, or whether to bring the discussion into the room by relating it to the therapeutic relationship. Partly this is a question of how to support and validate the feelings and issues that arise in young people's social relationships, including their love relationships, in the service of facilitating growth and development, and partly it is a question of the aim of the interpretation and its timing. Sometimes it is possible to achieve a 'both–and' situation where work is undertaken with regard to the social relationships and also relates to the therapeutic relationship. The therapist has to take a two-track approach in her mind, following parallel threads in the external, social world relationships and in the transference relationship.

Interpretations are part of an integrated way of working with the transference in TAPP. Many young people in therapy are fearful of their aggressive and hostile thoughts, impulses and phantasies and require containment of these and increased understanding, which is best achieved in most cases through thinking in and working with the transference. Sexual and erotic feelings are especially sensitive, though it is possible to address these thoughtfully; as discussed in Chapter 4, the therapist's fears and discomfort may also inhibit appropriately addressing these (Jackson 2017). This is true too of being able to talk about self-destructive feelings, and potential risks; it can be vital to ensure these are discussed. Interpretations are not necessarily the best way to work with some aspects of sensitive issues in the transference, particularly when the adolescent patient is fearful of his sexual, aggressive or hostile feelings, or if there is an oppositional quality to the relationship. The use of humour and irony can be facilitative for some patients in addressing these obstacles; for others humour makes it worse, adding insult to injury. The therapist must weigh up, based on the information available about the young person, as to whether naming a deep anxiety might bring some relief and a sense of feeling understood, or whether it would be preferable to suggest working or thinking together on the issue. Recognition of the importance of an issue and noting its complexity or suggesting that we "put our heads together to think" are ways of holding, in Winnicott's sense, a delicate but important issue. Some young people find it hard to tolerate a different point of view; the generational imbalance and the power differential for an adolescent in the process of becoming more separate are vital considerations; being separate means being different and anxieties about separateness lead to defences against difference. Differences in the room – age, gender, ethnicity – and the potential impact of these also need to be taken into account.

Linked to these thoughts are tensions about dependency and the defences against feeling small. It is easy to feel crushed and humiliated when in the process of developing from childhood towards adulthood. Britton (1998) developed a way of working with transferences that included these aspects for the patient who could not tolerate a different point of view. This involves first stating what they understood to be the patient's perspective and second, stating their own perspective. This was used in the example of Aretha in Chapter 7; there, Aretha's perspective was that she wanted the therapist to ask questions; the therapist's perspective was that she wanted Aretha to say what she was thinking. This approach is helpful in recognising the young person's thoughts, whilst also retaining a place for the therapist's, including the role of noticing unconscious communications. It also helps some fragile adolescents not to feel invaded by the therapist's mind and thoughts; as one 15-year-old said, he "gets freaked out by the idea of [the therapist] trying to get inside his mind and attach double meanings to things."

Conclusion

This chapter has discussed the therapist's priorities in the treatment phase; the emphasis has been placed on adopting and maintaining a therapeutic stance that facilitates making emotional contact with young people, working in depth and working in the transference–counter-transference relationship. Different aspects of the transference have been discussed, including current thinking about the potential for growth and discovery through working in the transference. Difficulties that occur when working with the erotic transference and regression have been discussed, along with considerations of issues of age, gender and ethnicity. The first priority, as in all psychoanalytic therapy, is self-reflection: exploring one's own thoughts, feelings and reactions. Working with adolescent states of mind involves being involved with the power of these processes that stir up one's own adolescence and feelings about adolescence, "taking us away from our comfortable equilibrium" (Mondrzak 2012, p. 93; see Chapter 4). In working with the counter-transference, the therapist aims to attune to the emotionality of the young person through self-reflection and to use the emotionality of the session as a tool for understanding the young person's inner world. Support for the therapist, through a seminar group or supervision, is important, as there is a great deal to think about, often infused with ambiguities, to understand the emotional pressures and maintain a time-oriented approach. There are tensions to manage: to not hurry in the face of limited time whilst also allowing the therapy to recognise development and the emergence of growth and new possibilities.

Chapter 9

Working with the developmental focus in the treatment phase

Introduction

Working with the developmental focus links together the elements of TAPP; it is through working with the developmental focus that the therapy engages with the central therapeutic idea of TAPP, that adolescent difficulties and symptoms represent disturbance of the adolescent developmental process. In Chapter 7, the process of identifying a focus and reaching a collaborative agreement with the young person was discussed; here the subject is how the therapist works with the developmental focus in the treatment phase of TAPP. In its essence, working with the developmental focus involves a therapeutic exploration of the young person's emotional experiences in the selected area of adolescent development, and of the disturbance that has been chosen as the focus for the time-limited therapy. Therefore, working with the focus is a psychodynamic process, the intensity of which is heightened by the time limit and the replication of the developmental issues facing the young person in the transference. The discussion here will include selected extended case examples to illustrate different ways of working with the focus for young people across the age range and the different kinds of difficulties they experience.

Relating to the developmental focus

In Chapter 7, we saw that the process of collaboratively agreeing upon the focus in the assessment and engagement phase of TAPP is through consideration of three elements: the therapist's psychodynamic formulations; the young person's narrative of themselves, their difficulties and their hopes and fears of therapy; and the emerging qualities of the therapeutic relationship. As the discussion of the focus represents two people – therapist and young person – coming to the process with different perspectives, backgrounds and roles in the therapy, it is expected that there will be differences between the two and probably a gap between them. The adolescent's anxieties, defences and expectations of therapy influence how the developmental focus is described and discussed in the assessment and engagement phase; it can be expressed in relatively simple terms, or it can be more elaborated. In the treatment phase, the understanding and articulation of the focus develop and change. The key considerations are as follows:

- The focus is not static: development in the therapeutic relationship, especially through the containing process, can lead to new ways of thinking about and articulating the focus.

In a well thought-through focus, the issues come alive in the therapeutic relationship and emerging clinical material continually elaborates the themes, casting new light, increasing depth and providing more opportunities for understanding the interplay between different aspects of the young person's experiences, relationships, problems, difficulties and disturbances in the developmental process. These are experienced in relationship with the therapist, so the therapy is grappling with the anxieties, defences and characteristics of the young person's internal world in the context of his current life, struggles and dilemmas.

Assessment in psychotherapy is a continuous process, and thus new, more detailed understandings of the young person's social and internal worlds are gathered throughout the therapy. Simple articulations of the focus are likely to become more elaborated and shared as the therapy proceeds. In some cases, new material may radically change one's understanding of the young person's difficulties and their therapeutic needs; these can include life events affecting the young person and members of the family or peers including disclosure of abuse, or the emergence of issues that heighten risks. If significant, these will require attention and probably some rethinking of the therapeutic approach.

Additionally, of course, this process is intrinsically one of growth and change; the therapy aims to develop in the young person the capacity to reflect and be aware of the reasons for distress and difficulties and this leads to more depth and texture in the young person's narrative. The therapist's holding and containing functions are important in developing depth in the relationship, and young people are more likely to be able to disclose abuse, for example, or discuss risks when they are more held and contained. On the other hand, the process of therapy is always one of discovery, and new information and ways of thinking about the young person and the therapeutic relationship continually emerge; these need to be thought about in relation to the focus; the therapist may find it is helpful to draw attention to new factors that significantly have an impact on the focus.

- Maintaining the focus: there can be tensions about deciding what clinical material is relevant or not relevant to the focus.

It is a potentially disconcerting aspect of working with young people that the material they bring to therapy can seem to change from week to week. Although in most cases the therapist will be able to link this new clinical material to what has gone before, and hence to the deeper structures of the developmental process and the adolescent's object relatedness, there are times when it can seem that a whole range of new leads are being introduced into the therapy, and following these could have a fragmenting effect. The therapist then has to think about how to address this material. The aim, with TAPP, is to work in depth and to possibly sacrifice breadth, but this should not mean that the focus is followed rigidly; certainly, the focus should not be treated mechanistically. In some cases, when the young person presents new material or new ways of discussing something, this may be a welcome sign of change to hitherto repetitive ways of relating. Stadter (2009, p. 152) refers to the need for flexibility in the focus; it should be a 'navigational beacon' rather than a 'road map' to be slavishly followed; in TAPP, the focus is inherently relating to a process of development, and thus it is likely to have a quality of flexibility and to be able to hold an important sense of the adolescent's developmental potentialities and disturbances over the course of the therapy. However, it is not helpful if the focus is so general and generalised that it can be all-inclusive; hence it is possible to go 'off focus.' The therapist can reflect on the clinical material, to ask whether and how it relates to the focus and whether it needs addressing and how. The therapist's counter-transference experiences can be helpful in guiding how the therapist responds.

- Should the therapist focus more on the focus, or on the relationship in the room?

The first priority in TAPP is to listen to the clinical material the young person brings to each session and to work with it. In the therapist's mind are reflections about what the young person is bringing and how it is experienced in the counter-transference so that the transference relationship can be better understood and responded to. Therefore, in most cases, the focus, once discussed and agreed upon, can be allowed to take a position in the background whilst the psychodynamic process of relating in the room to the patient's material takes place. There will be times when it moves more centrally into the therapist's mind. Thinking about the focus is a continuous process in reflections after each session. The supervision or reflective seminar can helpfully take on the role of thinking about the relationship between the material and the focus.

It is important to distinguish between the part of the focus that articulates an aim of reducing problems and symptoms, and the part that describes in dynamic terms developmental processes. Tracking and discussing changes in symptoms and problems, and any attendant risks, takes place throughout the therapy and will be discussed as relevant and appropriate. The dynamic aspect of the developmental focus is usually experienced, and hence followed, in the therapeutic relationship including the transference and counter-transference relationship; the idea of the focus in the transference can be helpful in working with this in TAPP. Thus the therapist can actively link aspects of the transference to the focus and vice versa; in practice this often involves issues to do with separation and separateness, and with feelings, defences and experiences of changes relating to the young person's emerging adulthood and loss of childhood; how these are experienced by the young person in relation to the therapist are considered at any point in the therapy. The relationship between the focus and the clinical material may be thought of as similar to the way the therapist uses theory; usually, the therapist will be able to access thinking about the focus when it seems important to do so, and this can then guide the way she thinks about and talks with the young person. This relationship might usefully be thought of as a kind of triangular space (Britton 1998), a relationship in the therapist's mind between the experience of the young person's clinical material and reflecting on its meaning.

- Working with the focus means working with time.

A key aspect of the developmental focus is that it relates to time: the present of the adolescent's difficulties that have brought him to therapy, the past of the childhood that has been – or is being – left behind through the changes of adolescence, the future of the adulthood towards which he is moving. As described in Chapter 7, the developmental focus is usually articulated as working towards a future event or experience that the young person will have as the therapy ends; the therapy is described as continuing until these events, such as the end of a school year, exams, a birthday, a transition to employment or university, a change of place, the family moving house, an anniversary and so on. The therapist will have in mind how the young person is experiencing these different dimensions of time, and the future orientation will be experienced in the transference relationship alongside the past and the present; the idea of development and the potentialities of the future will sit alongside experiences of loss and relinquishment and the emotions and relatedness to self and others that are thus involved.

How the therapist works with this sense of time in the developmental focus is important. In this, TAPP draws on the ideas of brief therapy discussed in Chapter 2, especially those of John Mann (1973), and Stadter's distinction between "time near" – clock time – and "time far," the timelessness of the unconscious. Whether time is experienced as rushing by, dragging or increasing fearfulness of or hope for the future will relate to the course of therapy and the number of sessions that have been used and remain; the time-limited therapy has a past, present and future that can seem to parallel the young person's social or external life; the parallel has a dynamic potential for the therapy, for growth and change. How the sense of time affects the therapist is an important aspect of the counter-transference. Much has been said about the pressures on the therapist to hurry, to try to cover ground in the limited time available (Mann 1973; Stadter 2009); the therapist's managing anxiety in the face of limited time is a key factor in all time-limited therapy. Especially if the adolescent seems stuck, unlikely to be able to separate at the end of therapy or not getting better and likely to continue to present risks and needs after the therapy ends, the therapist's sense of feeling under pressure to act on these anxieties is likely to be high. Osimo (1998) has developed a way of thinking that takes working with time beyond the binary of fast and slow pace. He uses a 2 x 2 matrix to distinguish what he calls good and bad slowness and quickness. Bad quickness is hurrying driven by anxiety; good quickness is recognising therapeutic change and development and being able to work with it, not to slow it down: for example, seeing the developmental aspect alongside apparent defensiveness. Good slowness is having a state of patience, returning to and working repeatedly with clinical material and working through: for example, repeatedly going over material relating to loss. The emotional experience is important, for it is usually possible to distinguish between the sense of working through and stuck repetitiveness. Perhaps there are sessions where not much is said, as the therapist stays with the patient's feelings. Bad slowness is where the therapist either does not recognise change and the patient's movement, and takes them back to this, or where she anxiously feels she must go over this one more time, to make sure, like an anxious parent. The therapist has to overcome and eschew the temptation to become caught up with an anxiety to work quickly and cover breadth. Instead, the aim is to work in depth, repeatedly returning to the key themes to explore them in greater depth and thus to understand the meaning of these for development.

- Working with the focus is affected by the young person's positioning in the developmental process.

The young person's age, social and familial contexts, gender, ethnicity and the kinds of problem he experiences influence the assessment of how he is experiencing the adolescent developmental process, as well as the identification of disturbances and difficulties for the focus for TAPP. The age of the adolescent is important; whether they are a young adolescent contending with the immediate impacts of the changes ushered in by puberty, or a young adult trying to find ways of entering a more adult world and relationships, makes a significant difference to how the developmental focus is thought about and worked with. The unifying principle of the developmental process, with the idea of adolescent states of mind across the age range, exists alongside the evident differences between an immediately post-pubertal teenager and a young adult at the beginning of the third decade; working with the focus is attuned accordingly to these contexts as well as to internal configurations and states of mind. Considerations of gender, ethnicity and culture and the changed and changing contexts of adolescence are important for working with the focus, as is the organisational context in which the therapy takes place, whether in a mental health service, an educational or primary health setting or in private practice.

Working with the developmental focus is best described through case examples which show the therapist holding and containing the conflicting states of mind about development and defences against this, in the complex adolescent field of social, familial and internal relationships. The following case examples describe working with the developmental focus for different kinds of difficulties; these are organised by age and gender, for younger adolescents, later teenagers and young adults. Illustration of working with the developmental focus here concentrates on the early and middle phases of therapy; working with the focus in the ending phase is discussed in the following chapter. The examples aim to illustrate the therapist working in depth, thinking in the transference–counter-transference and working with the TAPP structure.

Working with the developmental focus with younger adolescents

With younger adolescents, usually between 14 and 16 years old, the themes of the developmental focus often involve the anxieties and struggles of beginning to become more separate from parental figures, expressed through different states of mind and emotions; fragile, fledgeling subjectivities and a reworking of relatedness to self and others, especially parental figures, are involved. The specific qualities of these relate to experiences in families, past and present issues, conflicts and difficulties and the young person's internalisation of patterns of earlier relatedness. Symptoms and difficulties are thought about in relation to how the adolescent is experiencing and defending against the pains and anxieties of the developmental process, the changes following puberty. The developmental process in early adolescence is reflected in the therapeutic relationship, which is often characterised by tensions about dependency and separateness alongside a wish, perhaps a longing, for understanding. Two case examples – one female, one male – illustrate how the developmental focus is worked with. In the first case, Sasha, the focus is on anxieties about being separate, especially from her mother; in the second example, Peter, the problem of becoming more separate in adolescents is experienced in a different way. Peter feels he is separate, and overwhelmed, as the closeness of his childhood relationships feels lost to him.

Case example: Sasha

Sasha turned 15 years old during her TAPP; she presented in her assessment with anxieties that had increased, she said, since she was 11, coinciding with the move to secondary school, and she had developed compulsive checking behaviour especially before leaving home and at night. Sasha said she was very close to her mother, more distant from her father, but worried about upsetting them both. She found school unsatisfying; peer relationships were tense and difficult. Her problems seemed entrenched; previous therapeutic intervention had not had any effect. Sasha attended her assessment sessions, agreed to the offer of TAPP and contributed to formulating the problems and setting the developmental focus. The collaboratively agreed on formulation was that Sasha held herself back emotionally and developmentally for fear of upsetting her mother and herself. The focus was to help Sasha feel less anxious and to not have to obsessively check things, to work on becoming less entangled with and more separate from her mother and so to be able to engage more with her development. TAPP was planned over 16 sessions, taking Sasha into the next school year, in which she would take exams.

The first treatment session started with a tension sometimes encountered at this point in the TAPP process; Sasha said she had nothing to talk about, as everything was okay at the moment. Whilst the process of negotiating the treatment offer and the developmental focus in the assessment and engagement phase aims to address some of the ambivalences that arise at this point, the transition to therapy from assessment often has a meaning for the young person that needs to be attended to; anxieties about beginning, ending and time are always present. Here, the therapist talked about how Sasha was trying to keep things nice between them, and possibly protecting the therapist from Sasha's messy and destructive feelings. It then became possible to talk about Sasha's anxieties about starting her therapy, and where this might take both of them, whether she might not feel in control and whether 16 sessions might seem enough, too few or too much. Sasha talked in the first few treatment sessions about her intense anxieties; these took many forms, including a fear of burglars breaking into the house that could be triggered by the slightest noise, and then she could not sleep. The therapist spoke explicitly to the focus, that Sasha, by playing down her feelings and trying to smooth things over, was keeping herself small and limiting the knowledge she had of herself and her development. The fears of intrusion and aggression from outside were then talked about as a part of her internal world that she projected.

In the middle phase of the treatment, in sessions seven to ten, Sasha brought her anxieties more directly into the sessions, creating a tension in that she generated considerable concern, but she was also more alive her sessions; she talked more about interactions with others in school, her choice of subjects for the following year and her relief that the school year was nearly over. A break in her therapy would also occur whilst the therapist took her summer leave, and the therapist made a connection between Sasha's relief about the ending of the school year, the break in her therapy and the end of her therapy, which she was now halfway through. Sasha wanted to have everything neatly wrapped up when faced with the anxieties of these separations.

When therapy resumed after the break, Sasha spoke about having been ill; she was receptive to the idea that she was holding emotional things in her body during her therapist's absence. She said also that her checking had got worse over the break, and that her mother was more anxious about her. But Sasha began to be more spontaneous in talking, including about some angry and frustrated feelings towards her father, though she was still worried about upsetting her parents, and the therapist. Then, in the 11th session, she spoke about feeling things were better at school, about making new friends and about being interested in boys; growth was clearly taking place as she looked more 'adolescent' and there was a sense of emerging sexuality. She said she wanted to meet up with friends after school, and she was anxious how she would find this, and how her mother would respond; she expected her mother would be anxious. The therapist talked about her sense of having greater agency, and not holding everything inside, and how this increased her anxiety that she would not be in control, and not in control of others. This was linked to her therapy, the time that was left and the unknowns of the future and where this would take them – Sasha and her therapist – in the time that remained.

In the last phase of the therapy, between sessions 12 and 16, Sasha began to talk about the emerging conflict between herself and her mother; she expressed some irritation that her mother wanted to know every detail of what had happened when she went out with her friends. Sasha added, when the therapist asked her, that she spoke less to her mother now about what happened in her therapy. These movements towards greater separateness appeared important, if also difficult and conflictual, but Sasha said that though she felt less anxious now, and sought her mother's reassurance less, she still had compulsions and her checking behaviour; it was in the post-treatment review that Sasha reported that she no longer checked things. After meeting up with friends, Sasha said she would find her mother anxiously waiting for her return. The therapist linked this to whether she, the therapist, could let Sasha go, and how Sasha felt she would be kept in mind after the therapy ended.

Case example: Peter

This case example complements that of Sasha; in both, there is a disturbance of development during early adolescence, with different manifestations, symptoms and relatedness. The description of working with the developmental focus here shows a change in the quality of the therapeutic relationship in the middle sessions of the therapy.

Peter is 15; his parents initiated his assessment for psychotherapy as they were worried about him; he was not sleeping and was saying he could not cope with life. In his assessment, he tearfully described being under pressure, and feeling that everything was falling apart; he felt he was failing and having a complete breakdown. He was very worried about schoolwork, especially as exams were on the horizon, but also about not having a social life and not being able to communicate well with his parents. He had some suicidal thoughts but no plan to act on these. The formulation, which was shared and discussed, was that at this point in his life, when he was changing and growing, he felt he could not manage the demands of development and he felt trapped by his feelings of failure. The focus was shared in these terms: the therapy would aim to make sense of and try to reduce his distress and help him make sense of his feelings, so that he could feel more able to manage his tasks in the world, at this point in his development, including facing taking exams, and feel more able to communicate and relate to others whilst feeling more separate from them. The therapy of 16 sessions would take him up to just after his exams were due to finish.

When he began treatment sessions, Peter returned to a theme that had emerged in his assessment; he felt he should be able to sort out his own problems by himself and not have to rely on a therapist. He worried the therapist would not understand him, and that he would fail in therapy, as he felt he failed in other areas of his life. Alongside this was a fragility in having his own ideas and thoughts, which might not be the same as others'. His solution, he said, for now, was to try not to fall apart in his therapy; the therapist thought this was both a defensive avoidance of a painful situation and a desire to be more "grown up." The therapist wondered aloud whether Peter felt worried about her ability to understand his mind, and he said he was worried by the idea of the therapist trying to get inside his mind and 'attach double meanings to things'. These invasive fears led him to try to set a boundary between himself and his therapist, particularly between what was in his and his therapist's mind. Thus, he presented a particular dilemma for his therapy, which appeared to relate to anxieties about being separate, or becoming fused with another person. What can he share with the therapist, what is his and what is the therapist's? Where to set a boundary? On the other side was an equally difficult question – what does the therapist need to know about and what can be kept private? The therapist talked about the importance of what Peter was saying, and that they could try to think about how to manage these thoughts and feelings as they came up.

During the first six treatment sessions, Peter was often late and when in the room he was cautious and withholding. The therapist commented on this and also tried to find moments where there was some room for negotiation and moments when she could present Peter with a choice. One example was when the subject of Peter's exams came up; the therapist said that he might like to think about, and let her know, if he wanted to continue with weekly sessions during the exam period or have a break. The painfulness and delicacy of Peter's predicament arising from the attempt to be more separate stirred sympathy in the therapist for his struggles. When Peter mentioned, reluctantly, in the fifth session being in trouble at school for bullying younger children, a different aspect of his developmental struggles was brought into the therapy: his aggression and hostility to a younger version of himself, a small child who needed parental care. The therapist interpreted this and linked it to his feelings of having to be available when the therapist was, rather than when he felt he needed her.

Following this, from the sixth session, a more cooperative therapeutic relationship emerged. Peter was more open, talking about his fear of losing control and his fear of being separated from his parents. He seemed to be less fearful of closeness in his therapy. In the seventh session, Peter expressed discomfort with the idea of getting help from a teacher, and the therapist suggested this might be the same in his therapy. He disagreed with her, saying that he has made a choice to come to his therapy and he has realised that something happens here that doesn't happen elsewhere. He has found that talking in the way he talks here helps him to think clearly about things, so he has felt more comfortable about being more open. He followed this by expressing regret about the therapy time he has missed through being late, which he called a 'real shame'. The shift from feelings of persecution to gratitude and regret about time wasted appeared to be a significant development. The ending phase of Peter's therapy is described in the next chapter.

Working with the developmental focus with young people in their later teens

For older adolescents, between approximately 16 and 18 years old, the developmental focus reflects their being further into the adolescent process; the early turbulences after puberty may now have settled into patterns of relating to self and other, together with anticipation of transitions in the social world becoming closer in time. The imminence of the realities of these transitions into employment or higher education, leaving home, even if on a partial basis, and being involved in sexual relationships – and the anxieties these realities bring – can propel young people into therapy at this age; their immediacy can bring with them a need to gather agency, and perhaps take responsibility. In current social contexts, the pressures to constantly make decisions about pathways towards adulthood creates an anxiety-laden milieu.

Disturbances of the adolescent process may by this time be more entrenched and stuck. The symptoms and problems of this age group can appear more entrenched, especially amongst the more disturbed young people, though not without the hope or possibility of change, of getting back on to a more progressive developmental trajectory, and moving away from more disturbed or destructive relatedness (Waddell 2006; Flynn & Skogstad 2006). Practitioners can feel engaged with a problem of time or with a sense of regret or frustration that the young person has left it so late to seek, or be referred for, therapeutic help – that so little time is available before the realities of transitions will arrive; in mental health services and educational settings services where cut-off applies at 18, this also presents a time limit and challenge. The developmental focus therefore aims to reflect this aspect of time, and working with it can juxtapose two timescales: the longer-term nature of the difficulties and disturbances and the shorter amount of time available for intervention. Working with the developmental focus is complex in cases where mental health difficulties exist alongside social vulnerabilities and predicaments. The interplay of these processes is illustrated through two case examples illustrating working with the developmental focus. In the first of these, the focus is on containing and working through the depression felt by a young man, Luke, as his development has stalled; the therapy works with his identification with a father perceived as numb to emotions, and to help Luke find a pathway towards becoming a man. For Yasmin, the focus was on understanding the multiple levels of emotional and relational meaning of her self-harm by cutting in the context of her leaving school and preparing to leave home.

Case example: Luke

Luke began assessment for psychotherapy when he was 17 years old, when a worsening of his depression and a breakdown in his education led to his mother seeking help for him; his attendance and work at school was so poor that he was not allowed to continue into the following year. He said he had been depressed for some years, throughout his adolescence, but recently things had gone "off the rails." He had fallen out with his friendship group; he said he was not sure whether this led to him feeling more depressed, or whether he had been more depressed and consequently pushed the friends away. Whereas going out with his peer group had given him some relief, along with the alcohol he drank, now he was more alone and miserable. When Luke talked about his background it appeared difficulties had indeed been entrenched for some time. He had what he described as a very lonely childhood: his single-parent mother was also often depressed; she cared for him but kept herself busy with work, and several relationships, none of which lasted long. Luke had relatively briefly known one of these men in a stepfather role. His own father lived in a different country, was high-achieving, appeared to be limited emotionally and related in a distant way to him; Luke envied his father and was dismissive of him. In his assessment Luke was hard to engage, his misery uppermost; he did not expect anything to change through therapy, and he did not trust having better feelings, but he did feel desperate for some help and he was aware of the need to address his future education. He wished he could work and achieve, like his peers, and he did want to understand what was going on inside himself; he knew he turned away from his feelings and that this did not help.

The therapist felt that Luke would be challenging to work with, that his relentless negativism would be hard to bear and that he may need to try to defeat his therapy, though she did also warm to him. She formulated that Luke's loneliness, depression, the bleakness of his internal landscape and turning away from feelings and others was driven by his grievances about his childhood and parents, and that he seemed to feel he did not have a secure place in either parent's life or mind. Luke's state of mind indicated risks that needed to be attended to, though he said he was not thinking of suicide. Time-limited therapy was offered both because there was a limited amount of time available in the service, and it was felt the structure of TAPP could provide holding and cohesion, and a manageable time scale for him; there was a sense of him being trapped in the timelessness of his miserable feelings. Against this was the sense that his development was very stuck. The therapist suggested a developmental focus of trying to understand more about what was happening in his internal world to see if this would help him feel less depressed and help him find resources to deal with feeling derailed in his development, education, relationships with others and engagement with his own future. This was discussed in some detail with Luke as he thought about and disputed some of it. He said he would like to be less depressed, but he didn't feel he would become less miserable, as this was part of the human condition, and anyone who thought otherwise was self-deluding. However, he did say he wanted to have therapy and that he thought it should focus on how he feels he has lost his way, on his relationships and on planning his future. TAPP would be 16 sessions, taking him through the change in his education and until he might be settled in a new setting.

The first phase of treatment, whilst Luke was ending, mainly by not attending, his college, was characterised by stuck, repetitive and almost remorseless expression of his misery, exerting a fierce grip against anything more lively; he demanded that misery should be noticed, and expressed his irritation with anyone – amongst whom he included his mother – whom he thought looked for the cloud's silver lining rather than seeing the cloud. He stayed in bed and said he felt numb; he also described his distant father as numb. The therapist felt she was thus stuck between a maternal object that could not bear his anger and pain, and a paternal object that was numb, unfeeling and distant. She recognised he felt miserable and spoke about the sense of something happening to him, that he was subject to and could not influence, including his college excluding him from the following year. In the third treatment session, Luke offered that he felt things were quite bad at the moment and that he imagined being knocked down by a bus. He said he knew he would not do this deliberately, but if it happened, he would not be feeling miserable or angry anymore. The therapist commented on how intolerable things felt at the moment, to which he agreed. He added, referring explicitly to the focus, that his problems were more serious than being about his adolescent development and the therapist commented, using Luke's words, that development had gone seriously off track and his feelings were very distressing. He spoke of his fears of being mentally ill in the long term, and of his anger and violent feelings. At times the therapist felt warmth towards him, but helpless as he pushed this away, as his powerlessness was projected onto her. When she took up with Luke the suicide risks, he said he could not guarantee that he could keep himself safe and it was agreed the therapist would speak with his mother, who was concerned and said she would attend to Luke and the risks; the mother's mobilisation on Luke's behalf and link to the therapist appeared to be an important moment, and it was arranged for a colleague to meet with her. In the following fourth session, the therapist talked about how difficult it was for Luke to accept help. He was responsive, agreeing that he did hate himself for needing help.

In the middle phase of treatment, Luke began to be livelier and to have more engagement with the theme of dependence and independence. In the ninth treatment session, the therapist mentioned being halfway through the therapy, and that it may be easier for Luke to go numb on the therapy rather than being alive to the time that is left as well as to the fact that it will end. Luke spoke about how being alive was, for him, living on the edge, the margins, and involved a sense of having control rather than being subject to others' availability for his needs. He spoke of liking to walk around at night on his own when no one else was around. He had the feeling the whole world belonged to him. He would sit and watch the foxes play. His identification with the foxes held a meaning of suicidal danger; they seemed free to roam but were vulnerable to being killed on the road. The therapist named this risk and Luke agreed but said he would keep himself safe.

Luke usually began his sessions saying, "nothing has changed"; but he did change. He started getting out of bed and attending his new college; he made new friends and began a tentative relationship with a girlfriend. His mother encouraged him to take driving lessons and organised paying for these. This excited Luke, perhaps identifying with the aggressor – the fox killer – rather than the victim, but also, simultaneously, a sense of embracing aspects of adulthood. Luke spoke of having a new appetite, literally; whereas he had previously frequently not eaten all day, he was now feeling hungry a lot of the time. These new stirrings of life and development indicated Luke moving away from his identification with a numb father and finding some pleasure in feeling lively in the process of becoming a man. The ambiguities of meaning, hopes and renewed, if revised, risks required careful working through in the ending phase of TAPP.

Case example: Yasmin

For Yasmin, who was also 17 when she began therapy and in her last year at school, the focus that was shared and agreed upon during the assessment phase was to understand the meaning of her self-harm by cutting so she may be able to stop, which was her wish, and to feel more able to think about the changes ahead: exams, leaving school and leaving home to go to university. Yasmin had strong views on subjects which she expressed forcefully; she was committed to her education and expected to do well in her exams. Working with the focus meant aiming to understand her self-harm as a multi-layered communication of her internal conflicts; cutting as a metaphor appeared in much of the clinical material in the early sessions of her therapy. One level of meaning was that Yasmin cut herself off from her emotional life; in her second treatment session, she said she had no idea about feelings. She felt frustrated that she did not know herself and didn't know what was going on inside herself. She felt she did not matter to anyone, and that other people "cut her off" from their lives; the therapist felt that Yasmin might "cut short" her therapy, but also that, faced with Yasmin's stream of words in the sessions, she had to "cut in" to speak, as if cruelly making an incision.

Initially, Yasmin thought her self-harm was a secret, and that the therapist was the only person she had told; she hoped therapy would help her to stop before her parents found out. However, in the fifth treatment session, she reported that her mother did know; they had a conversation and Yasmin felt her mother had misunderstood why she felt the need to cut herself. She was furious with her mother, feeling shamed, embarrassed, exposed and vulnerable, and furious with her therapist for not solving the problem before it came out into the open. Yasmin's rage was difficult to withstand; she aimed to come out on top in any dispute and had the verbal and intellectual capacity to succeed in this. The therapist spoke about Yasmin not being able to share with her parents things that were important; Yasmin then spoke of being the victim of a sexual attack she had experienced in her early teens, and which she had also not been able to tell her parents. She felt ashamed, shaken up and vulnerable and yet rationalised not telling her parents as it was not really so important. The therapist questioned this; recognising the importance of Yasmin's pain and outrage at the abuse she had experienced became a key theme in these middle sessions of her therapy. This led to thinking about how Yasmin perceived her parents as fragile emotionally and that for some time she had ceased to think they would be able to cope with her emotional needs, so Yasmin managed by not talking about her worries and vulnerabilities, played down her difficulties in her mind and defended against the loss or absence of supporting parents by convincing herself she knew and was always right.

In the tenth and eleventh sessions, Yasmin was more able to ironically reflect on her defence of knowing and being right and to allow herself to hear her therapist's thoughts. This created a new situation, in which Yasmin began to talk more about her feelings and to allow herself to feel vulnerable, tinged with regret and sadness. In the 15th session, Yasmin talked about observing her parents' limitations; she compared being at her friend's and seeing her friend and her friend's mother cooking together, and said that never happened in her house because her mother could not

stand anyone being near her when she was cooking. The therapist talked about the
sadness about the mother she would have liked to have. Yasmin said her father had
recently said to her that Yasmin had been through a lot, and the therapist said that her
father seemed to be noticing now and some people never get to that point. Yasmin
replied that she "got that."

Working with the developmental focus with young adults

As discussed in Chapter 3, the extended period of adolescence is a key feature
of current social contexts. Attending to the developmental process is therefore
an important aspect of understanding the difficulties of young people who are
still in a process of making transitions to the adult world. These young people
present stuck or fractured transitions and their difficulties and disturbances often
reflect that past pains and losses, and defences against these, interact with current dilemmas and conflicts. Many if not most young people have had by now
experiences of living away from home; they present as being on the threshold of
adulthood, but not able to access a more fulfilling pathway to adulthood. They
usually have experiences of love and sexual relationships, either with an idea of
these enduring or not; alternatively, the world of relationships, sex and gender
can be experienced as involving complicated decisions about whom to be with,
whether to continue with or end a relationship, fearing and experiencing loss,
reactivating childhood losses or choices or dilemmas about sexual orientation.
The two case examples illustrating working with the developmental focus for this
age group represent young people struggling with a transition, of leaving home in
the first case, Aretha, and of having dropped out of university in the second case,
Eric. Working with the developmental focus involved, with Aretha, attending to
her fear of being separate and on her own which stirred up, powerfully, feelings
of self-hatred and self-destructiveness; with Eric, the focus was on his attempt to
toughen up as a way of managing the vulnerability that he felt overwhelmed and
humiliated him.

Case example: Aretha

Aretha, whose assessment was discussed in Chapter 7, was a 19-year-old not feeling
ready to leave home and go to university. The developmental focus was agreed on
as to work with her fear and panic of being alone, separate and being subject to difficult and self-destructive feelings and impulses; a significant difference, which was
named, was the therapist's view that feelings could be thought about, and Aretha's
wish to get rid of them.

In the first three treatment sessions, Aretha spoke about having better contact with her father than recently, and enjoying her work, an area of her life where she felt more adult and competent. In the fourth session, she reported an episode that showed a change in her experience of being alone. She spoke about a phone call from a friend that had left her anxious and annoyed; she felt alone and in a panic, and was on the point of rushing home, where she may have self-harmed. Instead, she managed to check this impulse and, finding herself outside a coffee shop, went inside. Calming down she said she actually found she enjoyed being on her own. As frequently occurred with Aretha, a new state of mind was discovered through a sudden decision or action; here she discovered, it appeared, some internal resources that allowed her to be alone and calm herself. The therapist sensed that, though it could not be said directly, Aretha had been able to draw on a thought about her therapy to sustain her capacity to resolve her panicky state in this way.

Instead of talking about these internal situations, to which she seemed not to have direct emotional access, Aretha told the therapist she felt better; she "knew" this must be due to her therapy, but she had no idea why. Initially, she portrayed a lack of curiosity about this lack of understanding. She liked coming to her therapy but could not see what the therapist was "doing" to make her feel so much better. "I feel better," she said, "but I don't know why." Work on the focus for Aretha's therapy then concentrated on the issue of knowing, or not knowing, what was happening in her mind, and how she could understand how events, including interactions in relationships, "caused" the feelings to which she was subject. Her therapist suggested that either she could accept the role of magician Aretha was ascribing to her, or she could wonder why Aretha chose not to know her own role in bringing about this change through her use of her therapy. Aretha was very reluctant to enter this discussion with its implications for giving up omniscience, in herself or in another, and being able to blame others for her difficulties, but her capacity for irony and spirited debate were attributes which were available to this process of negotiating difficult, angry and painful feelings.

Thus, two different positions were articulated between therapist and patient. One was a world of omniscience, where someone who knew, and who had power, "did" something to someone through her superior knowing, whilst the other was the passive recipient. The other position was one in which both contributed to experiences, and both had feelings, hopes and wishes in relation to each other, in which neither had complete control. In other words, both were separate individuals. Aretha's experience as the passive recipient of her parents' problems in their relationship, and particularly her father's unpredictable comings and goings, was discussed as contributing to her attempts to identify defensively with an omnipotent parental figure, a role which she wished to attribute to the therapist. In the therapeutic interactions, the aim of the therapist was to question these assumptions and to engage Aretha in experiencing greater separateness, and mutuality in relationships, whilst containing the consequently increased responsibility for bearing her feelings, thoughts and wishes, and her understanding of her impact on others in relationships and others on her.

Case example: Eric

Eric, 21 years old, had left university after the first year, feeling unable to cope with the academic work and student life. He came for therapy, somewhat reluctantly, to see if it would help him decide whether to reapply and return to university. In his assessment, he presented some disturbing aspects, along with risks to himself and others, but he would not consider longer-term therapy. He was emphatic that he wanted to reach a decision about university in time for the next academic year; he thought he would either get some help with this quickly, or not at all. He appeared articulate and to have a certain charm, but was depressed and anxious, and to an extent evasive; it was hard to disentangle in his narrative what felt authentic from a more rehearsed, defensive account of himself. He said he hated his university experience, had not made friends and had been reminded of difficult experiences at school, where he had been bullied; this he described as painful experiences that lasted from between when he was 10–13 years old. The absence of helpful, containing figures in his life was a notable feature; figures in his life seemed shadowy, or thinly textured. His father was described as tough, having no time for feelings; he thought his mother was conciliatory and described her as often tearful. As a response to being bullied, he had decided to toughen up and not show vulnerability to others, which he thought would prevent pain being inflicted on him. This included his relationships with girlfriends and, having felt rejected by one girl in his mid-teens, he aimed to not get hurt again. Eric agreed that his childhood and teenage years probably had a bearing on how he had experienced university and that reflection on and understanding these experiences might help with his decision about whether to return. The developmental focus, therefore, was to explore how his childhood experiences may have contributed to his difficulties at university, to help him decide whether to reapply, or to find other ways of furthering his development.

In the beginning phase of his therapy, a key theme was the relationship between vulnerability and toughness. In the first treatment session, Eric recalled from early in his childhood that his father, who had been in military service, had no tolerance for sadness or tears and would tell Eric to stop crying, or his father would "give him something to cry about." In the following session, Eric talked about a breakup in a relationship with a girlfriend; he had been hurt, but when she called and said she regretted breaking up he refused to think about getting back together; he felt he had trusted her too much and the only person he could trust was himself. In the following session, speaking about his difficulties when at university, he recalled starting a relationship, which ended when his girlfriend became frightened by him. At the therapist's prompting, he talked about intensely violent feelings, which he had tried to deal with, but which he also cultivated as a means of being frightening to rather than frightened by others. He wished not to have weaknesses that others could exploit, and he did not want to feel vulnerable again. Eric thus seemed to projectively identify with his father's approach to vulnerability and pain, as a defence against feeling hurt, bullied and rejected. In the fifth session he spoke about regularly using alcohol to dull the pain, and that the attempts to toughen up did not effectively remove his sense of being vulnerable, hurt and sensitive.

It appeared he felt increasingly able to trust the therapist with details about himself, despite his injunction to himself not to trust; in the middle sessions, the therapist commented on this and linked it with the time limit; she wondered how he would experience the ending, and in particular whether it would repeat the pattern in relationships of hurting–being hurt, or whether therapy may provide a different kind of experience. Eric's response was that he thought it would be different and that he saw his therapist as different from his parents: not critical, tough and violent, like his father, nor overwhelmed and frightened by him, like his mother.

In the ninth session, Eric had begun to work a temporary job; this was a tough labouring job and he came to sessions with cuts on his hands and arms. He seemed to be trying another way of being 'tough'; however, it was the first time he had shown a sense of being able to be more active in his life. The therapist was able to talk about a difference between toughness and strength, the latter stemming from relationships in the internal world, and to talk about Eric's intolerance of vulnerability and his need for others. Eric responded by saying that he had decided not to get into girlfriend relationships at the moment, as he felt not ready for them, and the therapist, recognising the idea of development in this thought, spoke again about needing to work to strengthen his relationships in his internal world in his therapy. This was followed by Eric showing a more generous and thoughtful approach to others; in the following session, he spoke about buying his mother a birthday present, over which he was taking some care. These signs of Eric beginning to take seriously his development sat alongside his continuing to have difficulties; he said he was sleeping badly and feeling increasingly troubled in himself. He also found he was less interested in philosophy, his university subject, and felt less inclined to return to university, but had no real ideas about what to do; the therapist said that though he had a time scale to make a decision about this, and though there was a time limit for the therapy, the therapeutic work that he had begun may well need to continue longer than this; Eric agreed and said he had been thinking this too.

Conclusion

Working with the developmental focus is the crucial aspect of the therapeutic process in TAPP. Case examples have been chosen to convey how developmental disturbances are experienced in different contexts and at different phases of the adolescent process. The therapist works with the focus through observing, reflecting and thinking in the transference, relating the underpinning themes in the focus to the nuances of the young person's social and interpersonal contexts. The cases describe some of the different ways in which the therapist works with a developmental focus and facilitates growth; they include young people with complex difficulties in order to clearly represent the kind of therapeutic work undertaken using TAPP. In complex cases, where there is a more severe disturbance of the developmental process, there is a tension between the aspect of the young person that is on the side of development, and that which, for many reasons, seems organised to resist and oppose development. These aspects of growth and change, and the struggles to achieve development, are further discussed in Chapter 11. Stuck and disturbed aspects of development can present formidable challenges to the therapist and the therapy; the discussion and examples in this chapter place these in context and emphasise the continual processes of assessment and readjustment that are needed when working with the focus. At the centre of this is the involvement of the therapist emotionally alongside the young person's difficulties. How the developmental focus is worked with in the ending is a powerful dynamic in the TAPP process and is discussed in the following chapter.

Chapter 10

Ending therapy

Introduction

This chapter discusses the important and complex processes involved in ending therapy. In TAPP, when worked with well, the ending is a powerful process for change and growth; experiences of loss and separation in the adolescent developmental process are mirrored in the therapeutic relationship. In the therapy, the ending is characterised by two processes which are the focus of this chapter: first, of working with the emotionality of the ending in the therapeutic relationship and second, of evaluating and reviewing where the young person is ending therapy, the changes that have occurred, current and future needs and how the therapy has had an impact on the young person's developmental process. Different states of mind and feeling in the ending process are discussed and illustrated with case examples. The role of the post-treatment review as part of the TAPP structure is discussed.

The importance of the ending

TAPP culminates in the working through of the meaning of the ending in each case. Discussion of a specific phase, the ending phase, is to an extent heuristic, for the ending is worked with throughout the duration of the therapy. Ending begins with the setting of a time limit, a limited number of sessions, and it is kept in mind throughout the therapy. At appropriate points the therapist will have reminded the patient how many sessions are left; around the midpoint, the young person's clinical material frequently refers to the ending, as discussed and illustrated in Chapters 8 and 9. Young people are often acutely aware of the number of sessions remaining, even if they do not overtly bring attention to this, and even if their material has a timeless feel. In TAPP, the ending 'phase' – usually including the last four to five sessions – brings together and intensifies the work on the developmental focus; the dynamics of the ending make for a powerful process for change and growth, if the intensities can be borne by both the therapist and adolescent patient, and if the communications and defences of various kinds can be understood and contained.

Ending therapy is always complex and a challenge, as Strupp and Binder (1984) observe: "Irrespective of whether therapy is short term or long term, termination represents one of the most critical challenges to the therapist" (p. 259). In TAPP the adolescent developmental process infuses the ending process with piquancy and implications. Ending TAPP becomes one of many experiences of ending, for young people, at various times across the adolescent process in contemporary social contexts; in adolescence endings at personal and organisational levels include moving school, changing class, family reconfigurations, moving house, friends moving away, separations in love relationships, and temporary and more prolonged separations from home. So, the gamut of experiences creates many potential configurations for the meaning of ending therapy. It involves, usually, a mixture of loss, sadness, anger and also hope and achievement, plus a sense of being set free from a structure, the therapy, and also left or abandoned by it.

The distinctive process of ending therapeutic relationships with young people is highlighted by the way that the ending of TAPP mirrors the adolescent developmental process, especially when that is conceptualised as involving the loss of childhood relatedness, dependency on parental figures and a movement towards the greater separateness and individuality of becoming more adult. The ending of TAPP can be significant for making sense of the other endings experienced during the adolescent years by addressing the emotions and problems of these endings and experiencing a new dimension to them, gaining new understanding and a different view of oneself. Facing endings, loss and separation and being able to process, and making use of, the knowledge gained from these experiences is, in and of itself, a core developmental task; earlier experiences of ending and how these have been internalised are repeated in the ending of TAPP; when these have been problematic, the ending of TAPP has to engage with defended and disturbed patterns of relating to self and others. Worked with well, the ending is crucial for accelerating and consolidating internal change and growth and for freeing the developmental process from the stuck, disturbed and unhealthy aspects that brought the adolescent patient to therapy.

The ending process of TAPP is therefore multi-faceted; it is primarily a process, involving both partners, the young person and the therapist, in exploring and managing the emotional experience of separating from each other alongside evaluating and reviewing the therapy and looking forward to the future. The process needs to be considered through discussion of its key components: the therapist's positioning or stance; understanding how the relationship develops in this phase; working with the developmental focus; and initiating a process of evaluation and review. These processes will be discussed alongside case examples that illustrate differences between individual young people.

The therapeutic stance in the ending phase

As throughout the treatment phase, when working with the ending the aim is to maintain a therapeutic stance that facilitates containment of anxieties, making emotional contact with the young person's conscious and unconscious communications and exploring his internal and social worlds relating to the developmental focus. In the ending period of TAPP, the therapist poses to herself the key question of how to optimise the young person's beneficial internalisation of the therapy process. Both participants, the young person and the therapist, are likely to experience anxieties; the therapist will have anxieties about the impact of ending therapy on the young person. Will he be able to manage? Or will there be a return to previous ways of relating? Will symptoms and risks persist, or worsen? In other words, will the gains from therapy be maintained and internalised or not, and will the young person's development continue to benefit from therapy after it ends? Young people's anxieties and defences feed into these concerns; meanings can be difficult to disentangle and understand.

The therapist uses the structure of TAPP as a framework for holding the young person and the anxieties about ending. A key emphasis when working with the ending is therefore protection of the setting, including the time frame, alongside maintaining a reflective approach to thinking about the emotionality in the therapeutic relationship. This involves wherever possible introducing a shared sense of thinking together about current emotionality and about future hopes and fears as the end of therapy draws nearer, and a reflective looking back on the journey travelled together in the therapy. The therapist will recognise the intensity of the process of ending for the young person, and that he will be likely to defend against the pains of loss and separation, including devaluing the therapy and therapist. The therapist will aim to recognise and appropriately talk about gains the young person has made in the therapy, and ways in which the developmental process has been strengthened or restored, referring back to where the young person started therapy and noting differences between then and now. It is important also to reflect on what has been difficult, and maybe remains stuck or problematic, and ways in which the young person has tried to work with these difficulties. The therapist will continue to work in a field characterised by ambiguities, where defence and development may be close together in the clinical material. For young people, the ending of therapy puts into action, in real time, the anticipation and preparation of the future: the future orientation of the adolescent process. Ending can be shocking and uncomfortably real – and really happening. One young person, speaking to these feelings in the final session added, poignantly, "It is just dawning on me just now!" This expressed simultaneously the ambiguity of, somehow, having avoided knowing about the ending and the immediacy and reality of the awareness; it *is* happening now, just now.

The ending phase requires binocular vision to focus on the process of evaluation and review, on the one hand, the emotionality in the therapeutic relationship, on the other hand, and the links between these. Perceptions of gains and changes, and also limitations and areas that appear not to be changing, will be thought about in relation to the specific focus for the therapy and its aim of freeing and supporting the developmental process. The therapist will have the developmental focus in mind throughout the therapy; reviewing how the issues were presented in assessment, how the focus was formulated and what has changed since will provide helpful information for the therapist to position herself when working with the ending.

This perspective is also important when facing the intensities of the emotional experiences of the ending. The therapist will need to observe, hear and think about the young person's communications about his own sense of change and growth or, alternatively, the anxieties and perceptions of not changing. This can be illustrated by referring briefly to the case example of Joshua, which was discussed in Chapter 8. The therapist worked with the feeling of repetition and Joshua's feeling stuck, including his dream and his anxieties and grievances that he was not changing or gaining the resources he felt he needed to make his transition to leaving home. Joshua's assertiveness – changing the subject – was a moment of change and newness within the therapeutic relationship whilst working with the meaning of the ending of the therapy. On the other hand, therapists may introduce the idea of thinking about development and need for support beyond the duration of TAPP as a contrast to, and a way of addressing, wishes for perfect, or magical, solutions.

The therapist aims to hold onto a perspective of realistically evaluating, identifying, noticing and emphasising areas of change and growth, whilst also keeping in view the realities first that development continues after TAPP and that there is an unknown, future dimension when ending. Second, some young people may need further therapeutic support after TAPP. Continuing risks need to be assessed, including those that are heightened by the end of therapy, which is recognised as a vulnerable moment (NICE 2011). The inclusion of young people with complex needs and risks as suitable for TAPP (see Chapter 7) has the implication that there will be different experiences of ending; some young people may continue to need support and care, as seen in Chapter 9 where the case examples illustrating working with the developmental focus contain dialogue about what may be resolved in the course of the TAPP and what may need further therapeutic input. As discussed in Chapter 6, when assessing continuing risks, it is important to relate these to the therapeutic process.

Working with the developmental focus during the ending

In the ending of TAPP the themes of the developmental focus intensify in the transference and counter-transference relationship; the meaning of individual experiences of loss, separations, a sense of growth and of becoming more adult are located centrally in the therapeutic relationship that is now ending, and which has been an important relationship in the lived experiences of the young people over the previous six months or so, for the duration of the TAPP. Therefore, it is important that the therapist thinks in the transference when working with the young person during the ending to understand his experiences of separating, how he experiences the loss of the therapeutic relationship and how this links other losses in his present and past relationships.

Thinking in the transference facilitates noticing the young person's communications about the therapy, however obliquely or opaquely these appear in the clinical material. In their stories and images, young people sometimes make vivid expressions of their feelings and states of mind; these might be thought about as dream imagery (Ferro 2015). For example, a fruitful exploration of one young person's feelings about her therapy, and her sense of disappointments in her life, was initiated by an apparently un-self-conscious description of a disappointing meal:

> Ali (17) spoke about not expecting too much from anything or anyone. She said she had been out for a meal and had been tempted by a pizza that, from its description on the menu, sounded really enticing. She expected a wonderful experience but instead, when it arrived, she was intensely disappointed finding she did not in fact like the toppings and the base was hard and inedible. The therapist wondered aloud if the pizza might be referring to Ali's therapy; and was it the therapy that was disappointing, or the thought of ending that soured the taste?

In most TAPP cases the developmental focus includes the process of becoming more separate from parental figures, engaging with more adult ways of relating and relinquishing childhood relationships. It is because of difficulties experienced in these processes, and the symptoms or problem behaviours that relate to these disturbances of the developmental process, that the young person has come into therapy. These issues are replicated in the ending process, intensifying it and highlighting ambivalence about development and the defences against it. Quite naturally a part of the young person will want to continue the therapeutic relationship and not to lose it; defences against separation and loss are brought into the therapeutic relationship. Pressure is thus brought on the therapist not to end the therapy.

Maintaining the time frame and the agreed-upon contract is a priority; this is not for reasons of technical rigidity, but to provide the young person with a reliable and robust experience. From the negative perspective, to not maintain the boundary of the time limit as it comes nearer risks the loss of credibility. The meaning of the pressure to change the frame is never straightforward or simple, and maintaining the boundaries, whilst offering to think about the young person's needs, offers the best way to make the most of the therapeutic opportunities for thinking and understanding. The time limit comes to stand for the irreversibility of time and development and the non-negotiability of facing loss. Inevitably, pressure to extend the sessions is inextricably interlinked with the young person's internal world, and how they relate in particular to separation and loss; these aspects of the young person's internal world and the developmental process are experienced and replicated in the transference–counter-transference relationship. Understanding the young person in the ending phase takes into account their phantasies about the reasons for ending (Lemma et al 2011). Though the time-frame may be clear, explicit and shared, this does not prevent the patient from holding an unconscious meaning about the therapist's reasons for ending; these usually involve ideas about other patients being more lovable, interesting and less trouble. Identifying where possible the specific meaning of these phantasies in each case is important in the ending process and links to the patient's internal difficulties, and hence to the disturbance of the developmental process.

Strupp and Binder (1984, p. 261) discuss how the patient, valuing the relationship with the therapist and wishing not to lose it, attempts to hold onto it by various methods; they identify four ways in which the patient defends against the anxieties, pains and difficulties of the process of separation in the ending phase, and aims to avert it. These accurately describe experiences of working with the ending in TAPP; they are:

- Bringing new problems that need to be addressed before the therapy can end
- Recurrence of the symptoms that brought the patient to therapy
- Clinging to the therapist and expressing hostility and blame towards her
- Actively trying to show mastery of the problems by leaving therapy early, before the termination date

Recognising these patterns as defences against separating and ending can help to contain the anxieties involved. The therapist may be able to say that she wonders if the feelings are linked to the ending or to anxieties about separating, and also about what will feel available internally after the ending.

Case example: Jenny

An example comes from Jenny, 14 years old, whose TAPP assessment phase was discussed in Chapter 7. Jenny began the assessment depressed; she said she felt bad. The developmental focus was to help her to bear the pains, disappointments and bitterness of her current predicament, whilst she was beginning her adolescence with the changes this was bringing to her relationships with others, including her peers. As her therapy proceeded, Jenny was less depressed, and she was embracing the changes of puberty and her emerging sexuality. In the 15th session, Jenny started to talk about feeling sad and down again. She talked about not sleeping well and not wanting to eat and feeling bad about herself. The therapist, recognising that the phrases Jenny was using were similar to those she had used at the beginning of the therapy, asked if Jenny might feel that this had to do with coming to the end of the therapy. Jenny thought for a moment and said "probably." She said it was frustrating, then she talked about how she had accidentally not saved something she had written on her computer; the therapist asked if it was like here, a worry about not saving the work she had done in therapy. Jenny said she will miss her therapy, as it is "different here," and, extending the computer imagery, she said she just wanted to press pause. This led into discussion of Jenny's experiences in her life of endings and separations as seeming to be sudden and as happening to her.

Quinodoz (1991), too, refers to the return of symptoms for the ending of psychotherapy. Aretha (see Chapters 7 and 9) also evoked a sense of returning to how she had been at the beginning of her therapy as the ending approached. In this example, accessing the meaning of the ending of TAPP was through linking the ending of therapy with Aretha's accounts of experiences in other aspects of her life; her phantasies about the reasons for ending seemed to be located in these relationships.

Case example: Aretha

In the 15th session, Aretha was depressed and tearful. The therapist wondered if her feelings were connected to the ending of her therapy. Aretha said she was anxious about leaving therapy, but direct discussion of this was less fruitful than linking material she brought about other situations to her therapy. Aretha talked about separating through her experiences of leaving work. She had expected work colleagues to be punitive towards her, and angry with her for leaving them. In fact, her work colleagues said to her that she had been a good colleague who was always willing to work for the team; they expressed gratitude for her work and wished her well for the future; this esteem came as quite a surprise to Aretha. The therapist noted the accuracy of the parallel between work and therapy, and that Aretha had been insistent on having a time-limited therapy that would end in time for her to start university. She said she wondered what Aretha thought that she, the therapist, would think about her leaving therapy, and, mirroring the comments of the work colleagues, said that in therapy she too had been very committed to this work and that the therapist was grateful that Aretha had shared so much about herself. Aretha said that this was a surprise too, and the therapist gave her first and only saturated transference interpretation, that Aretha expected and feared that the therapist, like her parents, would be angry with her for growing up and leaving them, just as she was furious that they had separated from each other and left her. The ending gave Aretha a very different experience from the expectation of hostility and attack with which she started her therapy.

In contrast to those young people who appear to regress when contending with the turbulence of the process of separating and ending, and repeat how they began the therapy, others show some new or different characteristics or states of mind. This can include a greater openness in expressing anger, hostility and defiance. On the other hand, there may be a sense of being more reflective, more alongside the therapist, or of introducing a moving, depressive capacity for guilt and remorse about destructiveness. In Chapter 9, the example of Yasmin shows her being more thoughtful, separate, observant of her parents and able to tolerate the pain of her parents' fragility, and that they had not been available for her in a way she would have liked and needed. Peter, whose therapy was also described in Chapter 9, moved in his ending from open defiance and hostility to regret for the ways he had attacked the therapy, a complicated process of saying goodbye, which included naming a phantasy about the ending.

Case example: Peter

Peter was late for his 14th session and was silent throughout the session, keeping his headphones in place; he did not respond to any of the therapist's attempts to engage him, except for a few one-word responses, like "maybe." In the following session, it was possible to think about this as being connected to the ending of the therapy, and Peter trying to take some control, of leaving rather than being left. He was 30 minutes late for this, the 15th, session. He sat quietly but apparently thoughtfully for a time, then said that he would like to apologise for last week. The therapist said that perhaps he felt angry towards her for making him feel vulnerable and exposed, and also for saying that therapy has to come to an end. He said he possibly did feel angry towards her. He said that he still felt ashamed about his behaviour, which he thought was childish, and wasteful of the therapist's valuable time.

In the 16th and final session, Peter arrived on time, in a cooperative state of mind and more able to face and talk about the ending; initially, this had a resigned feeling. He said that therapy had certainly been helpful, but even if he had it for years, there would come a point where he had to do it on his own. The therapist wondered whether the ending may feel hard because it reminded him that they are two separate people with separate minds. He nodded enthusiastically and said that he wanted to be able to take away how the therapist talked in this room. He would have a new part of himself that could watch over the other part of himself that got him into difficulties. The therapist commented that he was being reflective about what he would take away from his therapy.

The therapist added that they both seemed to be talking about therapy as a thing external to both of them and that the ending was also about them separating and then saying goodbye after the review; maybe this part of it felt the hardest to think about. After a struggle, Peter said that he didn't want to offend her, but he went through a phase of thinking about her as a person, but then realised that he started to care too much about what she thought about him. The therapist said that there was a time in Peter's therapy when he perhaps felt she was getting close to him, and that this made him feel quite anxious. She wondered whether this anxiety was partly about him actually telling her things she didn't want to hear, which meant that when she got to know the real Peter, she would not like him. He nodded and said that there are parts of him that he didn't like himself, and it would have been hard to let someone he cares about see those parts.

Peter's defence against closeness in relationships is apparent in this sequence; he connects anxiety about closeness with the fear or phantasy of not being liked or likeable, and in this final session it has become possible to talk about this.

Expressions of anger, hostility or defiance usually need to be present at some part of the ending process in order to work with the young person's experience of loss during the ending; these feelings are of course integral to experiencing loss. With some young people in TAPP, the ending process can be dominated by these feelings. This results in a stormy ending, with the therapist feeling bombarded by the young person's hate and fury at being left, experienced as abandonment.

This can present a real dilemma for the therapist especially when the young person is railing against the therapy stopping; as discussed earlier, the therapist can be under pressure not to keep to the boundary of the time limit whilst trying to find ways of containing the feelings and treading between rigidity and collusion. Intensification of depressed feelings stir up anxiety and concern, and the therapist has to work hard with these feelings in the counter-transference to find a realistic and appropriate way of ending TAPP, taking account of risks and exploring needs for further therapy. In some cases where the therapist's assessment coincides with the young person's demand, and where the pains of separating seem so difficult to bear, the therapist can soften the ending by emphasising the process of review and thinking together about what is next. This never gets around the problem or pacifies the angry young person, and the work of facing and containing the feelings involved stays at the heart of the process. It does, however, make use of the TAPP structure and provides a framework for thinking and an orientation towards future needs. Working with these cases is extremely testing of the therapist's own resources; support from a reflective seminar or supervision is important, as the following example illustrates.

Case example: Pauline

Pauline, 22 years old, began her therapy during her last year at university; the developmental focus was articulated as helping her with feelings of being alone, lonely and at times desperate, to understand why she has these feelings at this important and transitional point in her life. TAPP was planned to end at Easter before her final exams, with a post-treatment review to follow. In the 12th session, the therapist reminded Pauline of the number of sessions remaining; Pauline reacted as though the therapist had delivered a bombshell, adding, when the therapist asked, that she did know about the ending, but she had not counted the weeks. She said she wanted somewhere to go until she was ready to leave. This was difficult as the therapist could see, having worked with her to this point, that it could be an important issue for Pauline as, in other separations and ending she had spoken about, others had left her.

The therapist said Pauline is suddenly aware of how short her therapy time is now, and that she really does, as she puts it, feel dropped. She agreed and said she is worried about losing her structure; she has no home and university is ending. She can't sleep and lies awake thinking of all this. There was a pause and Pauline's next comments helped the therapist out of her predicament temporarily. Pauline talked about someone she thought of as a good friend who had one evening recently talked about being in love with her. Pauline said she did not want this, as she would lose her friendship with him. The therapist responded, in the transference, by saying how things can get very mixed up when people change the boundaries; though Pauline was saying how much she did not want to end her therapy, there would be a real problem if the boundaries of the therapy changed. Pauline then spoke about her uncertainties about the future, not knowing what to do after university, and the therapist said she and Pauline had been thinking about this together, and it was uncomfortable, and different from how things had been a few weeks ago. Pauline said, yes, she knew, not thinking. The therapist discussed, in a reflective seminar discussion after this session, how best to work with Pauline; maintaining the boundaries of the setting seemed crucial alongside attempting to contain Pauline's anxieties, pain and rage, and looking for opportunities to think with her about her future needs and wishes, including for therapy; would it be possible to hold on to some hope in this process?

In the following 13th session, Pauline talked about her difficulties separating from her parents and the therapist drew attention to the parallel between that and the angry feelings she had about ending therapy. Pauline said in a clear and steady tone that she did not want to end therapy. The therapist said she recognised she really meant this, and it was her wish, but it left them with a conflict. Pauline said that she felt her parents didn't care about her; she would probably have to lose a leg or something for them to care; she looked at the therapist and said, in a challenging tone, "What do you think of that?" The therapist said that Pauline was thinking that she, the therapist, would not care anymore; she would get to the end of the therapy and then be thrown out into the cold. Pauline said she would be OK for a couple of weeks and then go back to how she was, meaning not thinking and acting in self-destructive ways. Pauline checked herself and said she didn't mean it as blackmail, but maybe she did. The therapist said maybe she did, but she was really troubled by her feeling of needing her therapy and feeling dropped by her therapist, and that she felt she needed more. The therapist said she proposed that they both stick to the agreement to end the therapy at Easter, when there would, in any case, be a break, and then they would meet to review, where they could together discuss her need for support in the short term, for her final exams, and in the longer-term, her wish for more therapy. Pauline accepted this and appeared to relax.

However, Pauline continued to rage at her therapist; in the following session, she said she had not changed or improved and, moreover, now had new problems: she was not sleeping, and she had nowhere to go after she finished university; she needed support now while she was doing her exams; it was so stressful, and she wanted therapy. Her onslaught was interspersed with moments when Pauline said she knew she was being awful and not reasonable. The therapist said Pauline was complaining about her, about leaving her on her own and not overcoming the obstacles to her continuing the therapy.

In the 16th and last session, Pauline said she was worried the therapist would be angry with her for being so difficult. She talked about being exasperated with her mother, and about her father not caring. The therapist said Pauline was angry with her and thought she in response would be angry with Pauline; she also thought she, the therapist, didn't care; she was leaving Pauline on her own. Pauline looked directly at the therapist and said she had talked for weeks about the ending and hadn't said whether she would see her again. The therapist reminded her she had offered to meet again for a review to think about her future needs, adding that Pauline seemed to have forgotten this and wished to locate in the therapist all her difficulties about leaving and separating. Pauline said she realised it was about this, but she didn't want to have to think, and she didn't want to be left with something difficult to think about after the last session. The therapist said that it seemed unbearable, but however uncomfortable, thinking about her feelings was a real achievement of her work in therapy; Pauline said she did know this.

Although the therapist believed that withstanding Pauline's onslaught was important during the ending, she was left concerned and feeling that there had not been enough time, that the ending had stirred up so much pain and rage for Pauline and that it could have a destructive impact on the gains she had made during the therapy. On the other hand, the ending had provided an opportunity for Pauline to work with her rage and distress, for the meaning of this to be explored and for Pauline to have an experience of the therapist neither retaliating or colluding. One way of thinking about the dynamic in this ending is to refer to Winnicott's (1971) idea of the use of an object. Here Pauline is using the therapist as an object who can withstand and survive her attacks, whilst also showing her the value of the therapist and the therapy.

In contrast, in endings where the uppermost feeling is sadness, the final sessions can be painful but moving. Mann (1973) thought that sadness is the optimum feeling at the end of time-limited therapy, reflecting the realities of the loss of the therapeutic relationship. Reflecting and evoking earlier losses, and the loss in adolescence of childhood relatedness, can give the ending a powerful poignancy. The ending allows mourning to take place for these earlier lost relationships. This quality of emotionality in the ending is illustrated by the following case example; here, the sadness of the ending is directly faced and felt as the young person, David, experiences the pain of separating, alongside an appreciation of the changes he feels he has made in his therapy. David was able to express his gratitude and to appear generous in valuing her therapist.

Case example: David

In the first part of his last session, David, now 17 years old, spoke about how he valued his therapy and felt he had changed in being able to face rather than avoid his feelings; he said he felt more in control and less likely to be impulsive, and he hoped it would last. The therapist spoke about the process of therapy feeling helpful for David, and that he may, in the future, feel he may wish to have more therapy as part of his developmental process, to help with times when he can feel things are too difficult or painful. David agreed, but then became tearful; he said it is the end here, it feels the same as a relationship breaking up, like with his girlfriend. Through tears, he said he knows in the past he would have looked for something to put in its place, and not to let himself know he felt sad. But, he added, he did feel sad and had been thinking over the week about feeling left out when he was little. He used to try to rewind the clock, to go back. At the end of the session, there was a tangible feeling of sadness in the room and a warm goodbye. The therapist was moved by David's capacity to feel and to think.

David's recollections of feeling left out referred back to work in his therapy, to what the therapist had identified as the situation that comprised his core pain; working with being now "left out" of his therapy seemed to enable him to face this in a different way, with sadness and gratitude. The therapist was moved by this whilst also continuing to think that David's integration of the changes remained to an extent fragile.

There is a great deal to disentangle in the ending: the attachment to the thera-pist, the feelings aroused by separating and the feelings, defences and patterns of relating, or object relatedness, that the young person had brought from previous experiences. The ending stirs up, similarly, feelings the therapist has about end-ing and her past experiences. The young person is ending a specific relationship with the therapist, and, additionally, leaving a particular way of relating to another person, the therapeutic process. In the ending of TAPP, the therapist emphasises the importance of the therapeutic process, involving the experience of attention at a deep level, thinking about emotionality and relatedness, and articulating, com-municating and discussing experiences to understand meaning. The therapist will aim to discuss how the young person has found the process, in what ways it has been helpful or difficult. The process is identified as something that exists outside the specifics of the therapeutic relationship and that can be returned to, at a later date, and as the agent of change and growth; engaging in the process is the key to development and to the acquisition and enhancing of the capacities to reflect and become the subject of one's internal experiences. The young person's interest in the therapeutic process also means having an interest in his own internal processes and working with the emotionality of development. Referencing the value of the therapeutic process aims to transcend the specifics of time and place; it is some-thing the young person can take away with them, not split off from the person of the therapist, but as an activity that she has provided and of which both young person and therapist have partaken.

The ending also involves differentiating the therapist and the transference; this complicated process is managed in TAPP within the constraints of time; it is complicated by the intergenerational nature of adolescent therapy and the phan-tasies of adolescence. Defences against Oedipal feelings, especially in younger adolescents, make the therapeutic relationship a potentially fragile or tendentious arena; the 'R' word – relationship – can trigger a sexual meaning and immediate defensiveness with some young people. Seeing the therapist as a 'real' person can similarly be fraught with potential hazards, including stirring up erotic feelings. Adolescent patients can try to maintain a view of the therapist as simply someone sitting in the consulting room, rather than as someone with a life; being put in touch with the therapist's life outside the therapy room can feel catastrophic. In TAPP limited time means these dimensions of the therapeutic relationship often remain held in mind and not fully explored. However, at the end, when it comes to the fact of saying goodbye, the therapist becomes for a moment a person in a moment of time, and this can provide the final challenge in the process.

Further therapy?

In thinking about further therapy, the therapist has to differentiate her wishes for the young person to have access to and benefit from the therapeutic process from anxieties that can lead to underestimating the young person's capacities to continue his development after TAPP. There are different approaches in the brief therapy literature: Mann (1973) discouraged further therapy for at least a year after the end of time-limited therapy; he argued that the full effects of working with separation would be circumvented by returning to therapy earlier; Strupp and Binder (1984) were more flexible. In general, in brief therapy, more inclusive criteria for suitability lead to the need for more flexible approaches to the provision of further therapy. As TAPP applies inclusive suitability criteria, as discussed in Chapter 7, it is expected that young people will have a wide range of needs regarding further therapy. In TAPP the view is that time-limited and longer-term therapy are complementary and have different aims; it is possible in some circumstances that a young person may go on to long-term therapy after completing TAPP, and that this may constitute a good outcome. One strand of thought influencing this is that the experience of TAPP can increase the young person's interest in themselves and their internal world; the reflective processes of therapy develop a sense of their own subjectivity and a sense of being the subject of their emotional life, including unconscious aspects. Through therapy they may feel more engaged with their continuous project of development and awareness of their emotionality; they may seek further therapy for these reasons, or feel the need to continue to work with a therapist. Some young people come hesitantly and anxiously into therapy and are helped to engage by experiencing the time-limited nature of TAPP through the emphasis placed on engagement; they experience TAPP as overcoming fears of engagement in therapy and of learning from experience what a therapeutic relationship is like. This group of young people can evoke the thought that they have come to therapy late, prevented by barriers – internal or external – from accessing therapeutic help earlier. In more complex cases, it is important to carefully review future therapeutic needs at the end of therapy. Different outcomes for TAPP are discussed further in the next chapter.

Options for future therapy are often limited by constraints in services; as with access to many kinds of resources in current social contexts, young people may be dependent on parental support and this can be problematic for older adolescents and young adults who are in the process of becoming more independent of parental figures. The idea of following TAPP with longer-term psychotherapy, for those for whom it is indicated, presupposes its availability. This is clearly not the case in many settings and services where the duration of TAPP is a significant offering when mental health services are risk-assessment-led and operate threshold criteria for access. For those young people who have complex mental health problems and psychosocial vulnerabilities, it is expected that further therapeutic input will follow TAPP, especially where consideration of risks remains an important factor. The therapist who has undertaken TAPP with these complex cases is likely to be involved in mobilising further interventions, including in other services; for older adolescents, transfer to adult services can be an important consideration, involving the therapist and young person in referral and negotiation.

Stadter (2009) has the view that further therapy can be negotiated with the patient after completion of time-limited therapy. He introduced the notion of serial brief therapy and provides examples of some patients having repeated time-limited therapies, with gaps in between, over a period of several years. It is possible that, after careful review with the young person, a further period of time-limited work can be offered after TAPP; where resources are limited, this may be the only available option. There are some reasons for being cautious with this approach because, partly, there is an inherent contradiction in working with an ending and then not ending; partly, it is difficult to disentangle the more rational process of evaluating the need for further therapy from the unconscious motives, or phantasies, that the young person has about the time limit and the reason for ending, including phantasies of not being loved or interesting enough or of being too difficult. Another variation to consider is the example of whether the TAPP therapist can subsequently undertake long-term work with the young person; this option usually arises in settings where there is no other available resource, for example a psychotherapist working alone as a school counsellor. There are to date some examples of this being successful, though the process also requires paying careful attention to the unconscious meaning of ending and then re-engaging. In all cases, further therapy requires a robust process of review with the young person, including transferential aspects of the therapeutic relationship; the post-treatment review which is integral to the TAPP structure plays an important role in undertaking these assessments. Finally, and simply, some young people end TAPP feeling that they do not need further therapeutic help and that it has been sufficient for their needs; for these young people, having an awareness of the helpfulness of the process facilitates approaching a therapist in the future.

Post-treatment review

Several models of brief therapy include the concept of the post-treatment review; it was integral to Malan's (1976) approach, for example, and he also offered multiple reviews with some patients. Holding a review meeting six to eight weeks after the end of the therapy is integral to TAPP; the importance and scope of the review have increased as TAPP has been more widely practised in different settings. In current practice, the review has three main purposes: it allows for a trial separation at the end of therapy; it can be identified as a time and place where some issues can be further discussed, notably discussions of future therapy; and it is a space where therapist and patient can look back on the therapy from a vantage point of being now out of the weekly process, but whilst the therapy is still fresh in both minds. The review is thus part of a holding structure, allowing a sense of going on being, one that can be helpful for containing anxieties, and where practical decisions can be made.

During the ending phase of the therapy, the review date is set and flagged up as an opportunity to further think about some issues, an opportunity to look back at the therapy and a time to think about further therapeutic plans. The review therefore holds these aspects and allows time and energy to be focused on attending to the feelings generated by the ending and working to optimise change. Both the young person and the therapist may have anxious expectations of the review; therapists have anxieties about whether the patient will have maintained gains from the therapy, or whether the absence of the therapy has led to the emergence of further difficulties. Therapists may be anxious that the review will restart the therapeutic process without an ongoing structure to support it. Young people may be anxious about whether the review will disturb their equilibrium, open things up again, or whether future wishes for therapy will be met. Though Malan (1976) thought that the patient's unconscious accepted the therapy had ended in the last true therapy session, transference and counter-transference are still active in the review and the unconscious phantasies about why the therapy has ended may be rekindled.

The review can therefore present complexities to the therapist about how to manage it, to achieve a position which is close enough to the clinical material of the therapy to be able to draw on it, and distant enough to be able to observe and think reflectively. The therapist will need to structure the review to some extent, to enable the process, involving some distancing from the therapeutic process to take place. The content of the review will vary according to the individual's needs but should include a space for reflecting on the therapy, on the young person's current situation and on any future planning that needs to take place. The therapist will have in mind wanting to assess how the young person has found the gap between the end of the therapy and the review, what the experience of stopping regular sessions has been like and whether this shows the young person's capacity to hold on to the therapeutic gains, especially with regard to thinking about and sustaining feelings.

Although the review takes place a relatively short period of time after the therapy ending, the evidence that psychodynamic psychotherapies show benefits at follow-up can be held in mind (Fonagy 2015); this alerts the therapist to notice if new developments appear to be taking place. For example, it was at her review that Sasha (in Chapter 9) said she no longer had compulsive checking symptoms; she had sustained the gains from her therapy and she clearly related to herself as more separate from her mother, irritated by her mother's anxiety but not deterred by it from continuing her development, and at the same time not provoking or devaluing her mother. After being immersed in the intensities of relating in the ending sessions of TAPP, therapists can be surprised by how the young person's development presents in the review meeting. Pauline's greater equanimity, and her more reflective state of mind, provide an example.

Case example: Pauline

Pauline's ending has been discussed above; her therapist was pleasantly surprised by her state of mind in the review meeting. Pauline explained that she had not known what to do over the Easter holiday period after her therapy ended. She was determined not to simply go to her parents' homes feeling awful and furious with them.

She stayed on at university, worked in preparation for her exams and then went on holiday with friends. The therapist commented on how different she seemed; Pauline said she thought she had been very difficult in her therapy and was sorry about that and grateful that the therapist had put up with her. The therapist invited Pauline to review what she thought had occurred in her therapy, especially during the last few weeks; Pauline said this is what she had been thinking about, that she did feel very anxious, furious with her therapist and with her parents, but also that this had to do with having to think for herself, and she wanted to rely on someone else. She felt better in herself when she found she was able to make decisions. The therapist asked, humorously, if thinking was not so bad after all; Pauline, smiling, said she hates thinking, ironically recalling the phrase she had used so often during the therapy. When asked what her thoughts are now about further therapy, Pauline said she had no doubt she would want and probably need therapy in the future, but for now she was okay, as long as she could contact the therapist if she needed to.

Most reviews contain a mixed picture: positives, negatives and ambivalence co-exist in the accounts young people bring to this meeting. Young people feel they have a lot to tell the therapist about what has happened during the gap, and this can exert a strong pull in the session, with the feeling that all the time could be taken up by the young person bringing the therapist up to date. There are usually ups and downs and many kinds of events and goings-on in young people's lives so that there is no shortage of material; some structuring of the meeting is often necessary. There may also be a defensive wish on the part of the young person to not be left with difficult feelings after the meeting, and a tension between saying and not saying what is on their mind, which may feel difficult to talk about. The therapist can ask herself what and how much is possible in the meeting, what might it be possible to talk about. In the case example of Eve, discussed earlier in this chapter, the review was taken up with discussion of some current, complicated and engrossing peer activities; the therapist asked Eve as the end of the meeting approached if there was anything else she wished to say and Eve's reply, after some thought, was that she was proud that she was able to complete her therapy, despite finding it difficult and painful. The following example is a review meeting where the young person uses the meeting to talk about her current dilemmas and concerns, and the therapist attends to her whilst retaining in her mind the aim of reviewing.

Case example: Mia

Mia, 18 years old, was pleased to see her therapist at the review meeting, saying she had missed her regular therapy sessions. Mia began talking about several current preoccupations: her work and studying plans, and her relationships with her boyfriend and her family. She related as though in a therapy session, rather than a review, and the therapist felt herself, too, in the role of a therapist in an ongoing session. She listened as Mia continued, in a way that was richly evocative, and she noticed the emotionality involved. Mia said she was quite anxious; the therapist felt some concerns and thought it would be helpful to talk about further therapy. She said that as they had previously discussed, Mia does find the therapeutic process helpful and wondered if she had thought more about the ideas they had discussed about further therapy. Mia responded thoughtfully, saying that she felt she was in between feeling more mature, calmer and able to think, and at other times very anxious. Overall, she felt much better than when she started therapy. Mia said she would like to see how things go, for a time anyway, but she felt she would probably like to have more therapy in the future; the therapist confirmed Mia's request that she could contact her in the future.

Reviews, usually with younger adolescents, can and do include parents. It is usually vital to ensure that the review meeting is with the young person alone and, ideally, parental involvement is undertaken by a colleague to keep the two processes separate. Often, this is not possible, and meeting with parents separately has the aim of thinking with them about the impact of therapy on the young person, about their future needs and about parenting issues. Sometimes parents begin parent work after the young person has finished TAPP.

Summary

This discussion emphasises how crucial the ending process is in TAPP; the experiences are intense for both patient and therapist and provide opportunities for growth and understanding. The ending phase connects with, deepens and recapitulates themes and issues that run throughout the therapy; ending links closely and inextricably with the processes of separation in the adolescent process, and therefore with the developmental focus. In most cases, the focus is replicated in the dynamics of the therapeutic relationship, and the aim is to identify and work with this. Case examples have illustrated the different kinds of ending experienced in TAPP, and especially the range of emotionality involved, from sadness to rage. The therapist attends closely to the emotional experiences, to stay with painful feelings and to work with the developmental focus. The ending involves a process of review and discussion of future needs including for further therapy. The post-treatment review is an essential part of the TAPP structure to facilitate these discussions and to support the young person's internalisation of change and growth.

Chapter 11

Change, growth and outcomes

Introduction

In reflecting on change, growth and outcomes, this concluding chapter focuses on three distinct but interrelated questions. First, there is the question of how to characterise the qualities of change and growth that young people experience through TAPP. This is the primary focus for the chapter, involving several sub-questions including: which young people benefit from TAPP and in which ways? What changes can be expected within a time-limited framework of 16 sessions of treatment? Second, it is important to consider how therapists can provide TAPP in ways that optimise growth and change. This involves the development and adaptation of therapeutic skills for working in a brief, time-limited approach with young people and for the specific requirements of TAPP. Third, there is a question of how researchers can use this book as a protocol for evaluating the effectiveness of TAPP within the requirements for evidence-based practice. The chapter ends with a discussion of current knowledge about TAPP outcomes and the potential value of the book as a protocol for researchers undertaking evaluations of effectiveness.

The scope and limits of time-limited therapy

Growth and change for young people need to be considered within the framework of TAPP, as a time-limited therapy, and within its specific aims of providing a focussed therapeutic intervention to ameliorate the aspects of the developmental process that act against and/or restrict growth and development, and to support aspects of the developmental process that promote growth and development. This overarching aim of TAPP, described in Chapter 5, is applied to meet the specific needs of young people of different ages presenting difficulties. The developmentally led approach to TAPP is thought to make it suitable for a wide range of young people rather than a specific mental health condition, and the preceding chapters have discussed the application of TAPP when working with commonly encountered adolescent difficulties. These include: self-harm, suicidal thoughts and behaviours; depression and anxieties; obsessional and compulsive behaviours; risks of violence towards others; distress in and about relationships with parents, family members, and peers; anxieties about sexuality and gender and love relationships; and difficulties and anxieties relating to the social tasks of adolescence, including taking exams, leaving school and leaving home. Case examples have illustrated working with these issues; inevitably the examples do not comprehensively survey or give equal weight to all adolescent difficulties. The aim has been to illustrate the interplay between the difficulties young people experience, the adolescent developmental process, young people's internal worlds and the therapeutic relationship when working with TAPP. These examples focus on the core process in TAPP, that the young person's difficulties relate to disturbances of the adolescent developmental process and these become located, made visible and worked with in the interactions between the young person and the therapist in the therapeutic relationship. As a time-limited psychotherapy, TAPP works with parameters of time, termination, focus and suitability. TAPP does not aim to solve all problems and difficulties within the time limit; the aims of TAPP are limited to be commensurate with the limited time available. Through focussed intervention, the aim is to create the conditions whereby the young person's development, freed from the constraints of disturbance, will continue after the therapy.

As discussed throughout this book, TAPP is a focussed intervention; the developmental focus in each case is applied by providing attention to a specified area of difficulty. This leads to detailed work on a circumscribed area of the young person's life, located within a short passage of time in the young person's present life; the young person is engaged in thinking about his current preoccupations, anxieties, fears, aspirations, hopes and goals. These include, for example, details of distress or conflict in a relationship – with parents, peers, love relationships – feelings about the self, including depressed and anxious ones, and anxieties about the immediate future, including impending events like exams, leaving school, leaving home. The focus on development in TAPP links these specific details of the young person's life to larger themes that underpin emerging subjectivity in adolescence. These themes include questions of becoming more separate from parental figures; relating to others and having the capacity for intimacy from the perspective of gaining a more adult, embodied subjectivity, with its implications for sexuality; the expression of desires and recognising the limits of having an individual, finite life; and living in time. Change is therefore expected and experienced as the resolution – or part resolution – of the issues surrounding the specific events, circumstances and feelings about these, including problem and symptom reduction, and as changes in the underpinning, internal processes of development. The external, social events and contexts are profoundly connected through the process of development to internal patterns of relatedness: how anxieties are experienced and defended against and the qualities of internal object relationships. Change and growth is a process; adolescent development is a process (Waddell 1998).

The literature on brief therapy emphasises the interrelated factors of aims, outcomes and the criteria used for assessment of suitability. When suitability criteria are more inclusive, the aims are correspondingly broader and the outcomes more varied. Relational approaches and more recent applications of brief therapy tend towards greater inclusivity; current contexts for brief therapy in services with high demand for time-limited methods also exert pressure towards greater inclusivity. Inclusivity leads to differentiating outcomes based on the needs and difficulties that patients bring to the therapy and an open approach to discussing further therapy during the ending phase (see Chapter 10). The approach in TAPP to suitability is inclusive for three reasons. First, the rationale of TAPP is that the focus on developmental change makes it suitable for many young people, rather than for one mental health condition. Second, TAPP aims to meet the needs of young people in current social contexts, in which, as has been discussed in Chapter 3, development through the adolescent period is extended, and transitions to adulthood are often piecemeal, partial and unstructured. The idea of a time-limited therapy offers a structure that makes sense to young people and aims to increase engagement. It provides the opportunity of completing a process; this is illustrated by the case example of Eve, whose last treatment was discussed in Chapter 10. Eve said in her post-treatment review that though she had found therapy difficult, she was pleased and proud she had completed it. There is concordance in Eve's comments with achievement culture, and thus a discourse that young people relate to; experiences of competence counteract fears of failure in the process of becoming a subject and add to esteem (Briggs 2008). The experience has been that young people do engage, attend and complete TAPP; this is further discussed later in the chapter.

The third factor for applying inclusive suitability criteria in TAPP lies in the contexts in which TAPP is delivered. In mental health services, TAPP meets the need for structured time-limited psychotherapy for complex cases in which young people present with both mental health difficulties and vulnerable social circumstances. Often these young people have found it difficult to seek therapeutic help, and present as ambivalent and defended (Briggs et al 2015). These young people are represented in the case examples in Chapter 9; the therapist has to contend with the sense of regret that therapy was not sought earlier, the pressure of limited time and the imbalance between this and the young person's deeper problems that require careful attention and containment. There is all the difference in the world between purposefully working with intensely felt feelings to optimise the time-limited therapy, including and perhaps especially in the ending phase, and forcing change and development into a timeframe. The latter evokes Winnicott's thought of the perils of intrusions into the maturational process. Therefore, from its origins in the Brief Therapy Workshop, and repeated in many places and services since, TAPP has understood that when young people become interested in and valuing of the therapeutic process this can be in itself a significant change, representing the young person moving away from fearing thinking about themselves, especially their emotional lives, and from defending against being open with themselves in relationships with others, and towards valuing these processes. Therefore, as discussed in Chapter 10, the young person's wish for further therapy is seen in some cases as a positive outcome and as evidence of a developmental gain.

Wide and inclusive suitability criteria mean that there are diverse aims and outcomes for individual cases. Not many cases seen for TAPP can be characterised as simple; to this, both the complexities of the adolescent developmental process and the nature of cases referred for TAPP in mental health services contribute. Therefore, outcomes in TAPP cases can include one or more of the following:

- Being able to feel and be more separate from others
- Having greater capacity to think about feelings and states of mind, and to sustain emotionality rather than discharging it through actions
- Being more fully emotionally engaged and 'alive'
- Having an embodied sense of moving towards holding adult sexuality
- Having improved relationships, with greater texture and depth and understanding of self and other
- Showing symptom reduction, including anxiety and depression
- Showing reduction in (self) destructive relatedness
- Having greater coherence to narratives of oneself
- Having greater capacities to manage developmental tasks in the social world
- Being more tolerant of one's own emotions and difficulties
- Greater interest in self-reflectiveness; increased curiosity about self and interest in the therapy process
- Greater focus on a developmental approach to difficulties
- Having a greater sense of being able to make decisions and express agency

Change and growth

A well thought-out developmental focus articulates and holds the key issues for each young person's development at a point in time, and these come alive in the clinical material in the therapeutic relationship. The experiences of change and growth for young people in TAPP can be discussed through reflecting on the case examples discussed in Chapters 7, 8 and 9; key processes to be discussed are becoming more separate from parental figures; bearing and thinking about feelings and states of mind, rather than discharging them through impulsive actions and destructiveness; engaging with realities; being and feeling more alive; and managing the pains of growth and development.

Becoming more separate from parental figures and being able to manage the pains and anxieties this entails often form an important part of the developmental focus; it is, of course, a crucial aspect of the adolescent developmental process. Sasha, for example, in Chapter 9, gives a clear example of a young person who at the end of her therapy was more able to manage being separate from her mother; she was more engaged in peer relationships in an appropriate way for her age, more engaged at school and finding it more satisfying. Her embodied sense of herself also demonstrated development into adolescence. Processes in her therapy linked to these outcomes; Sasha had been more able to express her anxieties and to recognise her aggression, gathering this up to propel her to make changes in her relationships with her parents, to hold her emotions as states of mind rather than states of body (Williams 1997). Therapeutic processes that facilitate managing the pains and anxieties about feeling separate are also evident in Aretha's case; becoming more aware of what happens internally aided tolerating separateness from others, and she became more able to think about feelings rather than evacuating them. Feeling more able to be separate involved changes in ways of relating to dependence and independence; emerging interdependence and having less fear of feeling dependent were experienced as less of a threat to the need to become more independent, more separate. Peter illustrated this; he was more open and involved in his therapy where he felt less persecuted by the thought of his therapist taking over his mind and thoughts, and more able to communicate his thoughts to her without expecting to be not understood. The expectation of feeling understood makes feeling dependent and feeling separate more tolerable, along with increasing awareness of difference (Britton 1998). In a different way, Luke felt the connection the therapist made with his mother was helpful in responding to risks that stemmed from his unsafe feelings and contributed to a sense of being held by both his parent and his therapist together. In another case, a teenage mother was torn in many directions at the start of therapy, for which an astigmatism was an apt metaphor: "Noticeably, by the end of the treatment, her squint had gone; both eyes were focused, giving an embodied indication that for Beth things had come into focus" (Briggs et al 2015, p. 326).

Becoming more separate involves, when anxieties have become more contained, a reduction in relating through projective identification and a greater capacity to bear and think about one's own feelings and to encounter and engage with realities. For example, Yasmin was able to observe and think about her parents, recognising with the therapist her sadness about her parents not having the qualities she would have liked them to have; this allowed her to see how being superior was a defence protecting her parents from her aggression, which was related to her pain of not feeling noticed. She became aware and appreciative of moments when her parents did notice and recognise her. In another of the case examples, Eric assessed, with realism, that he was not "ready" for a relationship with a girlfriend. Outcomes of these internal changes are seen in the young person's capacity to relate to others and to manage the developmental tasks before them; Peter was able to take his exams, and Pauline was able to face her exams with greater equanimity. Being able to tolerate feeling more separate was the precursor to being able to contemplate and face actual separations, leaving school or home and endings in peer and love relationships.

The emergence of subjectivity could be observed – or felt – to occur in moments in the therapeutic process, moments of being more open to newness, discovery, feeling real and feeling alive. Aretha discovered the capacity to sit and be alone in a coffee shop, supported internally by a connection in her mind to her therapy. Luke became livelier and developed a new appetite as he became more alive internally. His sense of being alive moved from the margins of life, his need to feel like the only person in the universe, to being able to be more in the mainstream, relating to peers, thinking about having a girlfriend, planning his future. Having a sense of being alive can grow through containment of the idea of death and suicide (Ladame 2011), and feeling the pleasure, rather than fear, of desire, and making one's own desires of whatever kind and object. Subjectivity also emerges in moments of taking responsibility for one's life. Joshua, in Chapter 8, for example, indicated taking responsibility for his future when demanding to know what the therapist had in mind, in order to prepare himself.

The tensions and pains of development are vividly experienced in therapeutic relationships: developmental gains require emotional effort and a struggle between the desires to make changes, the hopes for growth and the wish to avoid or evade the pains of letting go of more familiar positions. Defences against the pains of growth in adolescence can be tenacious, either propelling young people into states of pseudo-maturity or into retaining childhood ways of relating. Defensively knowing, as demonstrated by Yasmin for example in Chapter 9, or wanting to not know and not discover, aims to shield the young person from the pains of growth. Pauline, for example, in Chapter 10, said she hated thinking, which meant feeling troubled and overwhelmed by the responsibilities for herself and her actions. Her rage against her objects powerfully expressed her difficulties in mourning and separating. Applying to these young people in TAPP, Bion's (1965) thoughts about catastrophic change and about the turbulence of psychic growth and the consequent disorganisation of previously held structures and ways of relating, the process of change in these therapeutic relationships can appear as intensely feared as disastrous before becoming profoundly helpful. These vulnerable young people can feel intensely troubled by becoming more reflective, more aware of depressive pains and open to new experiences; defences can be held onto more obstinately, or desperately, or the young people feel – and often complain about feeling – worse, or having new problems and symptoms. In the case examples, Eric, in Chapter 9, and Pauline, in Chapter 10, both talked about feeling more troubled internally, with new difficulties that required attention and containment. These new problems, including not being able to sleep and feeling troubled in oneself did speak to an increased awareness of the reasons for their distress. This contrasts with young people, whose retention of their symptomatic behaviour and risks instil anxiety in the therapist and the need to understand, contain and attend to the meaning of these communications.

Though in the case examples there is evidence of less self-destructiveness, continuing risks need to be assessed; however, in many cases, the problems encountered in the ending of TAPP are of being more troubled within oneself, of greater awareness of the causes of distress within the self and of more depressive pains and anxieties. As discussed in Chapter 10, this does suggest the relevance of further therapy for some young people after TAPP. For young people with complex difficulties, the weight of past deprivations, disruptions, losses and abuse do continue to be important considerations. The process of change and development in TAPP can evoke Blos' (1967) thought about uneven maturation during adolescence in which areas of emerging maturity and competence can co-exist with areas of immaturity or regression. TAPP works directly towards a partial development, in one area at a specific point in time, one which, however, through the developmental process, can transfer to other areas and over time.

How therapists effect change and growth in TAPP

In the above discussion, it is perhaps evident that the intensive therapeutic processes in TAPP generate change and growth in the context of internal conflicts in powerful emotional fields. The young person's development from projective, defensive or destructive towards more thoughtful ways of relating involves taking greater responsibilities for bearing one's own feelings; this puts pressure on the young person's internal resources, stirs up hatred and can lead to new defences against the pains of growth. Working through these issues in the time constraints of TAPP can be, to say the least, challenging. The therapist's role and stance have been discussed in detail in earlier chapters; the availability of reflective spaces for the therapist has also been described as important in helping to think about the process and retain sensitivity. Equally crucial is learning from experience about how to manage the time-limited structure of TAPP and how to work with the anxieties this engenders. Therefore therapists benefit from training to work with the specific demands of time-limited therapy. TAPP has some distinctive features: the process of engagement and the collaborative setting of the developmental focus during the assessment and engagement phase; working with the structure and the time limits, including linking interventions to these, for example by timely references to the timeframe and the number of sessions remaining; working with the ending; and the therapist's positioning when working with the focus and managing in herself the pressures of time and the need to not be caught up with anxieties about limited time, in order to reflect – using Osimo's (1998) distinction – good slowness (not rushing) and good quickness (responding to change). Perhaps above all is the demand for keeping much material of different kinds in mind, thinking in the transference, and selecting from this what can be talked about with the young person and how; there is often a sense of ambiguity in this material that complicates thinking about its meaning.

The therapist's approach to the young person in TAPP to create possibilities for growth involves being engaged in a process of recognition and exploration, holding the frame and structure of TAPP, working with time and containing anxieties. Close attention is paid to what feelings and states of mind can be managed and contained, and the therapeutic approach is adapted to the individual's capacity to bear strong feelings at any point in time. The process of thinking in the transference–counter-transference matrix has been discussed in detail in Chapter 8 and illustrated through the case examples in Chapters 9 and 10. Working with the therapeutic relationship in TAPP involves being open to newness, the potential of new experiences, symbolic moments, the developmental possibilities of irony, self-deprecation, self-assertion and discoveries at moments of awareness. Simultaneously, it involves containing anxieties and destructiveness, and mourning loss. As discussed in Chapter 8, it involves thinking about regressive and progressive trends in the young person and working with risks. Mutuality in exchanges with the young person in negotiable states of mind alternate swiftly with moments when the young person seeks and needs containment of anxieties (Anderson 1999). Case examples in Chapters 9 and 10 have illustrated these themes: for example, staying with Luke's misery rather than confronting it, so that liveliness could emerge; seeing Pauline's rage against the ending as her use of the therapist as an object, promoting an idea of development.

The person of the therapist becomes very important for the young person, even in – or perhaps especially because of – the time-limited nature of TAPP. Young people want to take their thinking away with them (Peter, Chapter 10), hold it in their minds in their absence (Aretha, Chapter 9) and recognise that relating to the therapist is a different kind of experience, providing a different quality of attention; Jenny (Chapter 10) referred to it as being "different here." Therapists can be seen by some young people as not replicating parental figures in significant ways, despite the power of transferential investments. When this occurs, the therapist becomes a new kind of object for the young person. The aim in TAPP during the ending is to highlight both the specific relationship that is important for the young person and the qualities of the therapeutic process that they value. As with all psychotherapy, there is a tension between the capacity of the individual to retain a good object in mind and the more destructive aspect that stems from hurts and grievances; this tension can be heightened in time-limited therapy. If the pain and anger of the ending can be tolerated and contained, the young person can take the process away with them as a bridge to use in their lives along with holding the potential benefits of further therapy in the future; the uniqueness of the relationship with *this* therapist enhances the value of the experience. Both the process and the person of the therapist contribute to internalisation of the individual's experience of therapy. What is internalised and retained by individuals after TAPP is not really known; the post-treatment review does provide some indicative evidence of how the young person begins to retain TAPP after therapy, and getting to know more about this is an important research task.

Outcomes: evidencing TAPP's effectiveness

A final aim of this book is that it should be useful for researchers as a protocol for evaluating the effectiveness of TAPP within the requirements for evidence-based practice. For this purpose, the guidance for practitioners described in Part II of the book provides a template for undertaking TAPP as an intervention for a research study. This can be read in conjunction with service evaluations and the new TAPP practice guidance, which identify criteria for assessing practitioners' adherence to the approach, and the kind of outcome measures that are appropriate for TAPP (Briggs et al 2018). Service evaluations of TAPP demonstrate indicative evidence of outcomes, including high levels of engagement (Briggs & Lyon 2012; Briggs et al 2018), and significant reduction in difficulties and risks (Briggs et al 2018).

Initial findings from service evaluations show that for periods up to 12 months after the end of therapy, young people value and have positive outcomes from therapy; young people's expressions of how they felt helped by TAPP include "It helped me sort out how to access my feelings" and "It got me out of a bad place... I do feel more comfortable now." Another young person conveyed the shared ownership of the therapy, using "we": "It was helpful to know what had changed and what we'd done to help." Some comments on the process of being in therapy authentically convey something of the intensity and difficulty of the emotional experience and are in accord with the emotionality expressed in the case studies in this book: "I hated it at the time, I felt very vulnerable. I didn't want to talk about certain things at the time." These anecdotal comments whet the appetite for systematic follow-up studies of the effects of TAPP, which are needed and important.

Conclusion

In summary, therefore, the clinical picture shows that in TAPP young people demonstrate some important changes that relate to its aims and objectives. These have been described as becoming more separate from parental figures; bearing and thinking about feelings and states of mind, rather than discharging them through impulsive actions and destructiveness; engaging with realities; being and feeling more alive; and managing the pains and anxieties of growth and development. These clinical experiences of TAPP provide a nuanced picture of young people engaged in therapeutic processes of working with the pains and emotional struggles, processes which lead towards gaining more sense of progressive developmental pathways through addressing developmental disturbances. Evidence from service evaluations supports the sense that young people, including those with severe clinical difficulties, do engage in TAPP to work with and reduce their problems and risks, and young people have provided feedback that indicates how they felt helped by their therapy.

Bibliography

Abbass, A., S. Kisely, J. Town, F. Leichsenring, E. Driessen, S. De Maat, A. Gerber, J. Dekker, S. Rabung, S. Rusalovska & E. Crowe (2014). Short-term psychodynamic psychotherapies for common mental disorders. *Cochrane Database of Systematic Reviews*, Issue 7.

Abbass, A., S. Rabung, Fr. Leichsenring, J. Refseth & N. Midgley (2013). Psychodynamic psychotherapy for children and adolescents: a meta-analysis of short-term psychodynamic models. *Journal of the Academy of Child and Adolescent Psychiatry* 52, 8, 863–875.

Alexander, F. & T. French (1946). *Psychoanalytic Therapy*. New York: Ronald.

Anderson, R. (1997). Putting the boot in: violent defences against depressive anxiety. In *Reason and Passion: A Celebration of the Work of Hanna Segal*, ed. by D. Bell. London: Duckworths/Tavistock Clinic Series.

Anderson, R. (1999). Introduction. In *Psychoanalytic Psychotherapy of the Severely Disturbed Adolescent*, ed. by D. Anastasopoulos, E. Laylou-Lignos, & M. Waddell. London: Karnac Books.

Anderson, R. (2002). Assessing the risk of self-harm in adolescents: a psychoanalytic perspective. In *Assessment in Child Psychotherapy*, ed. by M. Rustin & E. Quagliata. London: Duckworth/Tavistock Clinic Series.

Anderson, R. (2008). A psychoanalytic approach to suicide in adolescence. In *Relating to Self-harm and Suicide: Psychoanalytic Perspectives on Practice, Theory and Prevention*, ed. by S. Briggs, A. Lemma, & W. Crouch. London: Routledge.

Anderson, R. & A. Dartington (1998). *Facing It Out: Clinical Perspectives on Adolescent Disturbance*. London: Duckworths/Tavistock Clinic Series.

Anthony, J. (1975). Between *yes* and *no*: the potentially neutral area where the adolescent and his therapist can meet. *Adolescent Psychiatry* 4, 323–344.

Arnett J. (2000). Emerging adulthood: a theory of development from late teens through the twenties. *American Psychologist* 55, 469–480.

Baker, A. (2012). David Malan and the genesis of experiential dynamic psychotherapy in the UK. In *Theory and Practice of Experiential Dynamic Psychotherapy*, ed. by F. Osimo & M. Stein. London: Karnac.

Balint, M. (1957). *The Doctor, His Patient and the Illness*. New York: International Universities Press.

Balint, M. (1979). *The Basic Fault: Therapeutic Aspects of Regression*. London: Tavistock.

Balint, M., P. Ornstein, & E. Balint (1972). *Focal Psychotherapy: An Example of Applied Psychoanalysis*. London: Tavistock.

Baruch, G. (ed.) (2001). *Community Based Psychotherapy with Young People: Evidence and Innovation in Practice*. Hove: Brunner-Routledge.

Bateson, G. (1972). *Steps to an Ecology of Mind*. New York: Ballantine Books.

Beck, U. (1992). *Risk Society: Towards a New Modernity*. London: Sage.

Bell, D. (2007). Existence in time: development or catastrophe? In *Time and Memory*, ed. by R. Perelberg. London: Karnac.

Benjamin, J. (1988). *The Bonds of Love: Psychoanalysis, Feminism and the Problem of Domination*. New York: Pantheon.

Benjamin, J. (2004). Beyond doer and done to: an intersubjective view of thirdness. *Psychoanalytic Quarterly* 73, 5–46.

Benjamin, J. (2018). *Beyond Doer and Done to: Recognition Theory, Intersubjectivity and the Third*. London: Routledge.

Bick, E. (1968). 'The experience of the skin in early object relations'. *International Journal of Psychoanalysis* 49, 484–486.

Bick, E. (2002, first published in 1964). Notes on infant observation in psychoanalytic training. In *Surviving Space: Papers on Infant Observation*, ed. by A. Briggs. London: Karnac.

Bion, W. (1962). *Learning from Experience*. London: Maresfield.

Bion, W. (1965). *Transformations*. London: Maresfield.

Bion, W. (1970). *Attention and Interpretation*. London: Maresfield.

Bion, W. (1992). *Cogitations*. London: Karnac.

Bird, D. (1986). Crossing the boundary into psychotherapy: the process of assessment. *Tavistock Clinic Papers*, number 6. London: Tavistock Clinic Library.

Bird, D. (1989). Adolescents and negotiating treatment. *Tavistock Clinic Papers*, number 101. London: Tavistock Clinic Library.

Blakemore, S.-J. (2018). *Inventing Ourselves: The Secret Life of the Teenage Brain*. New York: Random House.

Blos, P. (1967). The second individuation process of adolescence. *Psychoanalytic Study of the Child* 22, 162–186.

Bradley, J. (2017). Some comments on "the experience of puberty" by Shirley Hoxter. *Journal of Child Psychotherapy* 43, 1, 108–112.

Brah, A. (1996). *Cartographies of Diaspora*. London: Routledge.

Bravesmith, A. (2010). Can we be brief? *British Journal of Psychotherapy* 26, 3, 274–290.

Brenman Pick, I. (1988). Adolescence: its impact on patient and analyst. *International Journal of Psychoanalysis* 15, 187–194.

Briggs, S. (2008). *Working with Adolescents and Young Adults: A Contemporary Psychodynamic Approach*. Basingstoke: Palgrave.

Briggs, S. (2010a). Time limited psychodynamic psychotherapy for adolescents and young adults. *Journal of Social Work Practice* 24, 2, 181–196.

Briggs, S. (2010b). Suicide prevention and working with suicidal people: the contribution of psychoanalysis. In *Off the Couch: Contemporary Psychoanalytic Applications*, ed. by M. Patrick & A. Lemma. London: Routledge.

Briggs, S. (2018). Working with troubled adolescents: observation as a key skill for practitioners. In *Observation in Health and Social Care Applications for Learning, Research and Practice with Children and Adults*, ed. by C. Parkinson, H. Hingley-Jones, & L. Allain. London: Jessica Kingsley.

Briggs, S., A. Chadwick, M. Maxwell, & A. Keenan (2018). Clinical audit and service evaluation: time-limited adolescent psychodynamic psychotherapy (TAPP). *Leicester Partnership NHS Trust*. February 2018.

Briggs, S. & H. Hingley-Jones (2013). Reconsidering adolescent subjectivity: a 'practice-near' approach to the study of adolescents, including those with severe learning disabilities. *British Journal of Social Work* 43, 1, 64–80.

Briggs, S., A. Lemma, & W. Crouch (eds.) (2008). *Relating to Self-Harm and Suicide: Psychoanalytic Perspectives on Theory, Practice and Prevention*. London: Routledge.

Briggs, S. & L. Lyon (2011). A developmentally focussed time-limited psychodynamic psychotherapy for adolescents and young adults: origins and applications. *Revue Adolescence*, number 76, 415–434.

Briggs, S. & L. Lyon (2012). Time limited psychodynamic psychotherapy for adolescents and young adults. In *Contemporary Developments in Adult and Young Adult Therapy: the work of the Tavistock and Portman Clinics*, ed. by A. Lemma. London: Karnac.

Briggs, S., J. Maltsberger, M. Goldblatt, R. Lindner, & G. Fiedler (2006). Assessing and engaging suicidal teenagers in psychoanalytic psychotherapy. *Archives of Suicide Research* 10, 4, 1–15.

Briggs, S., M. Maxwell, & A. Keenan (2015). Working with the complexities of adolescent mental health problems: applying time-limited adolescent psychodynamic psychotherapy (TAPP). *Psychoanalytic Psychotherapy* 29, 4, 14–329.

Briggs, S., T. Slater, & J. Bowley (2017). Practitioners' experiences of adolescent suicidal behaviour in peer groups. *Journal of Psychiatric and Mental Health Nursing* 24, 5, 293–301.

Britton, R. (1998). *Belief and Imagination*. London: Routledge.

Bronstein, C., & S. Flanders (1998). The development of a therapeutic space in a first contact with adolescents. *Journal of Child Psychotherapy* 24, 5–36.

Brunner, R., M. Kaess, P. Parzer, G. Fischer, V. Carli, C. Hoven, & D. Wasserman (2014). Life-time prevalence and psychosocial correlates of adolescent direct self-injurious behaviour. *Journal of Child Psychology and Psychiatry* 55, 337–348.

Butler, G., N. De Graaf, B. Wren, & P. Carmichael (2018). Assessment and support of children and adolescents with gender dysphoria. *Arch.Dis.Child* 103, 7, https://doi.org/10.1007/s00787-017-1098-4.

Bynner J. (2005). Rethinking the youth phase of the life-course: the case for emerging adulthood? *Journal of Youth Studies* 8, 4, 367–384.

Cahn, R. (1998). The process of becoming-a-subject in adolescence. In *Adolescence and Psychoanalyis: The Story and the History*, ed. by M. Perret-Catipovic & F. Ladame. London: Karnac.

Catty, J. (ed.) (2016). *Short-Term Psychoanalytic Psychotherapy for Adolescents with Depression: A Treatment Manual*. London: Karnac.

Cohen, S. (2002). *Folk Devils and Moral Panics*. 3rd edition. London: Routledge.

Coleman, J. & L. Hendry (1999). *The Nature of Adolescence*. 3rd edition. London: Routledge.

Coren, A. (2010). *Short-Term Psychotherapy: A Psychodynamic Approach*. Basingstoke: Palgrave.

Côté, J. (2014). *Youth Studies: Fundamental Issues and Debates*. Basingstoke: Palgrave Macmillan.

Cottrell, D. & A. Kraam (2005). Growing up? A history of CAMHS (1987–2005). *Child and Adolescent Mental Health* 10, 111–117.

CQC (Care Quality Commission) (2017). Review of children and young people's mental health services. https://www.cqc.org.uk/publications/major-report/review-children-young-peoples-mental-health-services-phase-one-report.

CQC (Care Quality Commission) (2018). Brief guide: transitions out of children and young people's mental health services. CQUIN. https://www.cqc.org.uk/sites/default/files/20 180228_9001400%20_briefguide-transition_CQUIN.pdf.

Dartington A. (1994). Some thoughts on the significance of the outsider in families and other social groups. In *Crisis at Adolescence: Object Relations Therapy with the Family*, ed. by S. Box. New York: Jason Aronson.

Dartington, A. (1998). The intensity of adolescence in small families. In *Facing It Out: Clinical Perspectives on Adolescent Disturbance*, ed. R. Anderson & A. Dartington (1998). London: Duckworths/Tavistock Clinic Series.

Davanloo, H. (1978). *Basic Principles and Techniques in Short-Term Dynamic Psychotherapy*. New York: Spectrum.

Davanloo, H. (1980). *Short-Term Dynamic Psychotherapy*. New York: Aronson.

Davanloo, H. (1990). *Unlocking the Unconscious*. New York: Wiley.

Davanloo, H. (2000). *Intensive Short-term Dynamic Psychotherapy: Selected Papers of Habib Davanloo*. Chichester: Wiley.

De Rementeria, A. (2017). How to grow up or (nearly) die trying: developing trust in one's own capacity for growth. *Journal of Child Psychotherapy* 43, 1, 66–82.

Della Rosa, E. (2016). The problem of knowledge in psychotherapy with an adolescent girl: reflections on a patient's difficulty in thinking and issues of therapeutic technique. *Journal of Child Psychotherapy* 41, 2, 162–178.

Di Ceglie, D. (2002). Castaway's corner. *Clinical Child Psychology and Psychiatry* 7, 3, 487–491.

Donaghy, M. (2014). *Collected Poems*. London: Picador.

Erikson, E. (1968). *Identity: Youth and Crisis*. London: Faber and Faber.

Ezriel, H. (1952). Notes on psychoanalytic group therapy II Interpretation and research. *Psychiatry* 15, 119–126.

Ferro, A. (2004). *Seeds of Illness, Seeds of Recovery*. Hove: Routledge.

Ferro, A. (2015). *Torments of the Soul: Passions, Symptoms, Dreams*. London: Routledge.

Flynn, D. & H. Skogstad (2006). 'Facing towards or away from destructive narcissism'. *Journal of Child Psychotherapy* 32, 1, 35–48.

Fonagy, P. (2015). 'The effectiveness of psychodynamic psychotherapies: an update'. *World Psychiatry* 14, 137–150.

Fosha, D. (2000). *The Transforming Power of Affect: A Model for Accelerated Change*. New York: Basic Books.

Freud, A. (1958). Adolescence: the psychoanalytic study of the child. 13, 1, 255–278. Reprinted in *Adolescence and Psychoanalysis: The Story and the History*, by M. Perret-Catipovic & F. Ladame (1998). London: Karnac Books. Chapter 3, 43–65.

Freud, S. (1905). Three essays on sexuality. In *The Standard Edition of the Works of Sigmund Freud, VII*, ed. by J. Strachey. London: Hogarth. 123–245.

Freud, S. (1909). Analysis of a phobia in a five-year-old boy. *Standard Edition* 10. London: Hogarth Press.

Freud, S. (1912). Recommendations to physicians practising psychoanalysis. *Standard Edition* 12. London: Hogarth Press.

Freud, S. (1914). On narcissism. In *The Standard Edition of the Works of Sigmund Freud, XIV*, ed. by J. Strachey. London: Hogarth. 67–102.

Freud, S. (1917). Mourning and melancholia. In *The Standard Edition of the Works of Sigmund Freud, XIV*, ed. by J. Strachey. London: Hogarth. 237–258.

Freud, S. (1923). The ego and the id. *Standard Edition* 19. London: Hogarth Press. 12–66.

Freud, S. (1933). The dissection of the psychical personality. In 'New introductory lectures on psychoanalysis'. In *The Standard Edition of the Works of Sigmund Freud, XXII*, ed. by J. Strachey. London: Hogarth. S.E. 22, 1–182.

Furlong, A. & F. Cartmel (1997). *Young People and Social Change: Individualisation and Risk in Modern Society*. Buckingham: Open University Press.

Gay, P. (1988). *Freud: A Life for Our Time*. London: Dent and Son.

Giddens, A. (1991). *Modernity and Self- Identity*. Oxford: Polity Press.

Gozlan, A. (2013). The virtual machine: a dis-intimacy at work. *Recherches en Psychanalyse* 16, 2, 196–205.

Gozlan, A. (2016). L'adolescent et les réseaux sociaux: quels impacts psychiques? *The Conversation*. May 19, 2016.

Graham, P. (2004). *The End of Adolescence*. Oxford: Oxford University Press.

Graham, R. (2013). The perception of digital objects and their impact on development. *Psychoanalytic Psychotherapy* 27, 4, 269–279.

Green, A. (1992). A psychoanalyst's point of view concerning psychosis at adolescence. In *International Annals of Adolescent Psychiatry*, ed. by A. Schwartzberg. Chicago: University of Chicago Press.

Griffin, C. (1997). Representations of the young. In *Youth in Society*, ed. by J. Roche & S. Tucker. London: Sage Publications.

Groves, J. (ed.) (1996). *Essential Papers on Short-Term Dynamic Psychotherapy*. New York: New York University Press.

Guerlac, S. (2006). *Thinking in Time: An Introduction to Henri Bergson*. New York: Cornell University Press.

Gunnell, D., J. Kidger, & H. Elvidge (2018). Adolescent mental health in crisis. *BMJ*, 361: k2608.

Gustafson, J. (1981). The complex secret of brief psychotherapy in the works of Malan and Balint. In *Forms of Brief Therapy*, ed. by S. Budman. New York: Guilford.

Guthrie, E. & A. Moghavemi (2013). Psychodynamic-interpersonal therapy: an overview of the treatment approach and evidence base. *Psychodynamic Psychiatry* 41, 4, 619–636.

Haley, J. (1973). *Uncommon Therapy*. New York: W. W. Norton and Co.

Hall, S. (2000). Conclusion: the multi-cultural question. In *Un/settled Multiculturalisms*, ed. by B. Hesse. London: Jed Books.

Hawton, K., K. Saunders, & R. O'Connor (2012). Self-harm and suicide in adolescents. *The Lancet* 379, 9834. 2373–2382.

Heimann, P. (1950). On counter transference. *International Journal of Psychoanalysis* 31, 81–84.

Hickey, C. (2017). *Understanding Davanloo's Intensive Short-Term Dynamic Psychotherapy: A Guide for Clinicians*. London: Karnac.

Hinshelwood, R. (1995). Psychodynamic formulation in assessment for psychoanalysis. In *The Art and Science of Assessment in Psychotherapy*, ed. by C. Mace. London: Routledge.

Hobson, R. (1985). *Forms of Feeling: Heart of Psychotherapy*. London: Routledge.

Hoxter, S. (1964). The experience of puberty. *Journal of Child Psychotherapy* 1, 2, 13–26.

Jacobs, T. (1990). The no age time: early adolescence and its consequences. In *Child and Adolescent Analysis: Its Significance for Clinical Work*, ed. by S. Dowling. Madison: International Universities Press.

Jackson, E. (2017). Too close for comfort: the challenges of engaging with sexuality in work with adolescents. *Journal of Child Psychotherapy* 43, 1, 6–22.

Johannsson T. (2007). *The Transformation of Sexuality: Gender and Identity in Contemporary Youth Culture*. Aldershot: Ashgate.

Jones, E. (1922). Some Problems of Adolescence. *British Journal of Psychology* 13, 31–47.

Jones, G. (2006). The thinking and behaviour of young adults (16–25). *Literature Review for the Social Exclusion Unit*.

Joseph, B. (1989). *Psychic Change and Psychic Equilibrium*. London: Routledge.

Kennedy, R. (1998). *The Elusive Human Subject: A Psychoanalytic Theory of Subject Relations*. London: Free Association Books.

Kennedy, R. (2000). Becoming a subject: some theoretical and clinical issues. *International Journal of Psychoanalysis* 81, 875–892.

Kernberg, O. (1976). *Object Relations Theory and Clinical Psychoanalysis*. New York: Jason Aronson.

King, P. & R. Steiner (eds.) (1991). *The Freud-Klein Controversies, 1941–1945*. London: Routledge.

Klein, M. (1922). On Puberty. In *Love Guilt and Reparation and Other Works*, by M. Klein. 1975. Hogarth Press.

Klein, M. (1952). The origins of transference. In *Envy and Gratitude and Other Works*, by M. Klein. 1975. London: Hogarth Press.

Klerman G. L., M. M. Weissman, & B. J. Rounsaville (1984). *Interpersonal Psychotherapy of Depression*. New York: Basic Books.

Kraemer, S. (2006). Something happens: elements of therapeutic change. *Clinical Child Psychology and Psychiatry* 11, 2, 239–248.

Kuhn, T. (1962). *The Structure of Scientific Revolutions*. Chicago: University of Chicago Press.

Ladame, F. (2008). Treatment priorities after adolescent suicide attempts. In *Relating to Self-harm and Suicide: Psychoanalytic Perspectives on Theory, Practice and Prevention*, ed. by S. Briggs, A. Lemma, & W. Crouch. London: Routledge.

Laor, I. (2001). Brief psychoanalytic psychotherapy: the impact of its fundamentals on the therapeutic process. *British Journal of Psychotherapy* 18, 2, 169–183.

Laufer, M. & E. Laufer (1984). *Adolescence and Developmental Breakdown*. London: Karnac.

Laufer, M. & E. Laufer (1995). *Adolescence and Developmental Breakdown: A Psychoanalytic View*. London: Karnac.

Laufer, M. (1998). The central masturbation fantasy, the final sexual organisation, and adolescence. In *Adolescence and Psychoanalysis: The Story and the History*, ed. by M. Perret-Catipovic & F. Ladame. London: Karnac. Chapter 7, 113–132.

Lemma, A. (2015a). *An Introduction to the Practice of Psychoanalytic Psychotherapy*. 2nd edition. Chichester: Wiley.

Lemma, A. (2015b). *Minding the Body: The Body in Psychoanalysis and Beyond*. London: Routledge.

Lemma, A., M. Target, & P. Fonagy (2011). *Brief Dynamic Interpersonal Therapy: A Clinician's Guide*. Oxford: Oxford University Press.

Luborsky, L., C. Popp, E. Luborsky, & D. Mark (1994). The core conflictual relationship theme. *Psychotherapy Research* 4, 3–4, 172–183.

Lyon, L. (2004). Very brief psychoanalytically-based consultation work with young people. *British Journal of Psychotherapy* 21, 1, 30–35.

McGorry, P. (2018). Tackling the youth mental health crisis across adolescence and young adulthood. *BMJ*, 362: k3704.

Malan, D. (1963). *A Study of Brief Psychotherapy*. New York: Plenum Press.

Malan, D. (1976). *The Frontier of Brief Psychotherapy*. New York: Plenum Press.

Malan, D. (1979/1995). *Individual Psychotherapy and the Science of Psychodynamics*. London: Butterworth.

Malan, D. & P. Coughlin Della Selva (2006). *Lives Transformed: A Revolutionary Model of Dynamic Psychotherapy*. London: Karnac.

Malan, D. & F. Osimo (1992). *Psychodynamics, Training and Outcome in Brief Psychotherapy*. Oxford: Butterworth-Heinemann.

Mann, J. (1973). *Time-Limited Psychotherapy*. Cambridge, MA: Harvard University Press.

Mann, J. (1991). Time-limited psychotherapy. In *Handbook of Short-Term Dynamic Psychotherapy*, ed. by P. Crits-Christoph & J. P. Barber. New York: Basic Books.

Mann, J. (1996). Time-limited psychotherapy. In *Essential Papers on Short-Term Dynamic Psychotherapy*, ed. by J. Groves. New York: New York University Press.

Meltzer, D. (1978). *Sexual States of Mind*. Perthshire: Clunie Press.

Meltzer, D. (1986). *Studies in Extended Metapsychology*. Perthshire: Clunie Press.

Menninger, K. (1958). *Theory of Psychoanalytic Technique*. New York: Basic Books.

Migone, P. (2014). What does "brief" mean? A theoretical critique of the concept of brief therapy from a psychoanalytic viewpoint. *Journal of the American Psychoanalytic Association* 62, 4, 631–656.

Molnos, A. (1995). *A Question of Time: Essentials of Brief Dynamic Psychotherapy*. London: Karnac.

Mondrzak, V. (2012). Reflections on psychoanalytic technique with adolescents today: pseudo-pseudomaturity. *The International Journal of Psychoanalysis* 93, 3, 649–666.

Moran, P., C. Coffey, H. Roamiuk, & C. Olsson (2012). The natural history of self-harm from adolescence to young adulthood: a population-based cohort study. *The Lancet* 379, 236–243.

Motz, A. (ed.) (2009). *Managing Self-Harm: Psychological Perspectives*. London: Routledge.

Mufson, L., D. Moreau, M. Weissman, P. Wickramaratne, J. Martin, & A. Samoilov (1994). Modification of interpersonal psychotherapy with depressed adolescents (IPT-A): phase I and II studies. *Journal of the American Academy of Child and Adolescent Psychiatry* 33, 5, 695–705.

NICE (National Institute for Clinical Excellence) (2011). Self-harm, longer term management. CG133. https://www.nice.org.uk/guidance/cg133.

O'Reilly, M., P. Vostanis, H. Taylor, C. Day, C. Street, & M. Wolpert (2013). Service user perspectives of multiagency working: a qualitative study with children with educational and mental health difficulties and their parents. *Child and Adolescent Mental Health* 18, 202–209.

Ogden, T. (1994). *Subjects of Analysis*. London: Karnac.

Ogden, T. (2004). On holding and containing, being and dreaming. *International Journal of Psychoanalysis* 85, 1349–1364.

Osimo, F. (1998). The unexplored complementarity of short-term and long-term analytic approaches. *Journal of the American Academy of Psychoanalysis* 26, 1, 95–103.

Osimo, F. (2003). *Experiential Short-Term Dynamic Psychotherapy: A Manual*. Bloomington: 1st Books.

Osimo, F. & M. Stein (eds.) (2012). *Theory and Practice of Experiential Dynamic Psychotherapy*. London: Karnac.

Patel V., A. Flissher, S. Hetrick, P. McGarry (2007). Mental health of young people: a global public-health challenge. *The Lancet* 369, 9569, 1302–1313.

Patton, G., C. Coffey, H. Romaniuk, A. Mackinnon, & J. Carlin (2014). The prognosis of common mental disorders in adolescents: a 14-year prospective cohort study. *The Lancet* 383, 9926, 1404–1411.

Patton, G. & R. Viner (2007). Pubertal transitions in health. *The Lancet* 369, 1130–1139.

Perelberg, R. (ed.) (2007). *Time and Memory*. London: Karnac.

Perret-Catipovic, M. & F. Ladame (1998). *Adolescence and Psychoanalysis: The Story and the History*. London: Karnac.

Pitchforth, J., K. Fahy, T. Ford, M. Wolpert, R. Viner, & D. Hargreaves (2018). Mental health and well-being trends among children and young people in the UK, 1995–2014: analysis of repeated cross-sectional national health surveys. *Psychological Medicine*, 1–11. doi: 10.1017/S0033291718001757.

Quinodoz, J. M. (1991). *The Taming of Solitude: Separation Anxiety in Psychoanalysis*, trans. by P. Slotkin (1993). London: Routledge.

Quinlivan, L., J. Cooper, D. Meehan, D. Longson, & N. Kapur (2017). Predictive accuracy of risk scales following self-harm: multicentre, prospective cohort study. *British Journal of Psychiatry* 210, 429–436. doi: 10.1192/bjp.bp.116.189993.

Racker, H. (1968). *Transference and Counter Transference*. London: Hogarth Press.

Rice, F., O. Eyre, L Riglin, & R. Potter (2017). Adolescent depression and the treatment gap. *Lancet Psychiatry* 4, 2, 86–87.

Rossouw, T. & P. Fonagy (2012). Mentalization-based treatment for self-harm in adolescents: a randomized controlled trial. *Journal of the American Academy of Child & Adolescent Psychiatry* 51, 12, 1304–1331.

Ruggiero, I. (2006). Consultation in adolescence: hurried, terminable, interminable'. *International Journal of Psychoanalysis* 2006, 87, 537–554.

Rutter, M., P. Graham, O. Chadwick, & W. Yule (1976). Adolescent turmoil: fact or fiction? *Journal of Child Psychology and Psychiatry* 17, 1, 35–56.

Salzberger-Wittenberg, I. (1970). *Psycho-Analytic Insight and Relationships: A Kleinian Approach*. London: Routledge & Kegan Paul.

Salzberger-Wittenberg, I. (2013). *Experiencing Endings and Beginnings*. London: Karnac.

Shaw, S. (2014). The elephant tied up with string: a clinical case study showing the importance of NHS provision of intensive, time-limited psychoanalytic psychotherapy treatments. *Psychoanalytic Psychotherapy* 28, 4, 379–396.

Schefler G. (2000). Time limited psychotherapy with adolescents. *The Journal of Psychotherapy Practice and Research* 9, 88–99.

Schmidt Neven, R. (2016). *Time-Limited Psychodynamic Psychotherapy with Children and Adolescents*. London: Routledge.

Shakespeare, W. (1611/1996). *The Winter's Tale*. Oxford: Oxford University Press.

Shefler, G. (2000). Time-limited psychotherapy with Adolescents. *Journal of Psychotherapy Practice and Research*, 9, 88–99.

Sifneos, P. (1967). Two different kinds of psychotherapy of short duration. *American Journal of Psychiatry* 123, 1069–1073.

Sifneos, P. (1968). Learning to solve emotional problems: a controlled study of short-term anxiety provoking psychotherapy. In *The Role of Learning in Psychotherapy*, ed. by R. Porter. London: J & A Churchill.

Sifneos, P. (1972). *Short-Term, Psychotherapy and Emotional Crisis*. Cambridge, MA: Harvard University Press.

Smith, J. (2006). Form and forming a focus in brief dynamic therapy. *Psychodynamic Practice* 12, 3, 261–279.

Smith, J. (2010). Panic stations: brief dynamic therapy for panic attacks and generalized anxiety. *Psychodynamic Practice* 16, 1, 25–43.

Spence, D. (1982). *Historical Truth and Narrative Truth*. New York: W. W. Norton and Co.

Stadter, M. (2009). *Object Relations Brief Therapy: The Therapeutic Relationship on Short-Term Work*. New York: Jason Aronson.

Stadter, M. (2016). Time, focus, relationship and trauma: a contemporary object relations approach to brief therapy. *Psychiatry: Interpersonal and Biological Processes* 79, 4, 433–440.

Stern, D. B. (2010). *Partners in Thought: Working with Unformulated Experience, Dissociation and Enactment*. New York: Routledge.

Stern, D. B. (2013). Field theory in psychoanalysis, part 2: Bionian field theory and contemporary interpersonal/relational psychoanalysis. *Psychoanalytic Dialogues* 23, 6, 630–645.

Stern, D. N. (2004). *The Present Moment*. New York: Norton.

Strupp, H. (1996). Psychoanalysis "focal psychotherapy", and the nature of the therapeutic influence. In *Essential Papers on Short-term Dynamic Psychotherapy*, ed. by J. Groves. New York: New York University Press.

Strupp, H. & J. Binder (1984). *Psychotherapy in a New Key: A Guide to Time-Limited Dynamic Psychotherapy*. New York: Basic Books.

Sukarieh, M. & S. Tannock (2011). The positivity imperative: a critical look at the "new" youth development movement. *Journal of Youth Studies* 14, 675–91.

Sullivan, H. S. (1953). *The Interpersonal Theory of Psychiatry*. New York: Norton.

Thomas, L. (1992). Racism and psychotherapy: working with racism in the consulting room – an analytic view. In *Intercultural Therapy: Themes, Interpretations and Practice*, ed. by J. Kareem & R. Littlewood. Oxford: Blackwell Scientific Publications.

Tisseron, S. (2011). Les nouveaux réseaux sociaux sur internet. *Psychotropes* 17, 2, 105.

Trevatt, D. (2005). Adolescents in mind. *Journal of Child Psychotherapy* 31, 2, 221–238.

UNESCO (2018). Learning to live together. http://www.unesco.org/new/en/social-and-human-sciences/themes/youth/youth-definition/ (accessed 29/11/2018).

Vanier, A. (2001). Some remarks on adolescence with particular reference to Winnicott and Lacan. *Pyschoanalytic Quarterly, LXX* 3, 579–597.

Waddell, M. (1998). *Inside Lives: Psychoanalysis and the Growth of the Personality*. London: Duckworths/Tavistock Clinic Series.

Waddell, M. (2002). Assessment of adolescents: preconceptions and realizations. *Journal of Child Psychotherapy* 28, 3, 365–382.

Waddell, M. (2006). 'Narcissism – An Adolescent Disorder?' *Journal of Child Psychotherapy*, 321, 21–34.

Watzlawick, P., J. Weakland, & R. Fisch (1974). *Change: Principles of Problem Formation and Problem Resolution*. New York: W. W. Norton and Co.

White, J. (2007). *Generation: Preoccupations and Conflicts in Contemporary Psychoanalysis*. London: Routledge.

Williams, A. H. (1978). Depression, deviation and acting-out in adolescence. *Journal of Adolescence* 1, 309–317.

Williams, G. (1997) *Internal Landscapes and Foreign Bodies*. London: Duckworths/Tavistock Clinic Series.

Winnicott, D. (1955). The depressive position in normal development. *British Journal of Medical Psychology* 9, 28, 89–100.

Winnicott, D. (1958). *Collected Papers: Through Paediatrics to Psychoanalysis.* Abingdon: Tavistock.

Winnicott, D. (1963). Struggling through the Doldrums. In *Winnicott; Deprivation and Delinquency*, ed. by C. Winnicott, R. Sheppard, & M. Davis. 2012. London: Routledge.

Winnicott, D. (1971) *Playing and Reality.* Harmondsworth: Pelican.

Wise, I. (2000). *Adolescence.* London: Institute of Psychoanalysis.

World Health Organisation (WHO) (2014). Preventing suicide: a global imperative. http://www.who.int/mental_health/suicide-prevention/world_report_2014/en.

World Health Organisation (WHO) (2017). Adolescents and mental health. http://www.who.int/maternal_child_adolescent/topics/adolescence/mental_health/en (accessed on 29/11/2018).

Young, L. & F. Lowe (2012). The young people's consultation service: a model of engagement. In *Contemporary Developments in Adult and Young Adult Therapy: The work of the Tavistock and Portman Clinics*, ed. by A. Lemma. London: Karnac.

Zac de Filc, S. (2006). Reflections on the setting in the treatment of adolescents. *International Journal of Psychoanalysis* 87, 2, 457–469.

Index

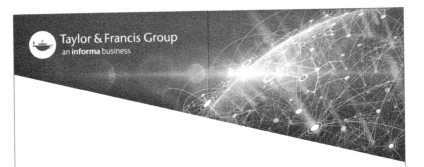

Made in the USA
Coppell, TX
10 September 2022

82936043R00111